Triple Compounding

Triple Compounding

by Kiana Danial

Triple Compounding For Dummies®

Published by: **John Wiley & Sons, Inc.**, 111 River Street, Hoboken, NJ 07030-5774, www.wiley.com

Copyright © 2026 by John Wiley & Sons, Inc. All rights reserved, including rights for text and data mining and training of artificial technologies or similar technologies.

Media and software compilation copyright © 2026 by John Wiley & Sons, Inc. All rights reserved, including rights for text and data mining and training of artificial technologies or similar technologies.

Published simultaneously in Canada

No part of this publication may be reproduced, stored in a retrieval system or transmitted in any form or by any means, electronic, mechanical, photocopying, recording, scanning or otherwise, except as permitted under Sections 107 or 108 of the 1976 United States Copyright Act, without the prior written permission of the Publisher or authorization through payment of the appropriate per-copy fee to the Copyright Clearance Center, Inc., 222 Rosewood Drive, Danvers, MA 01923, (978) 750-8400, fax (978) 750-4470, or on the web at www.copyright.com. Requests to the Publisher for permission should be addressed to the Permissions Department, John Wiley & Sons, Inc., 111 River Street, Hoboken, NJ 07030, (201) 748-6011, fax (201) 748-6008, or online at http://www.wiley.com/go/permissions.

The manufacturer's authorized representative according to the EU General Product Safety Regulation is Wiley-VCH GmbH, Boschstr. 12, 69469 Weinheim, Germany, e-mail: Product_Safety@wiley.com.

Trademarks: Wiley, For Dummies, the Dummies Man logo, Dummies.com, Making Everything Easier, and related trade dress are trademarks or registered trademarks of John Wiley & Sons, Inc. and may not be used without written permission. All other trademarks are the property of their respective owners. John Wiley & Sons, Inc. is not associated with any product or vendor mentioned in this book.

LIMIT OF LIABILITY/DISCLAIMER OF WARRANTY: THE PUBLISHER AND THE AUTHOR MAKE NO REPRESENTATIONS OR WARRANTIES WITH RESPECT TO THE ACCURACY OR COMPLETENESS OF THE CONTENTS OF THIS WORK AND SPECIFICALLY DISCLAIM ALL WARRANTIES, INCLUDING WITHOUT LIMITATION WARRANTIES OF FITNESS FOR A PARTICULAR PURPOSE. NO WARRANTY MAY BE CREATED OR EXTENDED BY SALES OR PROMOTIONAL MATERIALS. THE ADVICE AND STRATEGIES CONTAINED HEREIN MAY NOT BE SUITABLE FOR EVERY SITUATION. THIS WORK IS SOLD WITH THE UNDERSTANDING THAT THE PUBLISHER IS NOT ENGAGED IN RENDERING LEGAL, ACCOUNTING, OR OTHER PROFESSIONAL SERVICES. IF PROFESSIONAL ASSISTANCE IS REQUIRED, THE SERVICES OF A COMPETENT PROFESSIONAL PERSON SHOULD BE SOUGHT. NEITHER THE PUBLISHER NOR THE AUTHOR SHALL BE LIABLE FOR DAMAGES ARISING HEREFROM. THE FACT THAT AN ORGANIZATION OR WEBSITE IS REFERRED TO IN THIS WORK AS A CITATION AND/OR A POTENTIAL SOURCE OF FURTHER INFORMATION DOES NOT MEAN THAT THE AUTHOR OR THE PUBLISHER ENDORSES THE INFORMATION THE ORGANIZATION OR WEBSITE MAY PROVIDE OR RECOMMENDATIONS IT MAY MAKE. FURTHER, READERS SHOULD BE AWARE THAT INTERNET WEBSITES LISTED IN THIS WORK MAY HAVE CHANGED OR DISAPPEARED BETWEEN WHEN THIS WORK WAS WRITTEN AND WHEN IT IS READ.

For general information on our other products and services, please contact our Customer Care Department within the U.S. at 877-762-2974, outside the U.S. at 317-572-3993, or fax 317-572-4002. For technical support, please visit https://hub.wiley.com/community/support/dummies.

Wiley publishes in a variety of print and electronic formats and by print-on-demand. Some material included with standard print versions of this book may not be included in e-books or in print-on-demand. If this book refers to media that is not included in the version you purchased, you may download this material at http://booksupport.wiley.com. For more information about Wiley products, visit www.wiley.com.

Library of Congress Control Number: 2025946553

ISBN 978-1-394-34825-1 (pbk); ISBN 978-1-394-34827-5 (ebk); ISBN 978-1-394-34826-8 (ebk)

Contents at a Glance

Table of Contents

Introduction

I first found out about compounding the way most people do — through the promise of slow, steady growth over decades. But when I was secretly planning for a divorce, "slow and steady" wasn't going to cut it. I didn't want to depend on alimony or anyone else to secure my future, and I certainly didn't want my financial freedom tied to a marriage I knew was ending. I needed a way to create wealth *fast* — without gambling, without risky speculation, and without sacrificing my life to the grind. That's when I realized the problem: I was only compounding in one area.

So, I set out to compound more things, in more ways, at the same time. Within three years, I had tripled my portfolio to $5 million. In the next three years, it grew to more than $17 million, even as I raised my daughter and ran my business. My Triple Compounding system is what made it possible, and in this book, I show you how to use it to accelerate your wealth-building without relying on luck, perfect timing, or someone else's paycheck. You'll discover how to build an income engine you control, investments that grow while you sleep, and systems that keep you compounding no matter what's happening in the economy — or in your personal life.

And if you're wondering how my divorce story turned out — and the single decision I made that multiplied my results faster — read Chapter 1.

About This Book

If you've ever wondered why some people seem to grow their wealth, opportunities, and freedom year after year while others work just as hard but never break through, this book is your missing link.

Triple Compounding For Dummies is your playbook for building wealth faster than traditional advice can. Forget waiting 30 years for "slow and steady" growth to finally pay off. Instead, you'll discover how to stack three different layers of compounding so they work together — creating unstoppable momentum you don't have to restart from scratch every time life changes.

This isn't another "just save more" book. You discover

>> How to invest in yourself so your earning potential compounds before you
ever buy an asset

>> How to invest in your extensions — businesses, systems, and people that
multiply your time and income

>> How to invest in external assets — stocks, real estate, crypto, and more — so
your money works harder than you do

>> How to automate each phase so growth happens on autopilot, without
emotional decision-making

>> How to avoid the most common mistakes and reverse compounders that
sabotage progress

As you go through this book, you won't just understand triple compounding —
you'll have it running in your life, building wealth and freedom every single day.

Foolish Assumptions

I've made a few assumptions about you and where you're starting from:

>> You want more control over your financial future and don't want to rely solely
on employers, the stock market, or the government to secure it.

>> You may already be investing — in the stock market, real estate, your own
business, or retirement accounts — but you're not sure how to tie all your
assets, skills, and systems together for maximum compounding.

>> You've heard the advice to "start investing early" or "let your money work for
you," but no one's shown you a clear, step-by-step process to make that
happen in a way that also grows your income and lifestyle.

>> You may be a high-income professional, business owner, or someone who's
simply serious about building wealth, but you don't necessarily have the
time — or desire — to monitor markets every day.

>> You're comfortable using a computer and navigating the internet.

Icons Used in This Book

Throughout the book, you'll see icons to help you focus on what matters most:

The Tip icon marks tips (duh!), shortcuts, and simple actions to accelerate your progress.

Remember icons mark the information that's especially important to know. To siphon off the most important information in each chapter, just skim through these icons.

The Technical Stuff icon marks information of a highly technical nature that you can normally skip over.

The Warning icon tells you to watch out! It marks important information that may save you headaches and points out common traps and how to avoid them.

Beyond the Book

I've created extra resources to make sure you can keep compounding without having to flip through the book every time you need a quick reminder and to help you implement what you find out here even faster.

>> **Cheat Sheet** — Access the *Triple Compounding For Dummies* Cheat Sheet at www.dummies.com. Inside, you'll find quick-reference guides to

- The 3x3 Triple Compounding Framework at a Glance

- The most important "dos and don'ts" for investing in yourself, your extensions, and your external assets

- The common reverse compounders to avoid

- The key formulas, benchmarks, and action steps you'll come back to again and again

Find the cheat sheet by typing **Triple Compounding For Dummies** into the search field at www.dummies.com.

>> **Triple Compounding Masterclass:** Watch a free two-hour training session where I break down my Triple Compounding system in detail. You can also

download my Risk Management Toolkit and workbook for free. Go to
www.triplecompounding.com.

>> **Triple Compounding Live:** Join me at the Triple Compounding Live online
event, where I personally help you implement the exact strategy I used to go
from living paycheck-to-paycheck to building a $17,659,847.79 net worth —
even though I was a busy mom, couldn't afford to take big risks, and didn't
have a financial background. Click this link to look for upcoming dates:
www.triplecompounding.com/live.

Where to Go from Here

Triple compounding works best when you focus on the parts that match your current goals, challenges, and opportunities. Here are some ideas for where to jump in:

>> If you want the big picture first, start with Chapter 1 for an overview of my
Triple Compounding system, why it works, and how it's different from
anything you've seen before.

>> If you're ready to start investing right now, head to Chapter 6 for online
external assets like stocks and crypto, or Chapter 7 for offline external assets
like real estate and private equity.

>> If you need to figure out your risk tolerance and goals before moving forward,
go to Chapter 3, and to assess your starting point and design a plan that fits
your timeline, go to Chapter 4.

>> If you want to put growth on autopilot, check out Chapter 12, and for
automating your business income and external asset investments, flip to
Chapter 13.

>> If you suspect something is holding you back, flip to Chapter 20 to spot and
eliminate reverse compounders before they drain your progress.

>> If you want to see what success really looks like in action, jump to Chapter 21
to discover the daily habits of top triple compounders and how you can start
applying them immediately.

No matter where you begin, each chapter stands on its own — and you'll find
cross-references to other sections if you want to go deeper. You can dive into the
strategies that excite you now, then circle back later to fill in any gaps. The important thing is to start implementing because compounding rewards those who
act early.

1

Getting Started with Triple Compounding

IN THIS PART . . .

Discover what compounding means (and how it's different from investing or day trading), how to calculate your financial freedom number and why it matters, and what the three types of investment assets in the triple compounding system are.

See how triple compounding works in real life, with examples you can model.

Get clear on your personal risk tolerance and the different kinds of risks you need to navigate.

Chapter 1

Understanding Different Types of Compounding

So, you've picked up this book, and your first question is probably this: "What the heck is a triple compounding, anyway? Is it just a marketing buzzword? How is it different than normal compounding?" Simply stated, *triple compounding* is a method practiced by almost all self-made millionaires and billionaires like Robert Kiyosaki, Dave Ramsey, Grant Cardone, Cathie Wood, Kevin O'Leary, Oprah Winfrey, and even Warren Buffett to create generational wealth within their lifetime, even though they all have the same 24 hours as you and I.

It's the core philosophy that has helped them accelerate their financial growth. However, they rarely talk publicly about the details of the ecosystem they've created to help accelerate their financial success; instead, they point to only one element of their triple-compounding ecosystem — such as budgeting, real estate, index funds, media influence, or entrepreneurship — as the key to their success.

When you look into how the wealthy really make money, you realize they've all developed a sophisticated triple-compounding ecosystem. It's the ecosystem as a whole that creates accelerated financial growth, *not* any one product, service, investment strategy, or person. You can't try to take the ecosystem apart and measure its pieces in isolation.

Gone are the days when you could just go to college, get a good job, and retire on your 401(k) investment portfolio. If you're looking to accelerate your financial freedom, you should look into building a triple-compounding ecosystem that compounds multiple investment assets simultaneously. As you discover in this book, two out of three of these assets are not traditional financial instruments. In this chapter, I explain what compounding is and how compounding is different from traditional investing.

HOW I LEARNED ABOUT COMPOUNDING

I first heard this word during the 2008 market crash when I was studying electrical engineering in Japan and moonlighting as a guest on a popular Japanese TV show where we discussed current events.

It was a massive global economic recession. Businesses were going bankrupt, and people were losing their jobs. We were talking about the recession on one of our shows, and one of my panelists, an economics expert, said something I'd heard of without knowing what it meant.

He said governments are printing money to save the economy, which, to me, sounded like a good thing — more money! — until he explained what really happens when governments print more money. He said that when the government prints money to bail out corporations and hand out stimulus checks, inflation goes higher.

Inflation, which is why your parents paid way less for a gallon of milk than you do, is designed to lower the value of your money every year. So, every moment your money sits in the bank, you're losing money. That means leaving your money in the bank is kind of like setting your money on fire. He said the best way to prevent your money from losing value is to start compounding.

Defining Compounding

The word *compound* originates from the Latin word *componere*, which means "to put together" or "to combine."

Imagine that you have a small snowball. You start at the top of a snowy hill and roll that snowball down the hill. As it rolls, it picks up more snow and gets bigger. The longer it rolls, the more snow it collects, causing it to get bigger faster and faster. (See Figure 1-1.)

Compounding works like that, but instead of snow, the growth happens to money. Let's say you invest some money, and it earns a little bit of interest, which is like extra money. Now, the next time you earn interest, you earn it not just on your original money but also on the extra money you made before. So, just like the snowball gets bigger as it rolls, your money grows faster over time because you're earning more and more on top of what you already earned.

FIGURE 1-1:
The snowball effect of compounding.

Source: triplecompounding.com

I like to say compounding is kind of like making your money make money babies (see Figure 1-2), and then those money babies make money grandbabies, and the grandbabies make great-grandbabies, which helps your wealth grow bigger and faster over time.

The best thing about compounding is that it prevents your money from losing its value to inflation, so 20 years from now, you can still afford to live comfortably.

FIGURE 1-2: Making your money make babies with compounding.

Source: triplecompounding.com

Relying on Money Managers Won't Cut It Anymore

Once I found out about compounding during the 2008 market crash, I got very excited to start using it to stop the devaluation of my money. But I knew nothing about money. I had no idea how financial markets worked. It all sounded risky, and I was so scared I would lose everything.

I asked around a little bit and concluded that the best thing I could do was to find a financial advisor to manage my money for me and compound it on my behalf. I thought it would be better than having my money sit in the bank.

I thought these money managers with all their fancy C-level titles would not only have my best interest at heart but also be the key to me getting rich and making my money continuously grow so I could be set for life. With this in mind, I trusted a money manager with all my money.

As it turned out, it didn't work out the way I expected. Throughout the years, I noticed my portfolio was not only not growing but shrinking.

I got skeptical and started to look more into how money managers and financial advisors make money. What I found out absolutely infuriated me. I found out that the money managers had their partners' best interests in mind.

They invested my money in stuff that made *them* compounded income through commissions they get from their partners and companies they invest my money in, instead of what would make me money. Then, they were taking a commission off what little money I was making, too!

So, they were earning from compounding, and I was paying for compounding. This is called *reverse compounding*. It's when you pay compounded income instead of earning it. Flip to Chapter 5 to discover all the different things you could be reverse-compounding right now.

What I found to be very concerning about giving your hard-earned cash to money managers is that 96 percent of them underperform the market average. The *market average* refers to the overall performance of a group of stocks or other financial assets that represent a particular market or sector. The market average return is around 8 percent to 12 percent per year. Money managers underperform that, which means my money was barely growing with my money manager's fund.

What's even crazier about this statistic is that the other 4 percent of money managers who are supposedly doing okay change yearly! That means no money manager consistently does better than the market average. They're supposed to be the so-called financial experts, but they actually *lose* money compared to the market average and then charge you a commission for completely mismanaging your money.

Although this commission is typically only 1 percent to 1.2 percent over your lifetime, it can compound to over 28 percent using the same law of compounding. But instead of making your money grow, you're reverse-compounding, paying Wall Street bros at a compounded rate, which could add up to millions of dollars over time.

In addition, if you need to get your money out of the money managers' fund for any reason, you have to pay a hefty penalty. I found this out the hard way when, years later, I got fired from my job. I really needed my money back to pay rent. But when I called my money manager to pull the money out, he said — based on the 500-page terms and conditions agreement I had signed years before — I had to pay a 75 percent penalty if I chose to take my money out earlier than the date that was agreed upon.

Here's an example: If you'd put in $100,000, you would have come out with $25,000 thanks to this early withdrawal penalty. On top of that, they had also mismanaged my money, so what I left there with them was even lower than the initial amount I had given them.

Although the terms and conditions and the penalty rate may differ depending on the money management firm, this can be a huge blow to the security of your financial future.

This is why you will be better off investigating the triple-compounding methods I describe in this book to take control of your financial future and accelerate your freedom.

How I Discovered Triple Compounding

After getting fired from my job and facing the reality of how my money manager mismanaged my money, as I describe in the previous section, I finally decided to take matters into my own hands and learn how to manage my own money.

I studied for the Certified Financial Planning (CFP) degree and the Charted Market Technician (CMT) degree, among other financial and investing-related certifications, to deepen my understanding of financial planning, investment strategies, and market analysis.

I was never going to be taken advantage of again. In the following sections, I share an overview of my biggest takeaways from my studies and life experiences, which led me to discover Triple Compounding.

Understanding the Rule of 72

One of the first financial planning methods I discovered during my new journey was something called the *rule of 72*. It's a formula you can use to find out how many years it's going to take for your money to double or compound. For example, if you have $100 and want to know how long it will take to double, you can figure it out using the rule of 72.

Here's a simple formula to show you how it works:

Years it takes to double = 72/annual rate of return

The *rate of return* (ROR) is the percentage gain or loss on an investment over a specific period of time. It measures how much an investment has grown (or shrunk) relative to its original cost.

Following this formula, you can calculate how long it would take for your $100 to compound to $200 at a market average return of 8 percent.

The answer is 72/8 = 9 years.

This means that if you're investing your money in a financial asset that compounds your money at the same rate as the market average, it will take your money nine years to double.

This is certainly better than not investing your money at all. However, considering that inflation can sometimes be higher than the market average return, this method may not be suitable for those who want to accelerate their financial goals and retire early.

Considering Your Financial Goals and Financial Freedom Number

Why did you pick up this book? I'm guessing it's because you have some dreams and goals. What sets successful people apart is their definitiveness of purpose. In other words, successful people know where they're going. Napoleon Hill, the author of *Think and Grow Rich* (Tarcher, 2007), defines a goal as a "dream with a deadline."

I define goals based on what I've seen working for thousands of my students as a *measurable* dream with a deadline.

The clearer you are about your goals, the more easily you can find a strategy to reach them. That's why the first point of my Invest Diva Diamond Analysis (IDDA) is breaking down your goals. I explain how the IDDA works in Chapter 10.

What's cool about setting financial goals is that they are very easy to measure. If your goal is to become *financially free* or work-optional, you can calculate exactly how much money you would need in your portfolio to achieve it. This is called the *rule of 4 percent,* and it helps determine how much you can safely withdraw from your investment portfolio each year without running out of money. According to this rule, you can withdraw 4 percent of your portfolio in the first year of retirement and adjust that amount annually for inflation. This approach is designed to help your money last at least 30 years.

Based on the Rule of 72 I describe in the previous section, I knew it was going to take me years before I could become self-sufficient. But this method of basic compounding was not only what financial advisors were advising. It was what I was being taught when I was studying for various financial certifications. I felt stuck! No matter what I did, my portfolio was growing so slowly.

At this point, I had gotten married. But right off the bat, my marriage was suffering, and the only viable option seemed to be getting a divorce.

But I didn't want to rely on my husband for money. So, I had to figure out a way to be financially self-sufficient *before* filing for divorce.

Suddenly, my slow investment strategies were no longer an option for me.

Here's how you can calculate your financial freedom number:

1. **Find your total annual expenses (download the complimentary workbook for this at www.triplecompounding.com).**

2. **Divide your annual expenses number by 0.04.**

Voila! Now you know what you're aiming for! For example, if your total expenses amount to $60,000 annually, you will need $1.5 million in your portfolio.

WARNING

Investing involves a risk of loss. You must only invest according to your risk tolerance and financial goals. Flip to Chapter 3 to explore the different types of risk you can encounter when investing and/or compounding.

Discovering Triple Compounding

One day, I was complaining to one of my trading buddies about my slow growth and frantic search for something that would grow quickly and support me and my freedom in years to come. And he told me something that changed my life forever.

He said something along the lines of "I don't compound just one thing. I compound multiple things."

At first, I had no idea what he was talking about. But as I researched and looked around, I realized that all financial gurus were doing the same thing with their own money. But none were doing it for their clients or talking about it.

This included high-profile investors such as Robert Kiyosaki, Dave Ramsey, Grant Cardone, Cathie Wood, and even Warren Buffett. Even their mere definition of investing was different than the types of investments they talk about on investment channels like Bloomberg, CNBC, and Fox Business.

Discovering the Real Definition of Investing

Most people make the mistake of thinking the word *investing* only refers to monetary assets like stocks or real estate. But the truth is, investing has a deeper meaning. Understanding the root meaning of investing will help you utilize investing in a more profound way, like self-made millionaires and billionaires do; therefore, you'll accelerate your financial freedom.

The word *invest* comes from the Latin word *investire,* which means to "clothe" or "dress someone in official garments." Thus, to invest in someone is to endow them with a new role or responsibility.

So, one way to interpret *investing* is that you become the new version of yourself, permitting yourself to become more powerful, embodying the person you desire to become, the future you.

You can accomplish this by investing in different assets, the most important being yourself.

You can be an asset because no matter who the president is and regardless of the economic conditions, what is going on geopolitically, and where you go, you will always have access to *you*!

REMEMBER

If you become your most important value asset, you can get dropped off in the middle of a desert, and you'll come up with a way to create value, create something out of nothing, and make the world around you a better place. But of course, there are other assets you can invest in, and then if you put them together, also known as compound, you get to accelerate your financial transformation.

When it comes to investing in monetary assets, investing means *making your money work for you*. (See Figure 1-3.) But self-made millionaires and billionaires never rely on just one type of investment. They compound three types of investments on top of each other, and then they continue compounding these three investments over and over again. The following are the three types of investments (see Figure 1-4):

>> **Investing in yourself:** This is your most valuable asset.

>> **Investing in your extensions:** This is your career, business, or any other extension of you that generates income.

>> **Investing in external assets:** These are other people's assets, like their companies or other financial assets. In finance, they can come in different forms like private equity, stocks, cryptocurrency, real estate, and all other financial assets that would allow you to take a piece of other people's value creation.

FIGURE 1-3: Making your money work for you with investing.

Source: *triplecompounding.com*

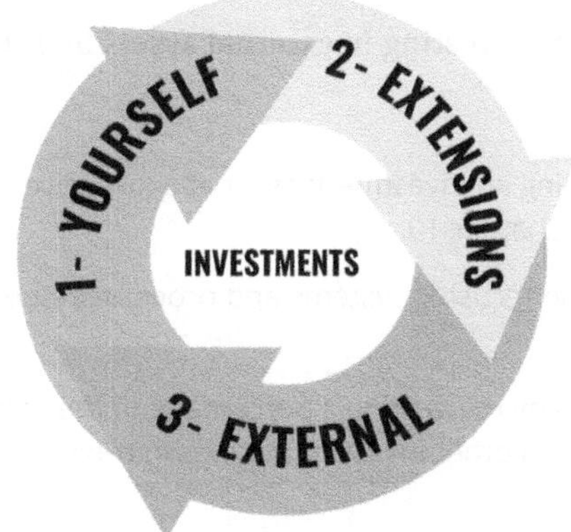

FIGURE 1-4: The three investments you compound in triple compounding.

Source: triplecompounding.com

Flip to Chapter 2 to get an overview of all the different assets you can invest in.

But my discoveries didn't end here. Not only do they compound three types of investments, but they also take it three steps further! At each investment level, they compound three actions (see Figure 1-5) that allow them to grow their investments much faster than people who don't take all three actions. This is how they maximize the same 24 hours you and I have.

The three actions they compound are

>> Generate

>> Automate

>> Accelerate

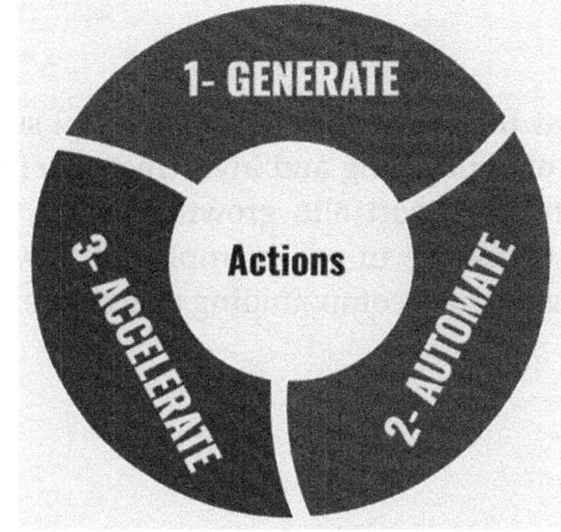

FIGURE 1-5: The three actions you compound in triple compounding.

Source: triplecompounding.com

For example, when it comes to investing in external assets like stocks, here's how this would work:

>> **Generate** income by buying an investment asset at a low price and selling at a high price, as I explain in Chapter 10.

>> **Automate** these investments using systems and processes (see Part 4 of this book).

>> **Accelerate** their portfolio by reinvesting a percentage of the income generated in the previous steps in other investment types in triple compounding.

When you put it all together, triple compounding for the purpose of wealth creation looks something like Figure 1-6.

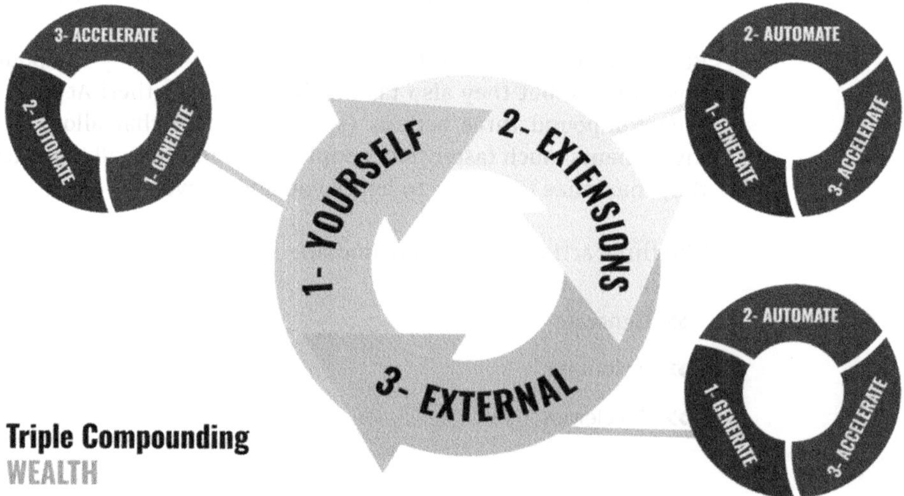

Source: *triplecompounding.com*

It became apparent to me that these role models of financial success all pretend that all their wealth comes from budgeting and investing only in external assets, but in reality, they accelerate their portfolio growth beyond the rule of 72 by triple-compounding. Flip to Chapter 2 to see examples of how these self-made millionaires and billionaires used triple compounding to accelerate their portfolios.

Using Triple Compounding to Change My Life

As I did more research on how self-made millionaires and billionaires actually make their fortune, I realized that if I actually wanted my financial freedom to become a reality, I needed to stop doing what Dave Ramsey was *saying* to do with *my* money and instead start doing what Dave Ramsey was *doing* with *his* money! I couldn't rely on just one type of compounding. Not even two.

I had to level up my game and start triple-compounding. I started to

>> Generate, automate, and accelerate my investments in myself by hiring high-level coaches, generating new skills, doing them over and over again until they became an automated habit, and unlocking a new version of myself. (I explain how this works in Chapter 4.)

>> Generate, automate, and accelerate my income generation by investing in my business, Invest Diva. (Flip to Chapter 5 for more on generating income.)

>> Generate, automate, and accelerate my portfolio by investing a fixed percentage of my income in external assets such as stocks and cryptocurrencies. (Flip to Chapter 6 for all the ways you can invest in external assets.)

Some savvy readers may see this and conclude that triple compounding is more focused on generating income with your business or selling courses online. If that is you, let me tell you a story.

As I started following the self-made millionaire's triple-compounding template, within a few years, in 2021, I hit a milestone of $1 million in cash flow generated in my business. I was a member of Russell Brunson's entrepreneurship Inner Circle. To celebrate this milestone, I received the Two Comma Club award (see Figure 1-7), which he gives to business owners who generate a million dollars in revenue using ClickFunnels, his software company.

However, after all my ad spending, expenses, travel, taxes, and staff payments, I probably only netted around $500,000.

Revenue and net income are different. *Net profit* (also called net income, bottom line, or net earnings) is the amount of money a business has left after deducting all expenses from its total revenue. It represents the actual profit a company makes.

FIGURE 1-7: When I received the Two Comma Club award from Russell Brunson.

Source: triplecompounding.com

When I lined up to accept my award, I was surrounded by other business owners who also had won the same award for generating a million dollars in revenue. As I started talking to them, I discovered something shocking: More than half of these entrepreneurs had a net profit of zero.

You may be wondering how that is even possible. The reason is that most people confuse cash flow with net income. Most people who generate a cash flow of $1 million may call themselves millionaires, even if they have a net-zero profit.

This is not the correct definition of a millionaire. Flip to Chapter 2 to discover the six types of millionaires and which one you should aspire to become.

REMEMBER

If you can't manage $1,000, you can't manage $1,000,000. But because I already knew how to accelerate my income by compounding external assets, in the same time frame, my $500,000 net income had triple-compounded to $1.5 million. (See Figure 1-8.)

This means that while other entrepreneurs were only growing their business income (but mismanaging their finances), I had already tripled what I earned from my business, using the third phase of triple compounding in my investment portfolio. (For more about this phase, flip to Chapter 10.) This means I've given myself the Golden Diamond award for reaching a million dollars in my investment portfolio — a more accurate measurement of your financial health than generating a million-dollar cash flow.

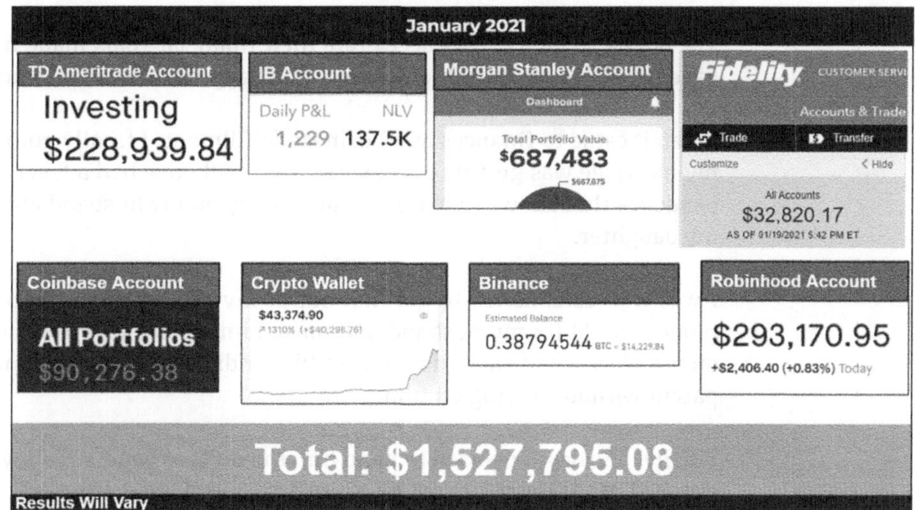

FIGURE 1-8: My triple compounding portfolio in January 2021.

Source: triplecompounding.com

This is when I started teaching the triple-compounding methods I share in this book with my Accelerator members, a group of high-level professionals — from doctors, lawyers, and corporate employees to stay-at-home moms, entrepreneurs, and artists — in many different countries who seek my expertise as their mentor. Using the same method, hundreds of my students have now received our six- and seven-figure portfolio Diamond awards as they reach their financial goals one after another. (See Figure 1-9.)

FIGURE 1-9: The Golden Diamond award.

Source: triplecompounding.com

The ability to help others accelerate their financial goals made my heart sing and gave me a level of fulfillment, pride, and happiness that I was not expecting.

When it came to finances and business fulfillment, I finally got it right. However, my marriage was getting even worse. I'd finally reached a level of financial independence that allowed me not to have to rely on my husband and also take care of my daughter.

I was well established to get him out of my life for good. Secretly, I hoped this money would fix my husband and make him behave how I wanted him to, but it didn't. Now, I had enough money to file for divorce and support myself as a single parent without relying on him.

Finally, one day, I decided to hand him the divorce papers. To my surprise, he was shocked. He asked if I would give him a second chance. I agreed but was convinced nothing was going to change. I did it for the sake of our daughter. What happened after that was crazy.

Inspired by my success, he quit his job, which was burning him out. This allowed him to focus on his new passion from home, and as we spent more time together, we were gradually able to heal our broken relationship.

Triple compounding not only gave me full control over my money and peace of mind about my financial future, but it also gifted us with financial freedom.

Then our financial freedom led to mobility freedom, career freedom, and time freedom for my entire family. Now we're each other's biggest cheerleaders, and we're building our empire as a team.

This is when I realized that triple compounding can actually be applied to more than just wealth. You can apply it to health and relationships as well.

Here's the full spectrum of triple compounding. (See Figure 1-10):

>> Investments you make:

- Yourself

- Your extensions

- External assets

» Actions you take at each phase:

- Generate

- Automate

- Accelerate

» Foundations you stake:

- Wealth

- Health

- Relationships

I occasionally host online live events to help people implement the triple compounding methods I teach in this book with me in real time. We call it Triple Compounding Live. Go to `https://www.triplecompounding.com/live` to see if there are any events coming up.

FIGURE 1-10: Triple compounding in life.

Source: triplecompounding.com

In Chapter 11, I reveal how triple compounding enables you to amplify your impact and harmonize your masculine and feminine energies, helping you reach ultimate fulfilment without burning out.

INTEGRATING THE NUMEROLOGY OF TRIPLE COMPOUNDING

If you're into numerology like I am, you may find it fascinating that the complete Triple Compounding system includes three sets of three, which brings the whole thing to the number nine.

Nine is the number of completion. It's the last single digit before the sequence resets (1 to 9), symbolizing the *end of a cycle*.

Nine is also the number of integration. It reflects the whole experience, the summation of your cycle. And it also happens to be my favorite number.

This is how, integrating all this from 2022 to 2025, I not only went from handing divorce papers to my husband to falling back in love with him while our net worth tripled from $5 million to $15 million, but I'm also healthier than I've ever been, living in my dream home.

Chapter **2**

Understanding Real-Life Triple Compounding

Gone are the days when you could go to college, get a good job, and retire comfortably on your government-backed retirement account. But I have good news: Building a comfortable retirement is now easier than ever, so it's no wonder the number of millionaires in the United States has tripled in the past decade. Nearly 6 percent of Americans now have more than $10 million net worth. The bad news is that most people are still following the old playbook, and it's failing them.

In this chapter, I explain how most self-made millionaires used triple compounding and how you can start applying the same framework to your life.

You can use triple compounding in any country as long as you have access to the internet. The principles of triple compounding are universal, and you can tweak any of the frameworks to make it work in your country.

REMEMBER

Examining Examples of Triple Compounding

When my marriage was going through a rough patch, I was desperately looking for a way to become financially independent quickly so I wouldn't have to rely on my husband for alimony. (Don't worry; as I share in Chapter 1, this is a happy-ending story.) Once I became financially free using the methods I share in this book, I was able to use that money to heal our relationship by investing in top relationship coaches. I also retired my husband from his corporate job, which was burning him out! It's a modern-day fairy tale story, if you will. *<Insert fairy dust.>*

When I was doing research to figure out ways to ensure my financial independence, I discovered a template that most self-made millionaires use.

WARNING

This template is powerful, but it may rub some readers the wrong way because it shows how the wealthy really make their money.

TIP

If you're serious about creating a comfortable financial future, you have two options. One is to get angry about the framework. The second is to model success without reinventing the wheel. This doesn't mean you have to do exactly what other people have done, but you can model their template.

I call this template Triple Compounding, and I've simplified it into three categories.

>> **Generating:** This is income generated from exchanging your time for money.

>> **Automating:** This is income generated from a *one-time* investment of time or money that continues generating automatic income indefinitely.

>> **Accelerating:** This is income generated from leveraging and combining your skills, money, and time with someone else's assets.

First, I want to showcase some millionaires you may know of, explain what they're famous for, and describe how they actually made their fortune.

Robert Kiyosaki: Real estate investor

Robert Kiyosaki came to fame with his bestselling book *Rich Dad, Poor Dad* (Warner Business Books, 2000). He's helped millions of people with financial literacy. Most people would attribute Kiyosaki's wealth to his smart investments in real estate, precious metals like gold, and *cryptocurrency*, a type of digital currency (like Bitcoin) that uses cryptographic techniques to secure transactions. However, when you dig into his wealth ecosystem, you discover it's deeper than most people think.

Here are the methods he *really* uses to make money. I've indicated their triple-compounding categories.

>> **Book sales and royalties (automating):** What Kiyosaki makes from his book is automated income generated from a one-time investment of time and money. He continues to get paid on the sales and royalties for the rest of his life on auto (as long as new copies of the book continue to sell).

>> **Speaking engagements (generating):** Kiyosaki generates income by physically doing something and exchanging his time for money. You can also call this *grinding* to generate income. See Chapter 11 to discover how grinding contributes to your financial impact.

>> **Rich Dad company (generating):** He invests time and money in his business to generate an income.

>> **Business ventures and partnerships (accelerating):** When he leverages other people's assets, talent, and time, Kiyosaki accelerates his income-generating potential.

>> **Licensing and franchising (automating):** When Kiyosaki creates something and then licenses and franchises it to get paid while others deliver on what he created, he's automating wealth building.

>> **Investments in stocks and commodities (accelerating):** He puts the money he generates from his other endeavors to work in the markets to accelerate his wealth creation.

>> **Real estate investments (accelerating):** He also accelerates his portfolio by investing in real estate.

Thanks to this triple-compounding ecosystem, Robert Kiyosaki has been able to amass a $100 million net worth even though he has the same 24 hours per day that you and I have.

Dave Ramsey: Budgeter

Dave Ramsey is a personal finance expert known for helping people manage debt and budget to build wealth. Most people assume he built his wealth using the same methods he teaches, focusing mainly on budgeting. But when you look into how he amassed his fortune of more than $55 million, you'll discover a different story.

Here are the methods he *really* uses to make money and their triple-compounding category breakdown.

>> **Book sales and royalties (automating):** The recurring automated income comes from a one-time investment of time and money into writing a book.

>> *The Ramsey Show* **(generating):** Ramsey generates income by putting time, money, and effort into his show.

>> **Financial Peace University courses (automating):** Ramsey created the course once and sells it over and over again on auto.

>> **Ramsey+ membership subscriptions (automating):** With this subscription-based offer to Ramsey's money tools and courses, he compounds the sales generated from each customer he acquired and maintains on auto indefinitely.

>> **Endorsed local providers program (accelerating):** This is a paid referral program that connects people with Ramsey's local providers; he gets paid because of other people's efforts.

>> **Live events and speaking engagements (generating):** Ramsey generates income by personally grinding as he makes public appearances.

>> **Business coaching (generating):** He exchanges his time for people's money to coach them.

>> **Product sales and merchandise (automating):** He creates products once and sells them repeatedly.

>> **Advertising and partnerships (accelerating):** Ramsey generates income by leveraging other people's assets, talent, and time, which accelerates his income-generating potential.

>> **Investing in mutual funds (accelerating):** Ramsey recommends investing in mutual funds, which allow you to invest in many companies at once. Chapter 6 explains why mutual funds may not be the optimal form of investing due to reverse compounding, something I dive deeper into in Chapter 5.

Budgeting isn't even one of Ramsey's top 10 ways of wealth creation!

Grant Cardone: Businessman

Grant Cardone is an American businessman known for his sales training programs and aggressive approach to business. Here are the additional methods he uses to amass his $600 million net worth and their triple-compounding category breakdown:

>> Sales and marketing training for Cardone University (automating)

>> Books and publications (automating)

>> Live events and speaking engagements (generating)

>> Online courses and coaching programs (automating)

>> Social media and content monetization (automating)

>> Merchandise sales (automating)

>> Real estate investments (accelerating)

>> Investments in other businesses (accelerating)

>> Grant Cardone license and franchising (automating)

>> YouTube ad revenue and sponsorships (accelerating)

>> Bitcoin investing (accelerating)

Aside from traditional investments like stocks, real estate, and private equity, Cardone also invests in alternative, less traditional investments like art and other collectibles.

Notice how he has much more automating and accelerating in his triple-compounding system than generating? This shows up on his bottom line! He has a net worth of $600 million with a $4.7 billion family portfolio under his management compared to Dave Ramsey's net worth of $55 million. I explain how automating helps you accelerate your freedom in Chapters 11 through 15.

Cathie Wood: Wall Street investor

Cathie Wood is an investor and the founder of investment management firm Ark Invest. She is known for her aggressive investments in disruptive technologies, particularly in emerging high-tech companies.

Here are the methods that show the full picture of how she's built her estimated $250 million net worth and their triple-compounding category breakdown:

>> ARK Invest management fees (automating)

In Chapter 1, I explain that money managers like Cathie Wood charge a management fee that can compound over the years. Although this would be reverse compounding and would cost you, it is forward compounding on auto for Wood, which is when compounding makes *you* — not others — money.

- **》** Ownership of ARK Invest (generating)

- **》** Book deals and media appearances (generating)

- **》** Direct investments in ARK ETFs (accelerating)

- **》** Selling ARK's research and data (generating)

- **》** Licensing and partnerships (accelerating)

- **》** Speaking engagements and conferences (generating)

- **》** Private investments in disruptive start-ups (accelerating)

- **》** Board memberships and advisory roles (generating)

Warren Buffett: Greatest investor of all time

Warren Buffett is an American investor known for his success in the stock market. He is often called the Oracle of Omaha. But even the greatest investor of all time hasn't made *all* his money from investing.

Here are the methods that show the full picture of how he built his $146.6 billion net worth and their triple–compounding category breakdown:

- **》** Ownership and leadership of Berkshire Hathaway (generating).

- **》** Stock investments and dividends (accelerating).

- **》** Insurance float (automating).

  Berkshire Hathaway owns multiple insurance companies (Geico, Gen Re), which collect premiums up front before paying out claims. They automatically generate an income for Buffett. Read Chapter 17 to discover how you can use insurance in your triple-compounding system.

- **》** Investing in private companies and start-ups (accelerating)

  Berkshire occasionally makes private investments or private equity. Flip to Chapter 7 to find out how this works.

- **》** Minimizing taxes (generating).

  Buffett uses long-term investing tax strategies to save on taxes. Chapter 18 explains how you can tackle your taxes and grow your income legally.

- **》** Books, speaking fees, and media influence (generating).

>> Modest personal expenditures (generating).

    Buffett and his family keep more of their money with frugal living, turning modest personal expenditures into a method to generate capital that can be invested and compounded over time.

Hah! Turns out that you can't make money you don't have work for you! Even Warren Buffett's most common technique is generating! He also has some automation on the backend, like insurance, that most people don't even know about.

Kiana Danial: Author

After I discovered the template for triple compounding, I started applying it to my own financial freedom journey. Since publishing my first book, *Invest Diva's Guide to Making Money in Forex* (McGraw-Hill Education, 2012), I have reinvented myself time and time again. It wasn't until 2021 that I finally put all the pieces of the triple-compounding puzzle together and achieved financial independence with a net worth of $1 million. Once I figured out the template, I was able to accelerate my portfolio quickly and achieve my financial freedom number of $5 million in 2022!

If you're not sure what your financial freedom number is, check out Chapter 1 to calculate it.

Here's what my Triple Compounding system looks like at the time of writing:

>> Ownership and leadership of Invest Diva (generating)

>> Stock investments and dividends (accelerating)

>> Cryptocurrency investments (accelerating)

>> Book deals and speaking engagements (generating)

>> Online courses and coaching programs (automating)

>> Social media and content monetization (automating)

>> Investments in other businesses (accelerating)

>> Insurance float (automating)

>> Minimizing taxes (generating)

I continue adding pillars to my Triple Compounding system. Every year, I focus on a new investment in myself, a new investment in my income-generating extension, and a new external investment category. For example, in 2025, I'm investing my time in writing this new book (generating), which will then contribute to my future automated income potential (automating). I'm also getting involved in private equity and using insurance as an external investment vehicle (accelerating).

This is exactly how I tripled my net worth in the past three years, from $5 million in 2022 to $15 million in 2025.

Can you see that I'm not teaching theory in this book? I'm telling you what I've done and continue to do!

FINDING ME ONLINE (AND AVOIDING MY IMPERSONATORS)

I routinely share my triple-compounding strategies and the latest updates on my website and social media channels.

There are thousands of scammers who create accounts using my pictures and videos to pretend to be me and lure people to fall for their scams. Some people have fallen for scams and lost up to $50,000 to these impersonators. Here are my *official* accounts and website URLs:

- **Instagram:** @investdiva
- **Facebook:** https://facebook.com/kianadanial
- **TikTok:** @kianadanial
- **YouTube:** https://youtube.com/investdiva
- **X:** @kianadanial
- **Bluesky:** @investdiva
- **Blog:** https://blog.triplecompounding.com/
- **Official website:** https://investdiva.com
- **Triple Compounding free Masterclass:** https://triplecompounding.com

Breaking Down the Different Types of Investment Assets

All the people I talk about in this chapter have three things in common:

>> They invest in themselves to acquire a success mindset that helps them generate more income.

>> They invest in an income-generating extension of themselves, like their own business or their job, and then they automate that process of generating income. Whether you have a business that automates your income-generation process or you're an employee who can figure out a way to increase your paycheck and commissions each month, you can find a way to generate more income.

>> They invest in other people's businesses and talents, whether through direct partnerships or private equity, stocks, and other financial assets.

They then compound all three to officially become a triple compounder!

Triple compounders often automate all parts of their system to accelerate their profits without physically being involved. See Chapter 9 to see how you can automate various elements of your triple-compounding system.

Investing in yourself

People who want to escape the rat race and achieve financial freedom often overlook the importance of having the right mindset. However, research shows that mindset is the foundation of one's ability to generate wealth.

In fact, in his research and study of the wealthiest people alive during his time, author Napoleon Hill came to two unique conclusions:

>> All self-made wealthy people have certain characteristics in common.

>> None of the people were born with these characteristics!

Isn't that an amazing insight? Every successful person develops this mindset by investing in themselves. Even though Napoleon Hill and the successful people of his time are all long gone, this stands true.

All self-made wealthy people admit that they first invested in themselves to acquire the success mindset. That gave them the confidence to bet on themselves so that they could generate more income, which is the first phase of triple compounding.

In Chapter 4, I explain the necessary steps to invest in yourself and develop a wealthy mindset.

Investing in your income-generating extension

The purpose of investing in financial assets like stocks and cryptocurrency is to make your money work for you. But you can't make money you don't have work for you!

Investing in external assets like stocks and cryptocurrency before investing in yourself to generate income involves huge risks. When you buy stocks without actually having money you've already generated, you're borrowing money to buy. Due to the volatile nature of such financial assets, investing with money you don't have can cause you to lose the little you may have and more. This is exactly why 96 percent of retail traders *lose* money in the stock market. Chapter 3 explains more about different risks and how to manage them.

Before starting to invest in online financial markets or other people's businesses, you must make sure of two things:

» You're generating an income.

» Your income is higher than your expenses.

Now, you may say, "But Kiana! That's easy for you to say! I'm already working three jobs and can barely make ends meet. How can I do this without burning out even more?"

You must become *resourceful*.

There are so many temporary things you can do to become resourceful and invest in yourself or in your extension. Here are some examples:

» Getting gig work, such as driving for Uber, delivering for Uber Eats or DoorDash, or doing personal shopping for Instacart or Shipt

» Babysitting

>> Waiting tables or being a barista

>> Writing AI prompts for ChatGPT (it can pay $30K per year as a side gig)

>> Mowing your neighbor's lawn

You're not trying to find something that will become your career. You're just trying to find ways to generate more income quickly. You want to reach your ultimate goal faster, like you're using a bridge.

Chapter 5 outlines the five income-generating categories you can consider.

A PERSONAL EXAMPLE OF BECOMING RESOURCEFUL

I got fired from my job, and my situation was so bad that I didn't even have money to pay rent. I failed every job interview, and I didn't speak English properly at that time, so I felt unemployable. A friend was away, so I was sleeping on her couch in exchange for looking after her five cats.

I'm not even a cat person, so while I stayed there, I was feeling sorry for myself while trying to keep the cats off my bed. Then, I came across this quote from Tony Robbins: "It's not the lack of resources that limits us, but the lack of resourcefulness."

That's when it hit me: I had to become resourceful to get myself out of the mess I'd created. So, I decided to snap out of playing victim, invest in myself, and learn a skill to generate income.

I had noticed a financial company was looking for a video news reporter, so I thought, "If I can read off a teleprompter, I can get that job."

I invested in a coaching program that taught people how to read off a teleprompter. That helped me get the side gig, and the side gig allowed me to increase my income potential, which was the steppingstone to my now multimillion-dollar Invest Diva business.

You may think, "But Kiana, if you were so broke, how did you pay for that program?!"

I became even more resourceful. I temporarily worked in a restaurant to save money so that I could invest in myself to learn a skill that paid me a lot more. I didn't aspire to be a restaurant server for the rest of my career. Good thing, too! I sucked at it so much that I got fired from multiple restaurants!

Investing in external assets

External assets are the final type of asset you need to invest in to complete your triple-compounding system. When you've already invested in yourself as an asset and invested in your income-generating extensions like your career, your business, or even side gigs as a steppingstone, you can start accelerating your triple compounding by investing in external assets. This means leveraging other people, businesses, or even governments' investment in themselves without having to be directly involved in the value creation. Here are some examples of what this can include:

>> Stocks

>> Crypto

>> Foreign exchange (forex)

>> Options

>> Index funds

>> Real estate

>> Private equity

>> Venture capital

>> Insurance

>> Alternative investments

Read Part 2 for information about different types of external assets you can add to your triple-compounding system.

Compounding the Three Types of Investment Assets

The word *compounding* essentially means "to put together." You'll first invest in your most important asset: yourself. Then you'll do your first compounding (1X) by also investing in your income-generating endeavor. Next, you'll do your second compounding (2X) by investing in external assets to accelerate your financial growth. At this point, you've completed the first round of three investment types, so you get to compound it by investing in yourself again (3X) to unlock your next level of financial growth.

As Tony Robbins says, if you're not growing, you're dying. Similarly, I say that if your money isn't growing, it's also dying. Triple compounding is the most complete framework to ensure that you're on the right path to reaching your fullest potential, both personally and financially.

IN THIS CHAPTER

» **Understanding the importance of risk management in triple compounding**

» **Determining your ability, willingness, and confidence to take a risk**

» **Considering compounding return versus risk**

» **Exploring different types of risks in the three triple-compounding phases**

» **Applying your risk tolerance to your investment strategy**

Chapter 3

Applying Essential Risk Management Strategies

You may be wondering whether triple compounding is really the winning formula you can use to accelerate your freedom, and you also may be wondering if the results outweigh the risks. Is triple compounding a "too good to be true" buzzword, or can you implement the formula of self-made millionaires and billionaires like Warren Buffett, Grand Cardone, and Dave Ramsey without taking more risk than you're comfortable with?

Or maybe you're excited to jump on the bandwagon, perhaps because you expect a gigantic *return* (profit) on your investment. That's basically the reward for investing. However, you can't consider return without also looking at risk. *Risk* is the uncertainty surrounding the return you generate.

In my Triple Compounding masterclass and investing books like *Cryptocurrency Investing For Dummies* (Wiley, 2023), I spend a lot of time speaking about risk and how everyone should approach it individually. What may represent a high risk for one person may not be as risky for you due to everyone's unique lifestyle and financial circumstances.

In this chapter, I cover the different levels of risk each phase of triple compounding can expose you to. I show you how to measure your exact risk tolerance. I also give an overview of methods you can use to increase your risk tolerance. This way, you get to decide which phase of triple compounding you can start with and manage your risk along the way as you build your triple-compounding system.

Measuring Exactly Where You Are Now

In Chapter 1, I show you how you can measure your financial freedom number, which is the first step of my five-step Invest Diva Diamond Analysis (IDDA) framework. (I dive deeper into that in Chapter 10.) The second step of the IDDA is called *capital analysis,* which helps you figure out exactly where you currently stand. This is kind of like using your GPS navigation system: For it to work, you must know your current location and where you want to go.

In the first step, you solidify where you want to go. In this chapter, you get to figure out exactly where you are, financially and emotionally, so that you can then move on to mapping how you will get to your goal!

This is also called measuring your current *risk tolerance* — that is, your personal ability, willingness, and confidence to take a risk. This helps you decide exactly how much you should start with and get an idea of what type of investments you should go for so that you can invest with confidence and minimize your risk.

Although most people associate their risk tolerance only with their own personal willingness to take a risk, the truth is, there's more to the story. You can't simply assume you have a low risk tolerance because you're scared of skydiving. You also can't simply assume you have a high risk tolerance because you enjoy gambling in Las Vegas.

Here are the three factors that collectively determine your real risk tolerance:

>> Your *ability* to take a risk

>> Your *willingness* to take a risk

>> Your *confidence* in the asset you're planning to invest in

Measuring your risk tolerance is the most important and foundational step you must take before starting your triple-compounding journey.

Not taking this step is the reason why 96 percent of traders lose money in the markets. They blindly follow the market noise without having a plan that is the exact fit for their ability and their willingness to take a risk.

You can find a free risk management toolkit to implement the steps I share in this chapter by attending the free Triple Compounding Masterclass at `https://www.triplecompounding.com`.

Calculating Your Ability to Take a Risk

Your ability to take a risk shows you your exact current financial strength minus any emotions or psychological factors.

There are different ways of calculating your financial ability so that you can basically become your own financial advisor and never have to rely on someone else for your financial statements. Because there are too many ways to cover in depth in this book, in the following sections, I focus on the two most important financial numbers you need to know to get a feeling about how you're doing:

>> **Your current financial snapshot:** This is what Wall Street bros would call a balance sheet, but it's really just a snapshot of your current financial situation.

>> **Your cash flow diary:** Wall Street bros would call this the statement of income and expenses, which is actually not as intimidating as their other lingo. It tells you how much money you're making *(income)* and how much you're spending *(expenses)* over a specific period.

Summing up your assets

Let's get into it without going into too much geeky stuff. Get a piece of paper and write down everything that you own that can be categorized as an asset.

An *asset* is anything you own that has value — something that can make you money now or in the future. As I mention in Chapter 1, you are the most valuable asset there is. You're priceless and not up for sale. So, for this exercise, let's leave you out of the equation and only focus on assets that you can put a monetary value on, including the following:

>> **Cash and equivalents:** Money in your bank's savings or checking account, anything you have in money markets (which is like a financial waiting room

where people and institutions park their cash temporarily while earning a little interest), and cash under your mattress (hopefully in a safe place!)

>> **Investments:** Stocks, bonds, mutual funds, real estate, retirement accounts like your 401(k), IRA, and education savings — anything that grows in value or pays you income

>> **Physical assets:** Houses, land, cars (sometimes), gold, luxury handbags, watches, jewelry, furniture, boats, private jets, collectibles — things that can be sold for cash

>> **Business assets:** Equipment, patents, trademarks — stuff that helps a business make money

Calculating your assets can also be an awesome family dinner discussion! I love talking about money with my daughter and my husband. It helps our family get on the same page about finances, and our arguments about money are now almost nonexistent. Even when we have a financial disagreement, we know exactly how to address it because we have our financial mindset right. So, use this exercise to open the dialogue with your family in a fun way. How fun is it to go through all the stuff that you own? And you may even find things you completely forgot about that you can now use to increase your risk tolerance!

Taking note of your liabilities

Once you get a general understanding of the total value of your current assets, you can move on to get a general understanding of your current liabilities — that is, everything that you *owe.*

Although most people consider liabilities to be bad things, you need to know that not all debt is bad. *Good debt* is the type of leverage wealthy people use to become wealthy! In fact, right now, debt is my favorite type of income!

Here's how to tell the difference between bad debt and good debt:

>> **Bad debt:** This is a liability on something that doesn't make you money. It is when you go into debt to buy things like luxury bags, a car that depreciates in value, televisions, and all the other things people go into debt for to give the appearance of having more money than they actually do. This is exactly the mindset I had a decade ago, and it pushed me into a welfare house. That's why I call this mindset a *Welfare Diva* mindset. (Welfare Diva is not to be confused with Welfare Queen, the slang term used in reference to people who supposedly try to defraud the government welfare system.)

The goal is to avoid compounding bad debt, which is a burden on wealth.

» **Good debt:** This is known as funding or leverage. It's money you may owe to acquire an asset that grows in value. For example, your investment in this book, even if you had to leverage the bank's money to get it, is actually an asset. Because this is going to put you and your family on the trajectory of taking control of your finances and making your money work for you, your initial investment in the book will keep on compounding for years to come as you become financially free. Once I snapped out of my Welfare Diva mindset and started using good debt to accelerate my financial freedom, I essentially transformed into what I now call a *Millionaire Diva*.

The goal is to leverage funding to create wealth. Leverage is the means to get to wealth. In fact, if it wasn't for leverage, most self-made millionaires and billionaires wouldn't even have had the chance to get started.

Although good debt is indeed better than bad debt, when measuring your ability to take a risk, you must add both good and bad debt under your liabilities column.

Evaluating your net worth

Once you have a rough draft of your good debt and bad debt as I describe in the preceding section, use a calculator to add all the values of your combined assets and the value of your combined liabilities. Then you're ready to calculate your net worth, which uses this formula:

Net Worth *equals* Total Assets *minus* Total Liabilities

All you have to do is punch in the total value of your assets from the first column and then subtract the total value of your liabilities that you got under the second column. (Figure 3-1 illustrates this idea.)

Your *net worth* is your financial scorecard — a simple way to measure how much you're really worth (in money, not personality!).

This number is going to be your first clue in your capital analysis and your risk tolerance. Here's an example:

If you own a house worth $500,000, have $50,000 in savings, and have $100,000 in investments, your assets total *$650,000*.

If you also have a mortgage of $300,000, student loans of $50,000, and $10,000 in credit card debt, your liabilities total *$360,000*.

$650,000 – $360,000 = $290,000

Your net worth is *$290,000*.

FIGURE 3-1:
Your financial snapshot. Assets minus liabilities equals your net worth.

Source: `triplecompounding.com`

TIP

If your net worth is positive by a lot, then your ability to take a risk is higher. If it's negative by a lot, and most of your liabilities are considered bad debt, then your risk tolerance is lower. If it's break-even or somewhere in between, then your risk tolerance is somewhere in between.

REMEMBER

Measuring your net worth gives you an insight into your current financial situation at any given time. You need to recalculate your net worth at least once per year or anytime something major happens in your life, such as if you receive an inheritance, get married, or make a huge lump-sum investment like buying a house.

Tracking your income

The next step in calculating your ability to take a risk is tracking your cash flow in a diary. To figure out the healthiness of your cash flow, you first need to identify all sources of income you receive during a specific period. Write them all down under an income column. You can go by a monthly or a yearly basis.

REMEMBER

Use the same time frame in all three columns of your cash flow diary.

Some examples of income include the following:

>> **Your salary or wages:** This is money you earn from your job.

>> **Your rental income:** This is income gained from any properties you own.

>> **Your business income:** This can include dividends and interest payments. If you have periodic capital gains income through swing trades or options trades, you can include them here. Flip to Chapter 5 to find out more about all the different ways you can generate income from within your investment portfolio.

>> **Side hustle or freelance income:** I include all my commissions from affiliate marketing, my payments from my books, and what YouTube and Instagram pay me for content.

>> **Government benefits:** If you're retired or receive any type of government benefits like Social Security, unemployment benefits, or food stamps, you can include them here.

If you are fresh out of college, just got fired, or are disabled with no income, you can put a big zero right there and not stress.

The purpose of this exercise isn't to make you feel bad. It's just to give you a solid understanding of where you stand financially. Also, in this book, you can find many alternative methods to increase your income. Flip to Chapter 5 to review some of the most common approaches.

Reviewing your expenses

Tracking your income may be exciting, but you can't consider income without also looking at your expenses. To complete your cash flow diary, you must add up your expenses over the same period of time that you calculated your income.

You can create categories for your expenses to make organization easier. Common expense categories include

>> **Your salary or wages:** This is money you earn from your job.

>> **Housing:** Rent/mortgage, property taxes, and utilities

>> **Transportation:** Car payment, insurance, fuel, and public transportation

>> **Food:** Groceries and dining out

>> **Debt payments:** Credit cards and loans

>> **Healthcare:** Insurance premiums and medical expenses

>> **Entertainment and leisure:** Movies, cable and streaming services, dining out, and your hobbies

>> **Savings and investments:** Any money you're putting away to save or invest over a set period of time

>> **Miscellaneous expenses:** Clothing, gifts, and personal care

Doing this exercise for the first time may shock you. I remember when I first did it as I was going through the Certified Financial Planning (CFP) program to earn my CFP certification, and I was so shocked to see how little things added up both in the income and the expenses columns. I remember getting super angry at my husband when I found out he was spending so much money on computer components.

Your spending habits can give you amazing tips when it comes to choosing the assets you'd like to invest in. For example, as I was going through our expenses, I found out that my husband (who's a huge gamer) was spending tons of money on buying stocks of computer gaming–related companies like Nvidia and AMD. I thought, *If he's spending this much money on them, I may as well invest in their companies.* And I did. We both bought AMD stock when it was just a dollar per share and bought Nvidia's stock when it was less than a dollar back in 2015. Over the next decade, we made hundreds of thousands of dollars on those investments. The profits even helped fund our dream home!

Why am I telling you this?

It's to start your transformation from a consumer to an investor, which is one of the essentials in becoming a triple compounder. As you're going through your expenses, see which companies you're spending the most with. Flip to Chapter 10 to explore how you can apply this to the third step of the IDDA: fundamental analysis.

Figuring out your bottom line

The number that is going to contribute to your risk tolerance is your net income. This is the money you actually get to keep after all the bills, taxes, and other costs are paid. It's also called your *bottom line* because it's the final number after all the financial math is done. You can calculate your net income by subtracting your total expenses from your total income (which is illustrated in Figure 3-2):

Total Income *minus* Total Expenses *equals* Net Income

If you have a positive net income, you can call yourself "cash flow positive," which indicates that you are living within your means and have a higher risk tolerance.

A negative net income is called "cash flow negative," which suggests that you are spending more than you earn, so your risk tolerance is lower.

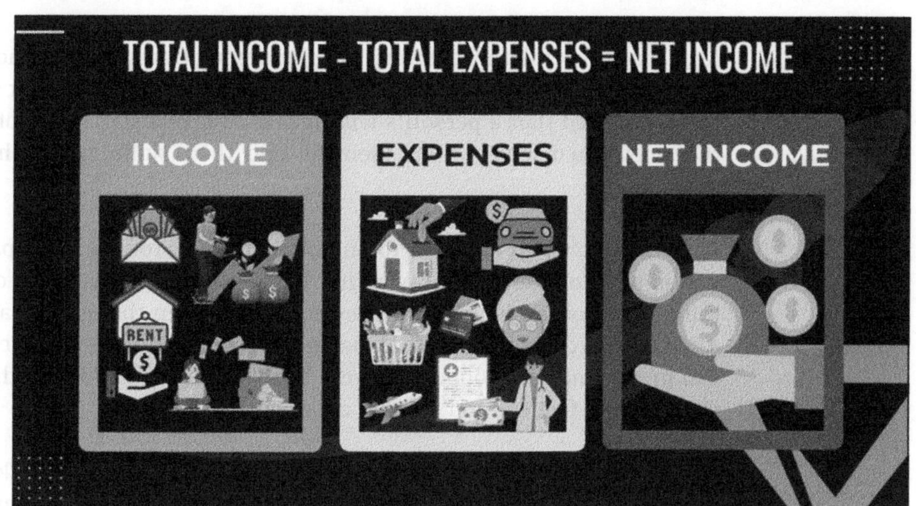

FIGURE 3-2: Your Cash Flow Diary. Total Income minus Total Expenses equals your Net Income.

Source: triplecompounding.com

REMEMBER

You may be upset because your expenses are currently more than your income and savings. Or you may be super happy because you were a big saver or had lucrative side hustles that you may have even forgotten about, so you feel great about where you stand.

There is no shame in either. The point of this is not to get you down or to fill you up with overconfidence. The point is simply to open your eyes so that you can take measured risks as you build your triple-compounding system.

Measuring Your Willingness to Take a Risk

The second component of your risk tolerance is your willingness to take a risk. This can depend on your age, family situation, health, and life cycle.

For example, between the ages of 25 and 45, you're probably more growth oriented. But even then, big life events can change your risk tolerance. For example, I was more willing to take a risk before I became a mom.

Between the ages of 45 and 60, you may identify as conservative and more protection oriented.

Some people see the years above 60 as their retirement years, so they may be concerned about generating income and protecting what they have — or maybe they are thinking about gifting to their grandchildren.

Age-based risk tolerance is very popular among traditional financial advisors, but I'm not convinced your age alone should dictate your investment strategy. In fact, I have realized that a person's willingness to take a risk has a lot to do with how they view themselves, their identity, and their skills rather than their age or personality.

For example, when it comes to outdoor activities, for the most part, I have a low willingness to take a risk. I wouldn't book a skydiving session. I don't like swimming in the ocean when the waves are rough, even though I'm a good swimmer. And I always drive in the slow lane on a highway. I don't even like changing lanes. I'm pretty much the opposite of my husband, who would race through the lanes in his super-fast car and take on a tsunami for fun.

Now, interestingly, skiing is when things flip. When it comes to skiing, I tackle the toughest slopes. I thrive on Double Black Diamonds — the mountain's steepest, most challenging, and downright scariest runs. The steeper the slope and the bigger the moguls, the more fun I have, even though skiing is one of the most dangerous outdoor sports.

Why does my willingness to take a risk suddenly change when it comes to skiing? It's because I have an expert skier *identity* that overshadows my natural risk aversion.

I've been skiing since I was three years old, and everyone in my family is an avid skier. You become the average of the five people you hang out with the most, so I adopted the avid skier identity. This identity allowed me to develop my skiing skills more easily, and as a result, I'm more willing to tackle the more high-risk slopes.

This is also true when it comes to your willingness to take financial risks. The cool news is that by adopting a new identity, you can change your willingness to take a risk and potentially say hello to your more financially secure future self. Chapter 4 can help you discover how to embody your future self now.

Measuring Your Confidence

The third factor determining your overall risk tolerance is your confidence in the asset you plan to invest in. This certainly applies to investing in yourself. If you have a habit of keeping your word to yourself, you will trust yourself more to follow through with the commitments you make to yourself.

Your self-confidence is directly impacted by your ability or disability to keep your promises to yourself. People often ask me how I have such high self-confidence. I certainly wasn't born with it. Just as you gain trust in someone who always keeps their word to you, you can establish trust with yourself when you keep your word to yourself.

When investing in assets other than myself, especially when investing in external assets like stocks and cryptocurrency, I use a method that I call my *Confidence Compass* — two questions that I ask myself. My honest answers typically reveal my exact level of confidence in the asset I'm buying and the price I'm paying for it.

Here are the two confidence compass questions:

>> If I invest at this price and the price drops by 50 percent tomorrow, will I freak out?

>> If I *don't* invest at this price and its price *skyrockets* by 50 percent tomorrow, will I beat myself up?

Of course, both scenarios kind of suck, but you have to be really honest with yourself as to which scenario sucks more and adjust your investment strategy accordingly.

If you freak out, beat yourself up, or panic, in most cases, your confidence in this asset is low. You can increase your confidence in a financial asset by researching more about it. Flip to Chapter 10 to explore fundamental analysis.

You can use similar confidence compass questions when deciding whether to sell an asset. Here's an example:

>> If I sell at this price and the price goes up by 50 percent tomorrow, will I regret selling too early?

>> If I *don't* sell at this price and its price *drops* by 50 percent tomorrow, will I beat myself up for not selling at a higher price?

Digging into Different Kinds of Risk

Risk is a part of life — especially when it comes to money. Whether you're investing, trading, running a business, or just deciding where to park your cash, you're always balancing risk and reward.

Don't let risk frighten you. After all, life itself is risky. Knowing your risk tolerance helps you decide what kind of risk you can confidently take so that you can reap the rewards while being able to sleep peacefully at night. Not all risk is equal. The following sections describe the various types of triple-compounding risks.

Compounding risk

Compounding is a powerful tool — when it works in your favor. The same rule of compounding I explain in Chapter 1 can come and bite you in the butt if you use it in reverse. I call this *reverse compounding*; it's when, instead of earning with compounding, you're paying. Common compounding risks include

>> **Bad habits multiplying:** If you repeatedly make poor financial choices (like overspending or ignoring your investments), those mistakes compound over time.

>> **Debt spirals:** High-interest debt compounds just like investments — but in the wrong direction. The longer you ignore it, the bigger it gets.

>> **Market downturns:** A downturn can erase your compounded gains if your investments are heavily exposed to risk without proper diversification.

>> **Interest rate cuts:** A news headline as harmless as "interest rates have dropped" can lower your ability to compound interest, especially if you've parked all your money in places that promise high-interest payments.

>> **Inflation:** When the price of everyday shopping, like groceries, continues to go higher, you're compounding in reverse by having to pay more for the same things month after month. Inflation means your money doesn't buy as much as it used to. So, if your money is sitting under your mattress, you're exposing yourself to compounded devaluation of your money.

Investing risk

Whether you're investing in yourself, your career, or external assets, there's always a risk that you will not only not gain the rewards you hoped for but also lose everything you have!

This is why it's so important that you first measure your own ability and willingness to take a risk using the risk calculation methods I share in the previous sections. Here are some investing risks to be mindful of:

>> **Financial risk:** The financial risk of investing is that you can lose your money. This type of risk is the most obvious because companies do go bankrupt,

cryptocurrency projects can go bust, and no matter how awesome you are as a value asset, your investment in yourself may not turn out as you had hoped. Check out Chapters 6 and 7 to explore how you can manage this risk by choosing your investments wisely.

>> **Market risk:** All the Wall Street bros and other market participants' mood changes cause the financial markets, such as stocks and crypto, to go up and down like a roller coaster. Flip to Chapter 16 to find out how you can use Wall Street bros' emotions in your favor and beat them at their own game.

>> **Security risk:** Scams! Hacking! Theft! I get way too many tragic emails from people who fell for an online scam on social media. Impersonators pretending to be experts reach out to individuals and promise the world. They're getting better at it every day, and with the progress of artificial intelligence, this problem can only worsen. Make sure that you triple-check everyone online before handing over your money.

Some assets have higher risks than others. For example, investing in yourself is always a lower risk, because even if you don't succeed on your first try, the knowledge you gain is invaluable. If you persist, you will eventually gain the rewards.

Other investment assets like stocks and crypto have higher risks. In my book, *Cryptocurrency Investing For Dummies,* I dive extra deep into crypto risk management, so if by reading this book you decide to add crypto to your triple-compounding system, make sure you read my other book, too!

Trading risk

Trading is like investing on steroids. It's faster, riskier, and — if you're not careful — it can burn through your money quicker than a bad weekend in Vegas.

If, based on the previous sections in this chapter, you discover you have a low or medium risk tolerance, then you may want to consider avoiding trading and stick to investing instead. Although traders aim to make quick profits, they face unique risks the following:

>> **Volatility risk:** This is the risk of unexpected market movements. Though volatility can be a good thing, it can sometimes also catch you off guard due to a sudden move in the opposite direction from what you expected. If you aren't prepared for the market volatility, you can lose the money in your trading account.

>> **Hype risk:** This is the danger of making investment decisions based on excitement, speculation, or media buzz rather than on solid fundamentals. When a stock, cryptocurrency, or asset becomes trendy, prices often

surge — not because of real value, but because of fear of missing out (FOMO). The problem? What goes up fast often comes crashing down even faster.

>> **Leverage risk:** Borrowing money to trade (margin trading) can amplify gains but also wipe out your account if the trade goes south. This is exactly how I lost all of my money in one trade when I was just getting started. That is when I created the IDDA framework to avoid making this mistake again.

>> **Tax risk:** Profits from selling stocks, options, or crypto held for less than one year are taxed as short-term capital gains, which are treated as ordinary income. This means you can be paying anywhere from 10 percent to 37 percent in taxes (depending on your income bracket) versus a lower long-term capital gains tax rate of 0 percent, 15 percent, or 20 percent for investments held over a year.

REMEMBER

The media thrives on creating fear emotions. That is how they make money, because people are more likely to click on negative headlines. Before falling for the market noise, arm yourself with knowledge of the specific asset you're considering adding to your triple-compounding system. You have plenty of opportunities to make lots of money in the markets. Be patient and acquire the right knowledge instead of betting on the hype. An investor who trades on the hype probably doesn't even have an investment strategy — unless you call gambling a strategy! You can find different methods of strategy development in Parts 2 and 4.

Business risk

As I mention in Chapter 2, the second investment asset of your triple-compounding system is typically an extension of you, which is your business. Entrepreneurs and business owners face a different kind of financial risk. Unlike investing in stocks, where you can buy and sell shares of companies that *other people* control, running a business gives you full control, but it also ties up your time, money, and energy. Here's where things can go wrong:

>> **Cash flow risk:** A business can be profitable on paper but still struggle if cash isn't flowing in at the right time.

>> **Competition risk:** A great business idea doesn't guarantee success — especially if competitors have a better offer or marketing system.

>> **Operational risk:** Mistakes in management, hiring, or supply chains can cripple a business before it even takes off.

You can learn from all of my business mistakes and set up your wealth-generating business the right way by exploring Part 5.

Tax risk

For an average person, taxes are one of the highest expenses. Although you can take advantage of the tax mitigation techniques I dive into in Chapter 18, there are also potential financial or legal consequences you need to watch out for. Here are some examples:

>> **Noncompliance risk:** This happens when taxpayers fail to meet their tax obligations, whether by accident or on purpose. Examples include filing taxes late, underreporting income (even unintentionally), and failing to pay taxes owed, leading to interest and penalties that will then reverse-compound.

>> **Audit risk:** This is the chance of being selected for a tax audit, which can be stressful, time-consuming, and costly. You can get audited for reporting large deductions or business losses that seem unusual, claiming excessive tax credits, and frequent changes in income that raise red flags with tax authorities.

>> **Investment tax risk:** This is the risk that taxes will reduce investment returns more than expected. Investors pay taxes on capital gains and pay even more if they sell stocks within a year of purchasing them (short-term gains). Dividend taxes can also eat into stock market earnings.

Tax-efficient investing, business structuring, and estate planning can minimize tax burdens. A tax advisor or Certified Public Accountant (CPA) can help you avoid costly mistakes. Flip to Chapter 18 for more details on taxes and mitigation strategies.

Missed opportunity risk

Not all risks involve losing money. Sometimes, the biggest risk is *not acting at all*. Although playing it safe feels comfortable, staying on the sidelines can cost you in the long run.

Although most people think taxes or their mortgage is their biggest expense, the truth is, your biggest expense is not knowing how to accelerate your financial freedom. If you've spent the past year thinking about learning a new skill to generate more income or starting to invest, then you have already missed out on a year of compounding.

Here's a list of some nonmonetary risks you could be compounding that will negatively impact your future net worth:

>> **Missed-out compounding:** The biggest component of compounding is time. The best time to start compounding was 20 years ago. The second-best time is today. Figure 3-3 demonstrates the importance of time in basic compounding.

>> **Being too conservative:** Avoiding all risk can mean missing out on high-growth opportunities.

>> **Fear of change:** Holding onto a failing business, job, or investment out of fear can keep you stuck.

>> **Ignoring financial education:** The biggest missed opportunity? Not learning how money works and how to make it work for you.

FIGURE 3-3: The importance of time in compounding.

Source: triplecompounding.com

REMEMBER

If, instead of purchasing every new high-end iPhone and accessories released since 2007, you had invested that same amount of money (about $1,600 per year) in Apple stock, reinvested dividends, and optimized your purchasing price based on the techniques I share in Chapters 10 and 16, your investment could have been worth more than $640,000 in 2025.

Now you may be saying, "But Kiana! I didn't start when I was 19! What to do now?" With compounding, you need time on your side. To accelerate this process and make up for the time you lost, you need triple compounding. That's how

I started in my thirties and became financially free before I hit 40. One of my Accelerators students started triple compounding when she was a 46-year-old empty nester and accelerated her portfolio to $1 million in just three years, before her milestone fiftieth birthday!

Understanding the Time Value of Money

When I was studying for my CFP certification, I discovered that one of the most fundamental principles is the time value of money (TVM). CFPs rely on this concept to make investment decisions, calculate retirement needs, and determine how much money should be saved today for future goals.

I believe that understanding TVM shouldn't be limited to financial planners. This needs to be taught in schools, and if you're serious about becoming financially secure, you must start playing around with it.

Simply put, TVM means that a dollar today is worth more than a dollar in the future because money has the potential to grow over time through investing or earning interest. Understanding TVM helps you create a unique triple-compounding system for yourself and make better financial decisions, whether you're planning for retirement, saving for a house, or comparing different investment options.

Breaking down TVM

The time value of money is based on two key ideas.

- **Money today can earn interest or be invested:** If you have $1,000 today and invest it at a 5 percent annual return, it will grow to $1,050 in a year. If you wait a year to receive that $1,000, you miss out on the growth.

- **Inflation erodes purchasing power:** Over time, the cost of goods and services rises. If inflation is 3 percent per year, that $1,000 will buy less next year than it does today.

Because of these factors, money has different values depending on when you receive it. You can use TVM to compare financial choices and evaluate investment returns.

The five key components of TVM

You can use TVM formulas based on the following five key variables:

>> **Present value (PV):** How much money you have today (or the current value of a future sum)

>> **Future value (FV):** How much money will be worth in the future after interest or investment growth

>> **Interest rate (r or i):** The rate at which money grows (also called the discount rate or required rate of return)

>> **Number of periods (n):** The number of years (or time periods) over which the money grows

>> **Payments (PMT):** Any regular contributions or withdrawals (like savings deposits or loan payments)

Once you have decided on these five variables, you can use websites like `www.calculatorsoup.com/calculators/financial/future-value-annuity-calculator.php` to calculate the following:

>> How much you need to save today for a future goal

>> How an investment will grow over time

>> The impact of different interest rates on financial outcomes

Making up for the time lost

Many people believe that if they didn't start investing early, they've missed their chance at financial freedom. But although starting early is ideal, starting late is still better than never. This is where triple compounding comes in. You can use the TVM formula to see how you can accelerate your retirement even if you start late.

The case study in Figure 3-4 shows the retirement outcome for Lisa and Mark, both 50 years old with zero retirement savings. They both want to retire at 65, but only one of them makes smart, consistent choices to reach $1 million.

Lisa follows one of the triple-compounding methods explained in this book to hit her $1 million retirement goal, whereas Mark contributes less and hopes for the best. Specifically, Lisa realizes she started late but makes up for lost time by investing $3,155 per month in a diversified portfolio that earns 7 percent annually.

Details	Lisa (Disciplined Saver)	Mark (Minimal Saver)
Starting Age	50	50
Retirement Goal	65	65
Starting Savings	$0	$0
Monthly Contribution	$3,155	$500
Investment Return	7% annually	7% annually
Investment Period	15 years	15 years

Source: triplecompounding.com

Using the TVM calculator to solve for FV, Figure 3-5 shows how Lisa makes up for lost time without even employing higher-risk investment methods that I cover in Chapter 6 and which could increase her rate of return.

Age	Lisa's Investment Value ($3,155/month)	Mark's Investment Value ($500/month
50	0	0
55	$225,875.6	$35,796.45
60	$546,082.57	$86,542.4
65	$1,000,016.05	$158,481.15

Source: triplecompounding.com

This is proof that starting late isn't the problem; inaction is. Lisa proved that even at 50, you can still hit $1 million by making consistent, disciplined contributions. Once you determine your risk tolerance, you get to choose the way that you feel comfortable with accelerating your financial freedom. In Lisa's case, she didn't increase her rate of return and only focused on increasing her contributions.

Mark started investing, but he didn't contribute enough, and he didn't increase his rate of return, and that cost him his financial freedom.

If Lisa applies the methods that I teach in Chapter 16 to maximize her investment returns, she could reach her financial freedom even faster like many of the triple compounders in our community.

This is proof that starting late isn't the problem, inaction is. Lisa proved that even at 50, you can still hit $1 million by making consistent, disciplined contributions. Once you determine your risk tolerance, you get to choose the way that you ... feel comfortable with ...

2

Investing in the Three Asset Types in Triple Compounding

IN THIS PART . . .

Discover why investing in yourself is important.

Grow your income through income-generating extensions like your career or business.

Explore online external assets, from stocks and index funds to crypto and forex.

Discover offline external assets, including real estate, private equity, and precious metals, for long-term growth.

Chapter **4**

Investing in Yourself

I have hit rock bottom more times than I can count, but the most severe tumble was when I seemingly lost everything within a week. It was especially painful because it came on a day when I thought I'd *finally* figured everything out!

I had a well-paying job on Wall Street. I had an apartment on the Upper East Side of New York City, just like I had envisioned when I used to watch TV shows like *Sex and the City* and *Gossip Girl* when I was younger. I had a boyfriend who was a surgeon — exactly like what my parents wanted — and I thought he was about to propose!

Little did I know, things were about to change. On a day I thought I had achieved an amazing performance, I got fired. A few days later, my boyfriend dumped me. Soon after, I ran out of money to pay rent.

I had bottomed out before, but this time felt like the worst one.

I'd always thought that by the time I was 27, I would have everything figured out. I had just tasted what it felt like to have it all, and *bam*. Just like that, it was all taken away from me — again.

What are my parents going to think? What are people going to say? Where am I going to live? What if I'm not married by the time I'm 30, and my immigrant community will label me as an old maid?

I felt like a failure. I still wasn't proficient in English, my third language. My financial advisor had taken advantage of me and was going to charge me a 75 percent penalty to give back the money I had invested with them that had barely grown. I felt unemployable. I was too heartbroken to make rational relationship decisions, and now I had a new problem: My family was breaking up with me to "teach me a lesson."

It was *humiliating*. I was so angry and felt so helpless.

Deep down, I knew this was an old pattern that I kept repeating over and over again — a pattern of achieving something and then ruining everything because I felt like I didn't deserve it. It was an old habit that had me falling to rock bottom repeatedly in the past.

In this chapter, I tell you how to recognize when you're caught in a repeating pattern (like I was) and how you can begin to break the cycle.

Going from Welfare Diva to Millionaire Diva

I now refer to this pattern of building some success before losing it all as my Welfare Diva stage. "Welfare Diva" is a nickname I've given to the version of myself before I discovered triple compounding, when I still carried a victim mindset, felt stuck, and didn't believe I had control over my future. She's the opposite of the "Millionaire Diva," who takes bold, elevated action. This time, I knew I had to snap out of it before I fell lower. I was tired of my old patterns of trying to follow the normal path everyone expected me to.

I declined multiple job offers that would have kept me in the rat race. Instead, I stepped into my future self, who I now call Millionaire Diva. I became *obsessed* with learning about finance and investing. I navigated through all the conflicting strategies among the Wall Street bros. I kept pushing through even when things got tough. The result was that I hit a million dollars in my portfolio within a decade.

This was all possible because I invested in my most valuable asset — myself — first.

Mindset versus skillset versus toolset

In this book, I share tons of tools and strategies you can use to create an investment portfolio system like mine. One thing I've learned from working with my clients, though, is that a toolset alone is not enough.

You have to have a skillset and, more importantly, a mindset to accompany your toolset, or you won't get results. If you have nails and a hammer without having the mental/creative/physical capacity to use them, you can't build anything.

You need to become the person who can use the toolset. Tripling your income, tripling your net worth, tripling your abundance has everything to do with investing in yourself.

With this book, I aim to help you build generational wealth. In fact, while other coaches teach people how to make $1 million in revenue (and possibly — or not — break even at the end of the year), I help people *triple*-compound and build a $1 million portfolio that will triple-compound for years to come and get them to financial freedom fast.

In the other chapters of this book, I give you all the tools you need to use when building wealth. But as I found out, and as you will find to be true, tools alone and knowledge alone won't help you become financially free. That's why, in the following sections of this chapter, I spend some time helping you develop the mindset that will allow you to use the toolset and to develop the skillset to become a triple compounder. Would that be cool with you? Yes? Then, keep reading the following sections.

Seeing yourself as the value asset

Throughout my years and years of learning, manifesting, and growing, I've learned the number one ingredient in accelerating success is *not* the information, the visualizations, or the affirmations that mindset gurus tell you about on social media.

The number one factor in accelerating your success is to invest in the most important asset you can ever access, which is *yourself*. How can you be an asset? Because regardless of the general economic conditions of the country or what is going on geopolitically, you will always have access to *you*!

If you become your own most important value asset, you can get dropped off in the middle of a desert, and you'll come up with a way to create value, create something out of nothing, and make the world around you a better place.

Developing a Vision

Before you can build wealth, achieve financial freedom, or leverage triple compounding, you need a clear, compelling picture of the future you want to create. Author Napoleon Hill called this *Definiteness of Purpose* — knowing exactly what you want and refusing to settle for anything less. Dr. Benjamin Hardy, coauthor of *10X is Easier than 2X* (Hay House Business, 2023), takes it further, arguing that achieving a 10X vision is actually easier than a small 2X goal because it forces you to eliminate distractions and focus only on what truly matters.

Here are just a few reasons why having a crystal-clear vision is crucial for your financial success:

- **Your mind needs a target.** Just like a GPS needs a destination, your brain works better when it has a clear financial goal.

- **Clarity eliminates distractions.** A strong vision helps you say *no* to things that don't align with your long-term success.

- **Big goals create big energy.** A 10X vision excites and motivates you far more than a 2X goal ever can.

When developing your vision, be as specific as you can. Don't just say, "I want to be rich." Instead, define a number and say it in the present tense: "I have a $5 million investment portfolio and work only 10 hours a week in 2035."

As you develop your vision, write down your six-month, one-year, five-year, and ten-year goals and place them somewhere you can see every day. Here are some methods I personally use:

- **Create a vision board.** This is a visual representation of your goals, dreams, and ideal future. It's a collage of images, words, and symbols that reflect what you want to achieve in your life — whether in wealth, career, relationships, health, or personal growth. Spend at least 30 seconds per day viewing your vision board.

- **Set reminders on your phone.** I have created notifications on my phone's calendar that pop up my goals, affirmations, and purpose every day at a certain time.

- **Create a future journal and read it every day.** Whenever I'm working on a brand-new vision, I take time to write a journal with my vision and the rules and principles that I know will help me achieve it. I then either record myself and listen to it every day or get my phone to read the text while I'm driving, going for a walk, or working out.

Check out and get inspired by my personal vision journal at `https://www.triplecompounding.com/abundance`.

Mastering Your Subconscious Mind

Your subconscious mind is the hidden powerhouse behind achieving your desired future. Your wealth starts in your mind before it appears in your investment portfolio. That is why it's crucial that you change your identity first and transform your mindset before you start your journey. When you do this, you can make decisions from the perspective of your future self and get on the right path to achieve your goal.

Your subconscious mind runs your financial habits on autopilot, and it influences your financial identity. If you grew up thinking "money is hard to earn" or "wealthy people are unethical," your subconscious will keep you playing small and prevent you from becoming wealthy to fit in your idea of "ethical."

Here's how to reprogram your subconscious mind to attract more wealth:

>> **Feed it the right input.** Don't just repeat financial affirmations. Get yourself in a state of gratitude and watch yourself become how you *feel.*

>> **Control your environment.** Surround yourself with wealth-minded people and cut out negative financial influences. Your subconscious mind absorbs the mindset of the people around you, and the news steals your attention and fuels fear. Both will keep you from achieving abundance.

>> **Take action that reinforces your new identity.** If your vision is to have a $5 million portfolio, start making investment moves like someone who already has it.

When your subconscious believes you are wealthy, your actions will naturally align to make it true.

Tapping into your imagination

If your vision is your destination and your subconscious is the engine, then your imagination is the fuel that helps you solve financial challenges and create wealth-building opportunities.

Zoroastrianism, one of the world's oldest belief systems, produced the ancient Persian proverb, "Good thoughts, good words, good deeds." This idea emphasizes that your inner world (thoughts), your spoken intentions (words), and your external actions (deeds) must be in harmony to create a righteous and fulfilling life.

In modern terms, this principle aligns with the power of mindset, language, and action in shaping your reality — especially in creating wealth and abundance.

Your thoughts, words, and actions determine whether you attract or repel opportunities, financial success, and abundance. The mind is a creative force, and when you master these three elements, you become the architect of your financial destiny.

Becoming your future self now

One of the most powerful ways to accelerate your financial success is to embody your future self today. I recommend the following exercise as a way to facilitate this transformation into your future self.

You don't have to understand exactly how this works just as you don't need to know how electricity works to still benefit from your fridge, microwave, and computer.

Here's a step-by-step guided meditation I hold for my students to invite their future selves to their presence.

1. **Center yourself.**

   Breathe in deeply, hold the breath for a moment, and slowly exhale. Let any tension in your body melt away. Slowly close your eyes and tilt your eyes toward the center of your forehead.

2. **Consider the future date you're stepping into.**

   For example, say, "It is July 21, 2035," and calculate how old you will be on this specific date.

3. **View the world from your future-self perspective.**

   With your eyes closed, look to your left, to your right, in your hands, and in front of you. Envision what your future self sees. Specifically, what stands out that shows you have achieved your dream? Maybe it's a number in your bank account. It could be an award hanging on your wall. It could be that special someone you're sharing the good news with. It could be the view from your dream home.

4. **Feel your future self.**

   With your eyes closed, answer this question: "Now that my dreams have come true, how do I feel?" The answer may put a smile on your face or a tear in your eyes.

5. **Anchor the feeling.**

   With your eyes closed, scan your body to find where you're feeling these emotions the most. You may be feeling a tingling in your tummy, in your throat, or on your cheeks. Tap on the area where you feel the most tingling. Then take a deep breath to anchor. When you're ready, slowly open your eyes and bring yourself back to the present moment.

I do variations of this guided meditation for client groups every week. To do one of the variations with me from one of my past events, go to `https://www.triplecompounding.com/abundance`.

TIP

You may be thinking, "Bro, I thought this book was about serious compounding stuff. What in the voodoo is this stuff about?" Don't get me wrong, I used to be super skeptical of this *voodoo* stuff when I first heard about it, too. But then I started hearing many successful people, including Tony Robbins, Mr. Beast, Oprah Winfrey, Richard Branson, and even Lady Gaga, practice the same principles!

Overcoming resistance

Have you ever noticed that every time you get excited about a new goal or commit to doing something that you know will help you grow, you feel or experience something that holds you back? Sometimes it's fear. Other times, it's skepticism. It may also be that something actually happens in your life to prevent you from moving forward, like getting into an argument with your spouse!

In his book, *The War of Art* (Black Irish Entertainment, 2012), Steven Pressfield describes this thing that holds you back as the *resistance*. He defines it as the invisible force that blocks you from achieving your goals. Every time your emotional mind comes up with a new goal to be excited about, the resistance comes and hits you to see if you're for real.

Here are the different forms of resistance you may experience once you step into your future self, as I describe in the previous section:

>> Self-doubt

>> Procrastination

>> Fear

» Distractions

» Self-sabotage

REMEMBER

Resistance will always try to stop you, but the fact that it's there means you're doing something important. So, if you feel resistance when taking bold financial steps, take it as a sign you're on the verge of a breakthrough — and push forward anyway.

REMEMBER

Resistance shows up whenever you try to level up — when you start a business, invest seriously, write a book, commit to a financial plan, or start your triple-compounding journey. It often disguises itself as logical excuses — such as *I need more research*, *I'll start next year*, or *What if I fail?*

Pressfield argues that resistance is strongest right before a breakthrough, which means the bigger your goal (like financial freedom), the stronger the resistance. Here are some methods you can use to overcome resistance:

» **Act first, feel ready later.** The best way to beat resistance is action — even small steps. Start investing, automate savings, and refine as you go.

» **Commit to daily progress.** Even if it's just one investment move a day, consistency weakens resistance.

» **Identify your excuses and challenge them.** Whenever you catch yourself delaying action, ask: *Is this Resistance talking?*

» **Embody your future wealthy self.** Think and act as if you're already financially free. Make decisions from abundance, not fear.

Reframing Your Past

Stepping into your future self is fun and all, but sometimes, the thing that's holding you back is your past. If you haven't taken care of your past, stepping into your future may become harder.

Can you think of a traumatizing experience in your past that is still haunting you to this day, and you feel like it's preventing you from moving forward? Maybe it's a mistake you made. Or a mistake someone else made that impacted you.

In this section, I teach you a *reframing* skill that allows you to turn your past "trauma" or failures into steppingstones for success.

Becoming better, not bitter

I was born and raised in Iran during the Iran-Iraq War, and they were literally dropping bombs on us when I was growing up. I remember being a four-year-old and hearing the *red alert* on the radio, a specific signal to warn citizens about incoming enemy aircraft and potential bombing in our area. I was young, but I knew that meant they could be dropping deadly weapons on us and that we needed to rush to a secure place.

Sometimes, if we found out about the bombing ahead of time, we would have time to travel to the suburbs of my hometown of Tehran to shelter. Other times, if we didn't have enough time, we would rush down to the basement.

During these stressful times, my family did something that I know has forever changed how I deal with challenges. Even during the bombardment and uncertainty of not knowing when bombs could drop on us, we still had *fun!* We would rush to the basement after the red alert, and my parents would put on music and start singing and dancing!

Maybe the idea was to distract us, but what I took away from it was that they took the challenge and turned it into an opportunity to have fun. What I learned from the experience has now become my life motto: "How can I turn this challenge into an opportunity?"

I could have used this traumatic experience to victimize myself all my life. I could have chosen to be *bitter* about my upbringing or maybe even blame my parents for having fun during a freaking war! Instead, I unknowingly put a *better* frame around that experience, not a *bitter* frame. This shift in framing could be one of the biggest reasons I never gave up despite all the curveballs life threw at me.

One of my favorite authors, Dr. Benjamin Hardy, explains this phenomenon in his book, *Be Your Future Self Now* (Hay House Business, 2022). Your future self is not limited by your past. It's shaped by how you choose to frame it.

Stuff that happened to you in the past can really mess with your head if you let it. You need to realize that it's not about what happened. The important thing is the story you tell yourself about it — the frame you put around it.

Your toughest times can teach you the most if you're open to it. Owning your experiences, instead of being owned by them, lets you create a story that helps your future.

Here's an exercise to help you reframe your past:

1. **Identify a past financial mistake or regret.**

   Maybe you missed an investment opportunity, overspent, or avoided managing money altogether. Or maybe you fell for a scam or media hype and lost all your money. Write the mistake down.

2. **Change the story you tell yourself.**

   Is there any way you can give a new positive meaning to your tragic experience? Think of at least one new way of reframing your past experience positively. Can you find a lesson? Or maybe even a blessing?

3. **Use your new story to build your compelling future.**

   Instead of using your past as an excuse, use it as evidence that you're evolving.

   You can ask yourself:

   - How can I use my past experiences to make better financial decisions now?

   - What strengths did those struggles develop in me?

You may have become more resilient, resourceful, or determined. These are assets that will help you become a triple compounder.

Instead of carrying the weight of regret, remind yourself that life is happening *for* you, not *to* you. Every challenge, every setback, every financial misstep was never meant to break you; it was meant to build you. The struggles weren't roadblocks; they were lessons disguised as obstacles, sharpening your resilience, wisdom, and financial intelligence. Add the following sentence to your daily mantra and witness your life change for the better:

The universe is conspiring in my favor.

Avoiding the fly's strategy

Have you ever heard that to succeed, you need to "try harder"? Okay, here's another question. Have you ever seen a fly at your window, trying super hard to fly *through* the glass?

Picture that scenario in your head right now. The fly keeps flapping and flapping, but it's just not producing a result. Basically, the fly's big plan is "I'll give it all I've got!" But that plan isn't working out. Even though the fly tries its best, it won't get through that window.

The saddest part? There's an open door right across the room! Instead of switching up its game plan, the fly is just being stubborn, sticking to what's not working. No one's forcing the fly to keep at it, but it's stuck on the idea that trying harder is the way to win.

Just trying harder with what doesn't work isn't the answer. If you keep doing the same thing over and over, expecting different results, you're probably setting yourself up for disappointment.

This doesn't mean you should sit on your butt doing nothing. You *do* need to work hard. But your effort needs to go toward things that are proven to work. If that little fly had a big fly mentor to model flying through the open door, the little fly wouldn't die.

The cool thing is, in your job, in your business, in your investments, in your bank account, in your life, you're not a gazillion steps away from achieving what you desire. You're likely three to five tweaks away from setting yourself up to reach that million-dollar portfolio that can compound and allow you to live your lifestyle once you decide to retire.

Developing a Decisive Nature

The word *decision* is rooted in the Latin word *decider,* which is the combination of two words:

> *de = off*
>
> *caedere = cut*

To *decide* means to *cut off* everything except the things that matter most.

This idea goes hand in hand with triple compounding, which requires you to cut off 80 percent of who you are and what you're doing right now and hone in on and automate the 20 percent that matters most. Making decisions is a very important component in your triple-compounding journey.

When I was stuck in my Welfare Diva mindset, I made all kinds of decisions that kept me stuck. Here are some examples:

>> I stuck with studying electrical engineering for seven years, even though I knew I had zero passion for it. I stuck with it because the Japanese government was paying me a scholarship. I wasted seven years of my life to earn $1,000 per month.

>> I listened to my parents encourage me to just get married to a rich guy so all my problems would go away. I ended up with a toxic boyfriend.

>> I took advice from a broke buddy of mine to partner up with a broke buddy of his who ended up scamming me.

>> I decided not to invest in Bitcoin in 2011 when my mentor told me about it because I was too lazy to put effort into really learning about it.

>> I kept making decisions about entrepreneurship through trial and error, including choosing to "budget" instead of going directly to people who had achieved what I wanted to achieve. When I decided not to pay them for that information to save a few bucks, the decision cost me almost ten years of my life.

My decisions were based on my values and beliefs and what I *thought* was correct. Now I know that instead of cutting off the 80 percent of the crappy stuff that was keeping me from achieving my big goal, I was cutting off the 20 percent shortcuts.

I was looking for instant gratification and had lost track of my big goal. Most important, I had a fear of being judged by the people around me who I most cared about and who thought that if I didn't do things their way, I must be crazy. Consequently, I kept getting stuck at the same place. My investments in Kiana Danial incorporated sucked.

But once I realized that my old way of thinking wasn't getting me anywhere, I started paying attention to what actually worked. I stopped modeling people who were stuck and started studying those who had already created the kind of success I wanted. That's when everything began to shift. I began building a new identity.

This is what helped me transform from a Welfare Diva into a Millionaire Diva. Here are some of the Millionaire Diva decisions I've made in the past decade that changed everything:

>> Writing my first book in 2012 (and getting myself published by McGraw-Hill against all odds)

>> Starting to compound even with low amounts (I started with $500 per month)

>> Hiring mentors who had already achieved what I wanted to achieve (so I could use their experiences as shortcuts and accelerate my progress)

>> Not going on a date for two years so I could focus on my investment in myself until my first book was published (even though my family was pressuring me to get married)

>> Once I was ready to get married, going on 400 first dates in three months

>> Deciding I was going to become a millionaire after my daughter was born

>> Creating investment strategies based on my unique risk tolerance and financial goals at every stage of my journey

>> Triple compounding

REMEMBER Becoming decisive in nature is one of the most critical traits for achieving success, wealth, and financial freedom. Indecision is the enemy of progress. It keeps you stuck in analysis paralysis; you second-guess every move while opportunities pass you by.

REMEMBER Successful people make decisions quickly and change them slowly. Unsuccessful people take forever to decide and then change their minds quickly.

When you're looking for financial freedom, you've got to evaluate your investments through the eyes of wealthy people. Ultimately, you have two resources for investing: your time and your money.

I probably don't have to ask you this, but what is more important: your money or your time?

Most people would answer time, and some may say "time is money." Here's the truth: Time is *infinitely* more valuable than money. You can always make more money, but you can never make more time.

Self-made wealthy people become financially free because they spend as much money as possible to save as much time as possible. Why?

Because the most important ingredient in compounding is *time*.

William Clement Stone, a self-made multimillionaire, entrepreneur, and co-author of *Success Through a Positive Mental Attitude* (Prentice Hall, 1960), built his fortune by embracing a simple yet powerful mantra: "Do it now."

He believed that *procrastination is the killer of opportunity* and that success belongs to those who take immediate, decisive action rather than waiting for the "perfect moment."

That's why he made himself and all his employees say, "Do it now," a hundred times a day!

Every time you hesitate, you allow resistance to creep in. (Read about resistance in the section, "Overcoming resistance," earlier in this chapter.) The faster you act, the faster you build momentum and the faster you step into financial freedom.

When you think about your next move — whether it's investing, starting a business, or making a big decision, ask yourself, "What would my future self want me to do?" Then, do it right away.

Surrounding Yourself with Like-Minded People

Your environment shapes your reality. If you want to build wealth, achieve financial freedom, and step into your 10X future, you must surround yourself with people who think bigger, act bolder, and are already living at the level you aspire to reach. Napoleon Hill called this the *Mastermind Principle* — the idea that success accelerates when you align yourself with those who elevate your thinking.

Success leaves clues. Instead of figuring everything out on your own, study the habits, mindset, and strategies of the people who have already achieved what you want.

>> How do they think about money?

>> What daily actions do they take?

>> What risks do they embrace that others avoid?

Surrounding yourself with wealth-minded people — especially other triple compounders — rewires your subconscious beliefs about what's possible. You start thinking, acting, and making decisions like someone who is already financially free because that's who you're becoming.

IN THIS CHAPTER

» **Using savings to generate income**

» **Working a job to generate income**

» **Earning from your portfolio to generate income**

» **Operating businesses to generate income**

» **Accelerating your triple compounding**

Chapter **5**

Investing in Your Income-Generating Extensions

I f you feel like you're late to the compounding game, there's only one way to catch up and speed your way to financial freedom: maximize your contributions. In Chapter 3, I break down the math of the time value of money (TVM). Your ability to compound wealth is directly tied to how much you put in. The more you contribute, the faster your money grows.

But here's the challenge: You can't contribute more if you don't earn more. That's why this chapter is all about expanding your income-generating extensions — the revenue streams that fuel your compounding engine. By increasing your income and positively influencing your cash flow, you're not just making more money; you're unlocking the ability to take higher-calculated risks, access better investment opportunities, and grow your wealth exponentially without losing sleep at night.

There's no such thing as truly passive income — not even if you win the lottery. In fact, one-third of lottery winners declare bankruptcy within five years, not because they didn't have enough money but because they never learned how to keep it growing. Even if you hit a financial jackpot, you won't stay ahead unless you're constantly investing in yourself, your income-generating extensions, and external assets.

When I first hit a million dollars in my portfolio, I thought I was done. That was my number — my "I made it" moment. But what I learned, and what you'll soon realize, is that every financial milestone unlocks the next goal. Growth isn't just about money. It's about momentum. If you're not growing, you're dying. And if your money isn't growing, it's dying, too.

Conversely, if you work through Chapter 3 and discover that you aren't cash-flow positive, what comes next is even more important. In the following sections, I help you find hidden money, generate new income streams, and transform your savings into an income-generating machine. This is where you expand your triple-compounding system and unlock your next financial breakthrough.

Generating with Savings

No, saving some money by giving up your morning latte will not make you a millionaire. But if you free up some cash and then use that cash to generate more cash, you're no longer just saving; you're compounding your wealth. In this section, I show you some easy ways you can generate income by saving on things that no longer give you joy. So, you won't be diminishing the quality of your life while finding money to contribute to your triple-compounding system.

Cutting the waste

Cutting waste is the easiest way to find money. Brainstorm all the things in your life that you could eliminate or reduce to cut your expenses, and enter them in a table like the one shown in Figure 5-1. For example, fly on a weekday rather than a weekend, cut down on the daily Pumpkin Spice Frappuccino, go out to matinée movies instead of evening shows, pack a lunch for work, and so on. These are small things that add up over time.

Now determine how much each of these items/activities cost. Fill in the amount for each and multiply it by the number of times per week you indulge in this expense to get a reality check about how much you are spending. Then ask yourself, on a scale from 0 to 10 (with 0 being none and 10 being extremely pleasurable), how much joy do you get from each of these items? Write this in the last column for each item.

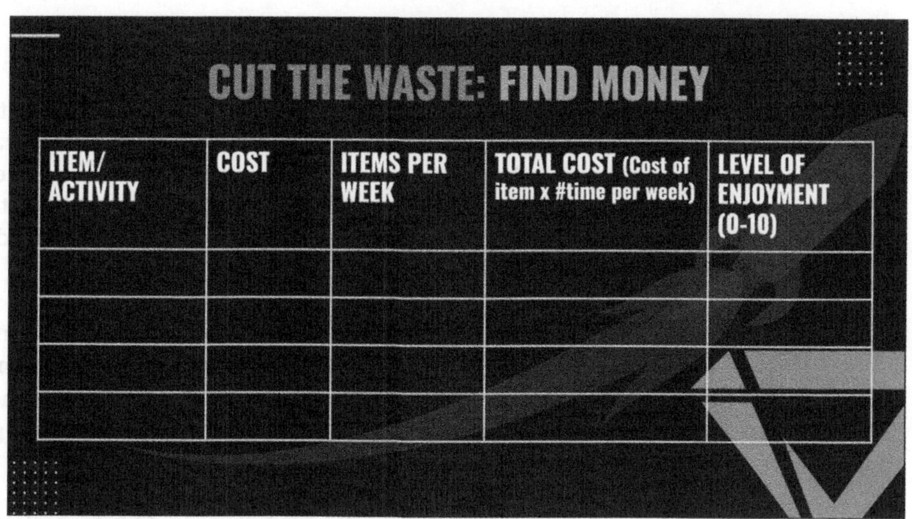

ITEM/ ACTIVITY	COST	ITEMS PER WEEK	TOTAL COST (Cost of item x #time per week)	LEVEL OF ENJOYMENT (0-10)

FIGURE 5-1: Cut the waste — find money.

Source: triplecompounding.com

TIP

Associate in your body the feeling of absolute financial freedom. How will it feel to be able to do whatever you want, wherever you want, whenever you want, with whomever you want? What will you be able to enjoy, have, do, be, or give? Now consider whether the expense you've included on your list will give you more joy or take you further away from your financial goals?

REMEMBER

Decide which is more important: the joy you receive from the items on your list or the feeling of absolute financial freedom. Also remember that life is a balance. You don't have to cut out everything you enjoy; rather, cutting the waste is about giving you more choices by reducing the things that truly do not give you proportional levels of joy.

Circle or mark at least three things in the list that you're resolved to eliminate from the list. How much money will this save you over the course of the next year?

This is found money.

WARNING

This is not about saving money and wasting it on something else that wouldn't accelerate your financial freedom. Here's a quick pop quiz:

Q. What are you *not* going spend this found money on?

A. Another liability.

Q. What are you going to do with it instead?

A. Contribute it to your triple-compounding system.

Eliminating liabilities

A liability is anything that takes money out of your pocket without generating income. That means your $5,000 Chanel bag, your leased car, or even that expensive couch that just sits there — they're all liabilities if they're not making you money. Although these purchases may seem harmless, they add up and compound over time, creating a negative wealth effect instead of fueling your financial growth.

Every dollar you're *not* spending on liabilities is a dollar that can be invested and compounded into more wealth. For example, the less I pay for my car lease each month, the more money I have to invest. That compounded income generation doesn't just stop there. It double-compounds as that money grows inside my portfolio, creating even more wealth.

It's time to shift your mindset. Every dollar you free from liabilities is a dollar that can be put to work. Small financial decisions, when compounded, create massive long-term wealth. Let's start redirecting your cash into income-generating assets today. Flip to Chapter 3 to discover the difference between good and bad liabilities.

Stopping reverse compounding

In the previous sections, I show how to invest in yourself, cut waste, eliminate liabilities, and generate income with savings — but there's one more silent wealth killer you need to stop: reverse compounding.

Reverse compounding happens when unnecessary fees and costs eat away at your wealth, compounding in someone else's favor instead of yours. It's what I was doing when I paid that shady money manager outrageous commission fees. He was compounding his own fortune, while my investments barely moved.

The same thing happens with the hidden fees inside your 401(k), IRA, and other retirement accounts. Most people don't even realize how much they're losing as, over time, these fees can add up to millions of dollars in lost growth.

Americans lose $5.7 billion every year just to 401(k) and IRA early withdrawal fees. That's $5.7 billion with a *b!!*

Now, you may be wondering, *Should I ditch my 401(k)?*

Not necessarily. The only time I'd consider keeping a 401(k) is if my employer offers a match — because that's free money. Even then, I'd take control of it and manage it using the triple-compounding method this book covers. That way, you can maximize returns, minimize fees, and eliminate reverse compounding wherever possible.

401(k)s have layers of hidden fees — so many that even most financial advisors don't fully understand them.

REMEMBER

Figure 5-2 reveals the ways that you're reverse-compounding without realizing it. Many of these stealth costs add up to over 28 percent compounded over time, which means you could be losing millions of dollars over your lifetime.

Things You Could Be REVERSE Compounding			
Bad Debt	Ignoring Maintenance	Poor Tax Planning	Leveraged ETFs
401K Hidden Fees	High-Expense Ratio Mutual Funds	Lifestyle Inflation	Non-Traded REITs
Late Fees	Actively Managed Funds	Annuities with High Fees	Private Equity Hidden Fees

FIGURE 5-2: Sneaky ways reverse compounding can occur.

Source: triplecompounding.com

If you stop reverse-compounding, you instantly free up more cash, increase your risk tolerance, and accelerate your triple-compounding strategy.

TIP

So, ask yourself: Do you want to be a reverse compounder or a triple compounder? The choice is yours, but once you see what's at stake, the answer becomes obvious.

I want to show you how to take back control of your money.

Using leverage

In Chapter 3, I break down the differences between bad and good debt. Bad debt is a liability that "reverse-compounds" against you — eating away at your portfolio and trapping you in financial stagnation. Good debt, on the other hand, is why 99 percent of businesses exist today. It's the tool successful entrepreneurs, investors, and corporations use to build real wealth.

If you're in a city right now, look out your window. What do you see? Hotels, car dealerships, malls, restaurants.

Now, let me ask you a question: How many of those businesses do you think were built with cash that was sitting under a mattress?

Almost none. Maybe 1 percent.

The truth is that nearly every successful business and investor uses debt strategically. They don't take on debt just to survive; they use it as leverage to build income-generating assets.

I used to think being debt-free was an achievement. I never had student loans because I took a scholarship from the Japanese government. However, there was a problem: I spent seven years studying something I didn't like in a language I didn't speak, and I didn't have a clear path to financial success — all because it was "free."

Was it really free?

No. Because what I lost was time — the thing that's infinitely more valuable than money. I could have used those years to invest in high-income skills like investing, marketing, entrepreneurship, sales, and public speaking — the very skills that later built my unshakable Triple Compounding wealth ecosystem.

Becoming debt-free is not the first step in your financial freedom journey. Most people believe that the first step to financial freedom is paying off all their debt. They focus on getting rid of their car loans, student loans, or mortgages, thinking that once they're "debt-free," they'll finally be in control. The hard truth is that *debt-free is still zero.*

If your only goal is to get out of debt, you're working incredibly hard just to get back to nothing — to a neutral financial position. You may feel relieved once you're debt-free, but relief isn't the same as freedom. And while you're focused on paying off every dollar, you're missing out on the most valuable asset you have: time.

The key isn't just eliminating debt. It's learning how to use leverage to your advantage.

There are three smart ways to borrow money that can generate more wealth for you:

>> **Borrow money to start a business** that creates cash flow and pays off debt.

>> **Use the bank's money** if borrowing is cheaper than using your own money.

>> **Leverage credit card rewards** to generate cash back and investment funds.

If I'm earning 40 percent on my money and the bank is offering me a loan at 10 percent, should I use my own money to pay for something? No.

If I use my own money, it's costing me 40 percent in opportunity cost. But if I borrow at 10 percent, my real cost is only 10 percent, and my money keeps earning 30 percent more.

That's why wealthy people use leverage strategically. They leave their money in income-generating investments and use cheap money from banks to pay for what they need.

Let your money work for you. Borrow at a lower cost and keep your cash compounding.

I charge as much as possible on my credit cards, but I pay them off in full every month. I use credit for

>> Facebook ads (business credit cards give higher points for marketing expenses)

>> Electricity and utilities

>> Groceries and dining

>> Flights, hotels, and business expenses

>> Amazon purchases

What happens when I do this? I earn points, cash back, and free money just for using debt.

If you can't pay your cards off every month, the solution isn't avoiding credit. It's borrowing the right way, building a business, and generating cash flow to eliminate bad debt while continuing to leverage good debt to your advantage.

Using bad debt can negatively impact your risk tolerance. See Chapter 3 to calculate your ability to take a risk.

Most people use debt to look rich instead of becoming rich. They put vacations, designer bags, and luxury cars on credit to impress people. They finance a lifestyle instead of financing income-producing assets. But once you shift your mindset and learn how to use debt as a tool, you stop playing defense and start playing offense. You start compounding your way to financial freedom instead of just escaping debt.

The real question isn't *Should I avoid debt?* The real question is *Am I using debt to build wealth or just to survive?*

When you use leverage wisely, you multiply your money, expand your compounding system, and accelerate your financial freedom faster than you ever thought possible.

Developing a spending plan

Most people create a spending plan (also known as a budget) with one goal: cutting expenses to avoid running out of money. But as a triple compounder, your spending plan shouldn't just be about saving money; it should be designed to make you money.

A wealth-building spending plan prioritizes cash flow, investments, and assets that generate income so that every dollar you spend has the potential to grow. Instead of just tracking where your money is going, you're going to redirect it into things that bring money back to you and turn your spending into a powerful tool for financial freedom. Here are a few ways you can create a wealth-building spending plan:

>> **Categorize your spending into assets versus liabilities:** If it's not generating income, you should question it.

>> **Question every purchase:** Ask yourself, *Does this expense get me closer to financial freedom, or is it just a liability?*

>> **Use a percentage-based system:** For example, dedicate 50 percent of your budget to necessities, 30 percent to income-generating investments, and 20 percent to fun.

Most people create spending plans to avoid going broke, but if you want to achieve financial freedom, your spending plan needs to be designed to generate income, not just cut costs. The goal isn't to spend less just for the sake of spending less; it's to spend smarter.

A bonus of developing a spending plan is that it reduces fights with your spouse! A spending plan will make family decisions much smoother because everyone has agreed how much money will be spent. As a triple-compounding family, you *must* know how much you're spending.

Cutting portions

If you know anything about marketing, you know that most stores deliberately price their largest portion only slightly higher than the medium one, so your brain automatically thinks, *Why not just go for the bigger one?* It feels like you're getting more value for your money.

The reality is that you're not saving money. You're spending more for something you don't actually need.

Not only is this bad for your body . . . but it is also bad for your income. If you're serious . . . portion. This doesn't just apply to food portions. It applies to the following ways that every company gets you to spend more without you realizing it:

>> **Streaming services** bundle extras you don't actually use into higher-priced plans.

>> **Gym memberships** offer "premium" packages when a basic plan would work just fine.

>> **Retailers** push "Buy More, Save More" deals that just make you buy things you wouldn't have purchased otherwise.

Every time you opt for the bigger portion, you're spending more without increasing value. That extra $2, $5, or $10 here and there may seem insignificant, but small amounts compound over time. You're giving that money away instead of putting it to work for you.

When you cut portions strategically, you free up hundreds, even thousands of dollars a year. You can reinvest and compound that money into income-generating assets and serve your triple-compounding system to accelerate your freedom.

Here's an example: Let's say you save $5 per day by cutting unnecessary spending. If you invest that $5 daily into an index fund earning 10 percent annually, you'll have $113,000 in 30 years — just from skipping the up-sized meal or premium subscription.

That's real money that can go toward your triple-compounding system, including your investment portfolio, income-generating business, or passive income stream.

Avoiding paying cost of convenience

Companies make millions — sometimes billions — because 97 percent of people are willing to pay a premium for convenience, even when that convenience adds no real value to their lives or financial future.

Most people overpay, not because they have to, but because they hesitate. They "sleep on it" when making a decision and think they're being careful by doing so. In reality, they're just delaying and letting opportunities slip away.

Here's the truth: For most decisions, no matter how long you think about it, the facts don't change, but the cost usually goes up. This is another reason why successful people like William Clement Stone are committed to "doing it now," as I explain in Chapter 4.

The following are some of the most common ways people overpay for convenience to their own financial detriment:

>> **Booking flights at the last minute:** Buying flights within a week of departure can cost two to three times more than booking months in advance.

>> **Shopping at convenience stores:** Markups on everyday items are often 50 percent to 100 percent higher than buying the same products in bulk at a grocery store.

>> **ATM fees:** Transactions that cost $3 to $5 at non-network ATMs compound into hundreds per year — just to access your own money.

>> **Precut fruits and vegetables from grocery stores:** You're paying up to three times more for something you can prep yourself in minutes.

>> **Bottled water instead of a reusable filter:** Spending $2 per bottle daily equals $730 per year, when a $50 water filter can last all year.

>> **Light bulbs that aren't energy efficient:** Traditional bulbs cost more in electricity over time compared to LEDs, which last longer and use less power.

REMEMBER

Time is infinitely more valuable than money, but that doesn't mean that paying for every convenience is a good investment. Some conveniences save time and are worth the cost, but most are simply draining your financial future. Every time you overpay for convenience, ask yourself these questions:

>> Am I really getting value, or just avoiding a small inconvenience?

>> Is this saving me significant time, or is it just feeding into my resistance?

>> If I invested this money instead, how much could it compound over time?

Generating More Income from Your Current Job

If you have a job right now, you already have a built-in opportunity to generate more income without starting a business or taking on side hustles. The key? Adding more value. The more valuable you become to your employer, the more leverage you have to increase your salary, commissions, and bonuses. Here are some ideas for how to earn more at your job:

>> **Add more value:** Invest in yourself by learning new skills that increase your worth to the company. If you can solve bigger problems, streamline processes, or improve efficiency, you become indispensable.

>> **Change positions within your company:** Knock your KPIs (key performance indicators) out of the park, take on bigger responsibilities, and position yourself for a promotion or leadership role.

>> **Earn commissions:** If your company offers performance-based pay, invest in sales, negotiation, and marketing skills to maximize your earnings. The better you are at driving revenue, the more you can compound your commissions.

You can also learn automation skills, organizational strategies, or even financial compounding techniques that make you an even greater asset. As a result, you gain the ability to negotiate better pay, higher bonuses, and improved benefits.

You need to bring value equivalent to what you're asking for. You can't do the bare minimum and expect a raise. This means becoming so valuable that your employer can't afford to lose you.

The key strategy for earning more money is figuring out how to add more value. Is it possible to earn twice as much money in the same amount of time? Three times as much? Ten times as much? The answer is yes, if you add two, three, or ten times the value.

Your income reflects the value you create. The faster you increase your value, the faster you can multiply your earnings without working more hours.

REAL-WORLD EXAMPLE: HOW MY ASSISTANT INCREASED HER INCOME

When my assistant first joined my team, she was just managing my calendar.

Then she leveled up and took over managing our events. Then she invested in learning tech and website development, and suddenly, she became the person running all of our digital infrastructure.

Now? She's essentially my right-hand person.

At that point, when she came to me and asked for a raise, I didn't hesitate. I happily paid her more because she had become too valuable to lose.

That's how you increase your earning potential at your job: by consistently leveling up your skills, solving bigger problems, and making yourself invaluable.

So, the question isn't *How can I make more money?* It's *How can I add so much value that my income grows automatically?*

Generating from Your Portfolio

The definition of *making your money work for you* is creating income by investing in external assets in your investment portfolio. Although my favorite type of external investment is long-term appreciation, there are several ways to make your portfolio work for you right now, producing cash flow that can be reinvested, saved, or used to fund other income-generating activities.

In this section, I point out some of the most effective ways to generate passive or semi-passive income from your portfolio.

Earning interest on your investments

One of the safest ways to generate income from your portfolio is through interest-bearing assets: investments that pay you simply for parking your money in them. This type of investment is especially popular when interest rates are high because it allows you to earn a steady return with minimal risk. Here are some examples:

> » **High-yield savings accounts:** These offer better interest rates than tradi-
tional bank accounts, keeping your money liquid while earning returns.

> » **Bonds and treasury securities:** Government bonds, municipal bonds, and
corporate bonds pay fixed interest over time.

> » **Money market funds:** These funds invest in short-term, low-risk securities
and provide steady, reliable interest income.

The time it takes to generate substantial income by earning interest is long. Interest alone won't make you rich unless you have significant capital invested. However, it's a safe way to earn while protecting your money from inflation.

Generating income with dividend stocks

Dividend stocks pay out a portion of their profits to shareholders regularly (monthly, quarterly, or annually). This creates a steady income stream, even when the stock price fluctuates. The risk level with this method is low to moderate, but without higher investment, you won't see meaningful returns, and it takes a while to generate substantial income.

Some of the best dividend-paying assets include the following:

> » **Blue-chip stocks:** Large, stable companies like Coca-Cola, Alphabet (Google),
Microsoft, and Procter & Gamble consistently pay dividends.

> » **Dividend ETFs:** Funds like Vanguard Dividend Appreciation ETF (VIG) or
Schwab US Dividend Equity ETF (SCHD) hold multiple dividend-paying stocks
to reduce risk while still generating income.

> » **REITs (Real Estate Investment Trusts):** These pay high dividends from real
estate income without requiring you to buy physical property.

Dividends can compound over time if you reinvest them into more shares, making them a powerful source of long-term passive income. Flip to Chapter 6 to explore different types of stocks.

Swing trading for short-term gains

As I explain in Chapter 6, swing trading involves buying and selling stocks, ETFs, or crypto over days or weeks to capitalize on short-term price movements. Unlike long-term investing, this strategy focuses on momentum, trends, and technical analysis, which means that you can generate substantial income in a short time, but the risk is high.

To be successful in swing trading, you need

>> **Risk management:** Knowing how to create a unique investment strategy that matches your risk tolerance. Read Chapter 3 to find out all about risk management.

>> **Emotional control:** Not making impulsive decisions based on market fluctuations.

>> **Chart reading skills:** Understanding the price action of an asset on the charts. Flip to Chapter 16 to find out how to master the charts.

Swing trading can generate quick profits, but it requires active monitoring, experience, and discipline to prevent big losses.

Earning crypto rewards through staking

Cryptocurrency (crypto) is a digital or virtual currency that uses cryptography for security and operates on decentralized blockchain networks. Unlike traditional currencies issued by governments (such as the US dollar or the euro), cryptocurrencies are not controlled by any central authority, such as a bank or government. In my book, *Cryptocurrency Investing For Dummies*, I dive deep into all the ways you can grow your portfolio with cryptocurrency investing.

One of the ways to earn with cryptocurrency is by *staking* — a process where you lock up your crypto to support blockchain networks and earn rewards.

Popular staking options include

>> **Ethereum (ETH):** Earn rewards by staking ETH on the Ethereum 2.0 network.

>> **Cardano (ADA), Solana (SOL), and Polkadot (DOT):** These offer staking rewards through various blockchain validators.

>> **Stablecoin staking:** Platforms like Aave, BlockFi, or Binance offer interest on stablecoins like USDC and DAI, reducing volatility risks.

Staking is a great way to earn passive income in the medium term, especially if you have a high-risk tolerance. However, the value of your crypto is still subject to market risks.

Generating income with options trading

Options trading allows you to generate income even when the stock market moves sideways. Unlike buying stocks, options let you profit from price movement without owning the underlying asset.

Two common strategies for income generation are

>> **Selling covered calls:** If you own 100 shares of a stock, you can sell a call option and get paid a premium, regardless of whether the option gets exercised.

>> **Selling cash-secured puts:** If you want to buy a stock at a lower price, selling a put allows you to earn a premium while waiting for the stock to drop.

Options trading can provide immediate cash flow, but the risk level is high, so without proper risk management, it can lead to significant losses. See Chapter 6 to find out more about options.

Generating with Businesses

One of the most powerful ways to generate income is through businesses. Real magic can happen when you add automation, accelerating your triple-compounder system even further.

When I say, "investing in business," I don't mean starting a company from scratch (although that's an option). You can generate income by leveraging other people's businesses, partnering with existing systems, or enhancing what you're already doing. Whether you work for someone else, run your own business, or are just getting started, there's a way to increase your cash flow right now.

And the best part? You can stack these income streams over time, making each dollar work harder for you.

Having your own business unlocks an ocean of tax loopholes that save you even more money.

In this section, I cover different ways you can generate income through business.

Becoming a contractor: Monetizing your skills as a freelancer

Not everyone wants to build a company, but that doesn't mean you can't profit from your expertise. You can offer services such as the following to other businesses that already exist and generate income as a contractor:

>> **Freelancing and consulting:** Provide specialized services like writing, coding, design, or marketing.

>> **AI and tech services:** Businesses are willing to pay for AI-generated solutions, such as writing AI prompts for ChatGPT or building automation workflows.

>> **Virtual assistance and operations management:** Many companies need help with back-end systems, website building, and event management.

If you're already skilled in a particular area, you don't need to reinvent the wheel — just offer what you know to people who need it.

Becoming an affiliate: Getting paid to share what you love

You don't have to create a product to generate business income. You can promote products you already use and love through affiliate marketing.

Affiliate marketing is a performance-based marketing strategy in which you earn a commission by promoting another company's products or services. Instead of creating your own product, you recommend and sell products you trust, using a unique referral link. When someone makes a purchase through your link, you earn a percentage of the sale.

One of the biggest advantages of affiliate marketing is that you don't need to create your own product. You're simply promoting an existing product or service. Unlike traditional businesses, start-up costs are minimal because you don't have to worry about inventory, shipping, or customer support. The income potential is also highly scalable. The more traffic and sales you generate, the more passive income you can earn over time.

Affiliate marketing works in virtually any niche, whether you're passionate about finance, health, beauty, tech, or business. It's a flexible and profitable income stream for anyone willing to put in the effort. Here are some affiliate marketing examples:

>> As a finance blogger, you can earn commissions by recommending investment courses.

>> As a YouTuber, you can review tech gadgets and links to Amazon's affiliate program.

>> As a business coach, you can promote software tools and get paid per sign-up.

>> As a fashionista, you can earn commissions by recommending your favorite skincare routine and fashion brands.

Some of our affiliates at Invest Diva make up to $20,000 per month simply by spreading the word about life-changing programs! You can join our affiliate program and start earning at `https://triplecompounding.com/affiliate`.

Earning income through insurance strategies

Insurance isn't just about protecting wealth. It can also be a powerful tool for generating income and building long-term financial security. There are two key ways to profit from insurance strategies:

>> Leveraging whole life insurance for wealth building and passive income

>> Becoming an insurance agent and earning commissions

Both of these methods allow you to use the insurance industry to your financial advantage — whether by growing your own money tax-free or earning a steady income helping others protect and grow their wealth.

Many of my Accelerators have found out how to generate income through insurance strategies — essentially becoming their own banks. Others have added insurance sales as a side income stream, leveraging their finance knowledge to help others while earning high commissions.

I had felt FOMO (fear of missing out) about this for over a year, and now I'm finally exploring how to add this income stream to my next level of the triple-compounding system. Chapter 17 explores all the different ways you can use insurance strategies in your triple-compounding system.

No matter the economy, people always need insurance, which means steady income opportunities. Top insurance agents easily earn six figures, and some even make seven figures per year.

Creating your own business

If you want full control over your income, financial freedom, and the ability to scale without limits, creating your own business is one of the most powerful wealth-building moves you can make. Unlike a job, where your earnings are capped by salary limits, running a business allows you to control how much you make, how you grow, and how you invest your profits.

Starting your own business requires vision, action, and persistence, but the rewards can be life-changing. Whether you're looking to replace your 9-to-5 income, build a side hustle, or create generational wealth, launching a business can put you on the fast track to financial independence.

All of the income-generating ideas in this section can be applied to your own business.

Most millionaires own businesses because business ownership allows you to scale income, automate systems, and invest profits into wealth-building assets.

Creating your own business is a fundamental phase of the triple-compounding system. As a business owner, you can reinvest your earnings in the following ways:

>> **Tax loopholes and write-offs:** Business expenses reduce taxable income.

>> **Investing in income-generating assets:** Stocks, real estate, and other wealth-building tools.

>> **Scaling and automating:** Hiring teams and leveraging technology to increase revenue.

Flip to Chapter 9 to find out all the tips and tricks on becoming a business owner.

Buying another business

Although starting a business from scratch is an exciting challenge, it requires time, effort, and often years of trial and error. But what if you could skip the start-up phase and step directly into a cash-flowing business that's already built, already making money, and just needs someone to take it to the next level?

That's exactly why buying an existing business can be one of the fastest ways to generate income and grow your wealth.

Many established businesses already generate revenue and profit, so you start earning from day one instead of waiting years for a start-up to become profitable.

For others, you can bring your up-to-date marketing and AI skills to old businesses, serve their existing customers with your updated offers, and take the business to the next level.

And the best part? You don't have to go knock on the doors of the businesses in your town to see if they're willing to sell. There are platforms dedicated to helping buyers connect with sellers. Here are a few:

>> `BizScout.com`: Lists Boomer-owned businesses for sale, many of which are profitable but need a new owner

>> `Flippa.com`: A marketplace for buying digital businesses, websites, and online stores

>> `EmpireFlippers.com`: Specializes in cash-flowing online businesses like e-commerce, Software as a Service (SaaS), and content sites

>> `BizBuySell.com`: A massive marketplace for brick-and-mortar businesses, franchises, and local service businesses

Before buying a business, ask yourself the following questions:

>> **Is the business profitable?** Check financial statements to ensure steady revenue and cash flow.

>> **Does it align with my skills or interests?** If you have experience in a particular industry, buying a business in that space can help you scale faster.

>> **Can I improve or automate it?** Look for businesses where you can increase efficiency, improve marketing, or streamline operations to boost profits.

>> **Why is the owner selling?** Understand the seller's motivation. Are they retiring? Facing competition? Losing money? Make sure the business doesn't have hidden problems.

>> **What financing options are available?** You don't always need to pay cash upfront. You can use seller financing, Small Business Administration (SBA) loans, or investor funding to acquire the business.

Finding money with tax loopholes

Most people think that they need to earn more to build wealth, but what if you could keep more of what you already make — legally? The tax code is filled with loopholes that business owners and investors use to lower their taxable income, keep more cash, and accelerate wealth-building. If you're not taking advantage of tax strategies, you're giving away money that could be working for you.

The wealthy don't pay less in taxes because they cheat the system. They use the system to their advantage. You can, too.

REMEMBER

The rich don't work harder; they work smarter. Wealthy people use legal tax strategies to redirect their income toward investments that generate even more tax advantages.

Here are some of the most common ways you can save on taxes:

>> Deduct business expenses (turn everyday costs into write-offs)

>> Use real estate for tax-free wealth growth

>> Pay yourself tax-free with the proper business structure

>> Hire your children for your business, pay them tax-free, reduce your taxable income, and keep wealth inside your family

See Chapter 18 to explore different tax strategies that you can discuss with your accountant.

BECOMING A DIVA MONEY COACH: GETTING PAID TO MASTER INVESTING

What if you could get paid just for managing your own investments?

At Invest Diva, we created a Diva Money Coach program, in which our Accelerators become money coaches for others. Here's how it works:

- You master investing and build your own portfolio through one of our coaching programs.

- You go live weekly with our community to share how you manage your investments or submit your analysis in written format.

- You get paid by us for helping others learn the triple-compounding system.

Many of our Premium and Platinum Money Coaches started exactly where you are, and now they earn while they invest. If you're interested in helping others take control of their finances, you can join us in scaling this mission. You can start at https://www.triplecompounding.com.

IN THIS CHAPTER

» **Clarifying your risk tolerance and defining your portfolio goals**

» **Choosing an asset allocation that reflects your triple-compounding goals**

» **Investing in cryptocurrency**

» **Exploring online-accessible external assets and understanding the strengths, risks, and strategies for each**

» **Building a system that supports long-term wealth through diversification and automation**

Chapter **6**

Investing in Online External Assets

Most people hear the word *compounding* and instantly think of investing in external assets — stocks, real estate, crypto, or gold. But here's the truth: This is actually Phase 3 of the triple-compounding method I outline in this book.

Why is it last? Because investing in external assets is about making your *money* work for you, and you can't make money work if you haven't made any yet. That's why you start with the other two phases: Phase 1, investing in yourself (read Chapter 4) and Phase 2, investing in your extensions (read Chapter 5).

Once you've completed those two phases, you're ready to put your money to work in external assets — and that's where the third compounder kicks in.

In this chapter, I introduce you to some of the most popular online-accessible external assets — from Wall Street favorites to new digital opportunities — and explain how to decide which ones deserve a place in your triple-compounding portfolio.

You don't need a financial advisor, trust fund, or market predictions to start investing in external assets. But you do need a process.

The goal of external investing is not to beat the market. It's to build a life of financial peace, freedom, and choice — on your terms.

Considering Your Risk Tolerance

Before you choose any external asset to invest in, you need to check in with a critical piece of your financial profile: your risk tolerance. I go deep into how to calculate your exact ability and willingness to take a risk in Chapter 3, but here's a quick refresher tailored specifically for external investing.

Risk tolerance is more than just your gut feeling. It's a combination of three factors:

>> Your *ability* to take a risk (your current financial strength)

>> Your *willingness* to take a risk (your mindset, goals, and life stage)

>> Your *confidence* in the asset you're planning to invest in

All three of these factors directly shape how much volatility, loss, or uncertainty you can handle, especially when the markets turn against you.

This process of evaluating your financial position and emotional readiness is part of my five-step Invest Diva Diamond Analysis (IDDA) framework, which I outline in more detail in Chapter 10. The second step of this framework, called *capital analysis*, helps you figure out exactly where you currently stand so you can align your investments with your personal situation.

Before investing in any external asset, ask yourself these questions (which I call the Confidence Compass questions):

>> If this asset dropped by 50 percent, would I panic or hold steady?

>> If this asset soared by 50 percent and I hadn't invested, would I regret it?

Your honest answers reveal your true confidence level.

Although traditional advisors often adjust portfolios based on the investor's age alone, I believe your identity, education, and emotional resilience are just as important. As Warren Buffett puts it, "Risk comes from not knowing what you're doing."

REMEMBER

Knowing your risk tolerance upfront doesn't just help you pick the right assets; it helps you avoid emotional decisions when markets get bumpy.

Skipping this step is one of the top reasons investors lose money. They chase returns without a plan that matches their tolerance, goals, and circumstances.

WARNING

I offer a risk management toolkit to attendees of my free Triple Compounding Masterclass. Visit https://www.triplecompounding.com to find out more.

In the rest of this chapter, I show you how to evaluate each external asset class through the lens of risk, reward, and suitability so you can invest with clarity instead of guesswork.

Considering Your Portfolio Goals

Once you've clarified your risk tolerance, the next question is, *What is the purpose of your portfolio?*

This is where intentional analysis comes into play. It's the first step of the IDDA framework. In this step, you define exactly *why* you're investing in external assets and what outcomes you're looking to achieve.

In other words, are you investing for long-term wealth? Early retirement? Passive income? Saving for a down payment? Legacy building? Your intentions shape everything, from the assets you choose to the strategy you use to manage them. Without clear portfolio goals, you risk chasing shiny objects or reacting emotionally to short-term market movements.

Here are a few common portfolio goals to consider:

>> **Wealth accumulation:** Building long-term wealth through steady growth. This often includes a mix of stocks, ETFs, and real estate held over many years.

>> **Income generation:** Earning steady payouts from dividends, rental income, or bonds. This is common for those who are preparing for or already in retirement.

>> **Capital preservation:** Protecting the money you've already earned, often with lower-risk assets like Treasury bonds, dividend stocks, or precious metals.

>> **Aggressive growth:** Taking on higher risk for the chance at higher reward. This may include growth stocks, options trading, or early-stage investments.

>> **Tax efficiency or legacy planning:** Structuring your portfolio to minimize taxes or pass on wealth to future generations.

If you're not sure what your goals are, think in terms of milestones. Do you want to replace the income from your employment? Retire early? Buy your dream house in five years? The more clarity you have, the better your portfolio can support that vision.

The most successful investors aren't chasing random returns; they're building a system that supports their lives. A portfolio without a goal is like a GPS without a destination.

If you copy someone else's strategy without knowing their goals, you could end up with a portfolio that's totally wrong for you. It's not about what's "hot." It's about what's *right* for you.

Selecting Your Asset Allocation

Once you clarify your risk tolerance and your portfolio goals, it's time to answer the million-dollar question: *Where should you actually put your money?* This is where *asset allocation* comes in — the strategic mix of different asset types you include in your portfolio to balance risk and reward.

Your allocation acts as your portfolio's blueprint. It determines how much of your money goes into stocks versus bonds, real estate versus crypto, or index funds versus private equity. A well-crafted allocation reflects your personal financial goals, timeline, and comfort level with volatility — not what's trending on social media.

Asset allocation is more important than individual investment picks. In fact, research shows it accounts for more than 90 percent of a portfolio's long-term performance. In this and the following sections, I help you build a personalized strategy for choosing the right mix so you can invest with confidence rather than guesswork.

Think of asset allocation as building a plate at a buffet. If you pile it with only one type of food (or asset), you will get either bored or sick. A smart portfolio includes a healthy variety.

There's no perfect one-size-fits-all formula. Your asset mix should evolve as your goals, income, and risk tolerance change.

In the following sections, I break down the most common *online* asset classes — starting with stocks — and explain how to decide which ones align with your goals, risk tolerance, and freedom timeline. To find out about offline assets that you can add to your triple-compounding system, turn to Chapter 7.

Stocks

Stocks are one of the most popular — and accessible — external assets in any portfolio. When you buy a stock, you're buying a tiny slice of a publicly traded company. If the company grows, your slice becomes more valuable. If it pays dividends, you also get a piece of the profits along the way.

In triple compounding, stocks play a critical role because they offer both *growth potential* and *passive income* opportunities, depending on the type of stock you choose.

Not all stocks are created equal. Some are undervalued and overlooked. Others are pumped up by hype. Some are consistent income generators. Others are built to ride economic trends. The five common stock types you're likely to encounter are

>> **Value stocks:** Often overlooked, sometimes underpriced, but full of potential. These are the kinds of companies Warren Buffett loves.

>> **Dividend stocks:** Steady income generators that pay you just for holding them.

>> **Pump-and-dump stocks:** Flashy, risky, and often manipulated. These may look tempting but are usually traps.

>> **Cycling stocks:** Follow predictable economic trends and can be powerful tools if you know when to ride the wave.

>> **Growth stocks:** High-risk, high-reward companies with the potential for rapid price appreciation.

In the following sections, I walk you through each of these stocks to explain how to evaluate whether they deserve a spot in your portfolio.

Just like you diversify your income sources in the first two phases of triple compounding, you also want to diversify the types of stocks you invest in to balance stability, growth, and opportunity.

Buying a stock means buying into a business. So, before you invest, ask yourself: *Would I be proud to own this company?*

Value stocks

Value stocks are the underdogs of the investing world; they're companies that are often trading for less than they're really worth. They may be out of the spotlight, temporarily struggling, or simply misunderstood by the market. But for investors who know how to spot them, they can offer incredible long-term upside.

This is the style of investing Warren Buffett made famous. He looks for businesses with strong fundamentals that are on sale — not because they're broken but because the market hasn't caught up to their true value yet.

You can think of value stocks as Black Friday deals on quality companies. The trick is knowing the difference between a deal and a dud.

What makes a company a *value stock?* Buffett says to approach stock picking as if you're buying the *entire company*. Would you want to own the whole thing and be proud to call yourself the CEO? That mindset changes everything. Consider the following when picking stocks:

>> The stock price is low compared to its earnings, sales, or assets. Two popular ratios used to measure this are

  - **P/E (price-to-earnings) ratio:** Shows how much investors are paying for each dollar of a company's earnings. A low P/E may signal a bargain *or* a business in trouble.

  - **P/B (price-to-book) ratio:** Compares the stock price to the company's book value (what the company is worth on paper). A lower P/B often suggests the stock is undervalued.

>> The company still shows strong fundamentals: solid cash flow, brand strength, or a competitive edge.

>> It may be in a boring or "unsexy" industry the market has temporarily overlooked.

>> The business is stable but currently undervalued due to market fear, economic cycles, or negative headlines.

I take it one step further. Instead of getting lost in short-term financial reports and thousands of quarterly earnings statements, I look for a different kind of signal. I ask, *Is this company making the world better?*

As a triple compounder, you don't just buy stocks you heard about from your brother-in-law and hope for the best. You buy the *right* ones and hold onto them with intention — not just to avoid unproductive screen-scrolling but to build a system that compounds both financially and energetically.

Here's what I look for in a true value asset.

>> **Category kings:** Companies that dominate their niche

>> **Efficiency creators:** Businesses that help people do things better, faster, and cheaper

>> **Mission-driven brands:** Companies that do good for humankind

Published growth trends, profit margins, and P/E ratios matter, but not as much as understanding how a company creates long-term value. The goal isn't to predict the next quarter. It's to invest in companies that *last*.

I developed this lens after reading the book *Play Bigger: How Pirates, Dreamers, and Innovators Create and Dominate Markets* (Harper Business, 2016) while building Phase 2 of my Triple Compounding system. That's when I realized that great entrepreneurs make great value investors because the qualities that make *your* business valuable are exactly what you should look for in *other* businesses. That mindset shift is one thing that makes triple compounding so powerful.

A value stock doesn't rise overnight. But over time, when the market catches up to its true worth, it can deliver consistent and compounding returns, especially when paired with dividends.

Dividend stocks

Imagine getting paid just for owning something. That's exactly what dividend stocks do, and they're my favorite alternative to renting out real estate because there's much less hassle involved in earning. These are shares of companies that distribute a portion of their profits to shareholders — usually every quarter. It's one of the most accessible forms of passive income and a core component of many triple compounders' portfolios.

Dividend stocks are especially popular among people who want

>> Steady, predictable income

>> Lower volatility compared to growth or hype stocks

>> The ability to reinvest dividends and compound wealth over time

These companies are often well established, profitable, and stable — think blue-chip companies like Coca-Cola, Johnson & Johnson, or Procter & Gamble. Although their value may not double overnight, they tend to be resilient during market downturns and offer a level of consistency that many investors appreciate.

The best part? Dividends can be automatically reinvested, allowing you to compound your returns over time without lifting a finger.

Here's why I love dividend stocks inside a triple-compounding system:

>> They align beautifully with Phase 3, investing in external assets, especially when paired with automation.

>> You can set up DRIPs (dividend reinvestment plans) that buy more shares for you every time a dividend is paid.

>> They can supplement your income in retirement — or sooner if you build your portfolio with intention.

>> Reinvested dividends can significantly boost long-term returns, even if the stock itself doesn't grow much.

Not all dividend stocks are created equal. Some companies pay high dividends because they're desperate to attract investors. If a yield looks too good to be true, it may be. Always check the company's health and dividend payout ratio.

The goal of dividend investing isn't just income. It's *compound income* — income that grows on autopilot when you reinvest it smartly. Dividend stocks are like your portfolio's loyal employees. They keep working and paying you — even while you sleep.

You can discover the amount of dividend a company pays on websites like Yahoo Finance.

Pump-and-dump stocks

If value stocks are the wise old sages and dividend stocks are your loyal employees, pump-and-dump stocks are the shady restaurant customers who promise the world and disappear before the check arrives.

These are stocks that get artificially inflated — *pumped* — through hype, manipulation, or social media buzz only to be *dumped* once enough unsuspecting investors buy in. The result? The stock price crashes, leaving latecomers holding the bag.

You've probably seen this happen in real time, even if you didn't realize it. A stock skyrockets overnight because of a viral Reddit thread, a Twitter (I mean X) influencer, or a "leaked" stock tip and then drops like a rock days (or even hours) later. The problem isn't just volatility. It's that the price has nothing to do with the company's actual value.

Signs of a pump-and-dump stock include

>> Massive price spikes with no news or fundamental reason

>> Heavy promotion on forums, in chat rooms, or in spammy newsletters

>> A small, low-volume stock that's easy to manipulate

>> Sudden surges in volume followed by silence

Pump-and-dumps are common in penny stocks, microcaps, and even crypto, especially when there's low liquidity and low regulation. If it feels like gambling, it probably is.

In my early investing days, I lost thousands chasing hyped-up stocks that had no business being in my portfolio. That's one of the reasons I created the IDDA framework — to help investors *avoid* the noise and make confident, independent decisions.

Just because a stock is being talked about online doesn't mean it's a scam, but hype should never be your reason to invest. The moment you hear, "It's going to the moon!" ask yourself, "Based on what, exactly?"

Triple compounders don't fall for shortcuts or speculation. They build portfolios based on real companies, real value, and long-term vision. They don't invest in hype. They invest in purpose.

Cycling stocks

Some stocks move in waves — and not the kind you catch at the beach. These are called *cycling stocks* (or *cyclical stocks*), and they tend to rise and fall in sync with the economy.

When the economy is booming, people spend more on things like travel, new cars, and fancy furniture, so companies in those industries thrive. But when the economy slows down, those same companies often see a drop in profits, and their stock prices usually follow.

This isn't necessarily a bad thing. In fact, if you understand how business cycles work, cyclical stocks can be a powerful addition to your triple-compounding strategy, especially as part of your long-term plan.

Common examples of cycling stock industries include

>> Travel and hospitality (like airlines, hotels, and cruise lines)

>> Automotive and transportation

>> Retail and luxury goods

>> Construction and home improvement

>> Energy and materials (like oil, gas, and metals)

How do you know when to buy cycling stocks? It starts with understanding where the economy is in its cycle.

>> **Early expansion:** People are cautiously optimistic; markets start to rise.

>> **Full-blown boom:** Spending is high; cyclical stocks usually perform best.

>> **Slowdown or recession:** Spending pulls back, and these stocks tend to drop.

Although cyclical stocks rise and fall with the economy, defensive stocks do the opposite. These are companies that tend to remain stable even during economic downturns — think groceries, utilities, and healthcare. Many defensive stocks also pay consistent dividends, which can help cushion the blow when cyclical stocks are taking a hit.

Because of their predictable behavior during market cycles, many cyclical stocks make excellent *swing trading* candidates. Their price movements often follow patterns that technical traders can spot and capitalize on — whether that means holding for a few days, weeks, or months. I expand on swing trading in Chapter 13.

"

Growth stocks

If value stocks are the slow-and-steady types, *growth stocks* are the overachievers. These are companies that are expanding fast, disrupting industries, and reinvesting most of their profits (if they even have profits yet!) to keep growing even faster.

Growth stocks are typically not cheap because investors are betting on the company's *future potential* rather than its current financials.

Think of tech giants like Apple, Amazon, or Tesla in their earlier days. These were once high-risk bets, but over time, they proved their growth trajectory. Today's growth stocks may be in sectors like

>> Artificial intelligence

>> Clean energy and electric vehicles

>> E-commerce and cloud computing

>> Biotechnology

>> Fintech and emerging markets

Unlike dividend stocks, most growth stocks don't pay dividends. Instead, they reinvest everything back into innovation, hiring, or expansion. That means the only way you make money is through *capital appreciation,* the stock price going up.

Here's why growth stocks can be powerful inside a triple-compounding portfolio:

>> They have the potential to significantly outperform the market — if you choose wisely and time your entry right.

>> They're ideal for younger investors or anyone with a longer time horizon and a higher risk tolerance.

>> When paired with more stable assets, they can give your portfolio the "rocket fuel" that accelerates long-term returns.

Growth stocks often look overpriced on paper (they usually have high P/E ratios), but that's because the market is pricing in future earnings. Your job is to determine whether those expectations are realistic or hyped.

I like to combine growth stocks with value investing, meaning that I buy growth stocks when their price temporarily drops due to market sentiment.

You can find my hottest stock picks every month in my monthly newsletter: www.triplecompounding.com/newsletter.

Growth stocks tend to be more volatile than cycling or value stocks, especially in down markets. That doesn't make them bad; it just means you need a strategy, not just hope.

When chosen wisely, growth stocks can transform your portfolio over time, but they're not lottery tickets. They're businesses that need time and execution to fulfill their potential.

Unlocking Cryptocurrency

Cryptocurrency is one of the most hyped — and misunderstood — asset classes in modern investing. It's volatile, unregulated, and polarizing. But for triple compounders who know how to approach it strategically, it also offers unique opportunities for growth, diversification, and long-term freedom.

I wrote an entire book on this topic — *Cryptocurrency Investing For Dummies*, 2nd Edition (Wiley, 2023) — because I believe crypto is more than just a speculative asset. It's a new layer of the financial ecosystem. In this section, I show you how to explore it as one of your external investment options.

Defining cryptocurrency

So, what is cryptocurrency, really? It's a decentralized form of digital money that operates without a central bank, powered by *blockchain* technology — a decentralized digital ledger that records transactions across a network of computers in a secure, transparent, and tamper-proof way.

Unlike traditional currencies like the US dollar or the euro, most cryptocurrencies have a fixed supply and are controlled by code, not governments. That makes them potentially resistant to inflation and government interference — two factors that heavily influenced my personal journey into crypto investing.

After watching my father lose his business and assets to a corrupt government, the idea of financial sovereignty hit home for me. Bitcoin and other decentralized assets offer something many traditional systems can't: freedom and control over your own money.

Here's why cryptocurrency can be a compelling part of your external asset strategy:

>> It diversifies your portfolio beyond traditional assets like stocks and real estate.

>> It may provide capital appreciation through price growth (if chosen and timed wisely).

>> Some cryptos allow for yield generation, such as staking or earning interest.

>> It can serve as a potential hedge against inflation and currency risk.

>> It fuels emerging technologies like decentralized finance (DeFi), non-fungible tokens (NFTs), and the metaverse.

NFTs are unique digital assets stored on a blockchain representing ownership of something unique, like art, music, or virtual collectibles. *Metaverse* is a virtual, interconnected digital world where people can interact, work, play, shop, and invest using avatars, often powered by blockchain, cryptocurrencies, and virtual reality technologies.

Before you get starry-eyed, here's the truth: crypto is not magic. It comes with serious risks — from volatility and scams to regulatory uncertainty and tech vulnerabilities. That's why I dedicate an entire section to risk management in Chapter 3 and use the IDDA framework to evaluate each crypto's fundamental, technical, and sentimental health.

Crypto is not about getting rich overnight. It's about getting smart, intentional, and strategic about how you enter this space — as you do with any other asset class.

The price of a coin may catch headlines, but what really matters is what's *behind* that coin: the blockchain, the use case, the adoption, and the community. In other words, don't invest in symbols; invest in substance.

If you don't understand how a crypto project works, don't invest in it. That's not just one of my rules. It's your protection against being the exit liquidity for someone else's pump-and-dump.

Understanding coins, altcoins, and tokens

Before you go crypto shopping, it's important to understand the difference between coins, altcoins, and tokens because they're not interchangeable.

>> **Coins:** These are digital assets that operate on their own independent blockchain. Examples are Bitcoin (BTC), Ethereum (ETH), and XRP.

>> **Altcoins (short for "alternative coins"):** These include any coin that isn't Bitcoin. Most run on their own blockchains and offer specific use cases beyond just "digital money."

» **Tokens:** These are digital assets that don't have their own blockchain. Instead, they operate on top of an existing blockchain network. Ethereum and Solana are examples. Tokens can represent anything: ownership in a project, access to a platform, or even digital art.

Think of coins as the infrastructure and tokens as applications built on top of that infrastructure.

Bitcoin

Bitcoin is where it all began. Launched in 2009 by the mysterious Satoshi Nakamoto, Bitcoin (BTC) was the first-ever cryptocurrency. It remains the largest, most recognized, and most widely held digital asset in the world.

But Bitcoin isn't just a first mover. It's the foundation of the entire crypto ecosystem. For many investors, it still serves as the "digital gold" of the 21st century.

Bitcoin was created as a decentralized alternative to government-issued currencies. It runs on its own blockchain, has a fixed supply of 21 million coins, and is not controlled by any central bank, government, or corporation. This makes it immune to inflationary policies that devalue traditional currencies over time.

Here's why many triple compounders consider Bitcoin an essential part of their external asset allocation:

» It's seen as a **store of value,** similar to gold, especially during times of currency debasement or economic uncertainty.

» It's **scarce** by design, with only 21 million coins ever to exist — a feature that increases its appeal as digital hard money.

» It's **borderless and permissionless,** meaning you can send it to anyone, anywhere, without a bank or intermediary.

» It's becoming **more mainstream,** with adoption by companies, hedge funds, and even governments.

Although Bitcoin is no longer the fastest or most innovative crypto out there, it's the most battle-tested and widely adopted. For many, it serves as the entry point to crypto and the core holding in a diversified digital portfolio.

If you're new to cryptocurrency, Bitcoin is a great place to start. It's the least risky of the bunch — not because it's safe but because it's proven. Owning Bitcoin doesn't mean betting on a trend. It means investing in a system of money that's decentralized, deflationary, and global.

Bitcoin can still be extremely volatile. Don't invest more than you can afford to hold through wild price swings.

Altcoins

Altcoins are any cryptocurrencies that aren't Bitcoin. Some try to improve on Bitcoin's limitations. Others launch entirely new ecosystems around smart contracts, DeFi, and next-gen tech.

Here's a breakdown of three of the most important altcoins in the market at the time of writing:

>> **Ethereum (ETH):** Ethereum introduced the concept of smart contracts, enabling developers to build decentralized apps (dApps) that run without middlemen. Ethereum is used to pay for transactions and services on the Ethereum network.

   Blockchain: Ethereum

   Primary use: Smart contracts, dApps, DeFi, NFTs

   As of March 2025: Approximately $1,993 per coin, about $375B market cap

>> **Solana (SOL):** Solana is built for speed. It can process thousands of transactions per second thanks to a unique system called proof-of-history (PoH). It's popular among developers building fast, scalable applications in gaming, NFTs, and finance.

   Blockchain: Solana

   Primary use: High-speed DeFi, Web3 apps, NFTs

   As of March 2025: Approximately $129 per coin, about $120B market cap

>> **XRP (Ripple):** XRP focuses on cross-border payments, aiming to make international money transfers faster and cheaper. It's not mined like Bitcoin; instead, it uses a consensus protocol that reduces transaction time and energy usage.

   Blockchain: XRP Ledger

   Primary use: Global payments and remittances

   As of March 2025: Approximately $2.38 per coin, about $138.7B market cap

Altcoins can offer more upside than Bitcoin, but they also come with more complexity and risk. Use the IDDA framework to evaluate both the vision and viability of each project.

Just because a coin is "cheaper" doesn't mean it's a better deal. Price per coin means nothing without understanding market cap, supply, and utility.

Tokens

Tokens are digital assets created and hosted on an existing blockchain. The most common platform for tokens is Ethereum, but others like Solana, BNB Chain, and Avalanche also support them.

Unlike coins, tokens don't function as native currency for their networks. Instead, they represent

>> Access to a product or service (utility tokens)

>> Ownership or voting rights in a project (governance tokens)

>> Real-world assets like dollars or gold (stablecoins)

>> Unique digital collectibles (NFTs)

Here are some common types of tokens:

>> **Utility tokens:** Give you access to services, discounts, or tools on a crypto platform

>> **Governance tokens:** Allow you to vote on decisions related to a decentralized project

>> **Stablecoins:** Pegged to traditional currencies like the USD (for example, USDC, USDT) to reduce volatility

>> **NFTs:** Represent ownership of unique assets like art, music, or in-game items

Tokens are like apps on your phone, where the blockchain is the operating system. You don't need to build a new operating system to build something useful. You just need to use the tools already available.

Many of the most exciting projects in crypto aren't coins; they're tokens. But their value depends on adoption, not hype.

Staking

If you've ever wished your crypto could earn income while you sleep — without having to sell it — staking may be your new favorite strategy.

Staking is the process of locking up your cryptocurrency to help support the operations and security of a blockchain network. In return, you earn rewards, usually in the form of more crypto. It's kind of like earning interest at a bank but for participating in a decentralized system.

You can stake certain cryptocurrencies that run on proof-of-stake (PoS) or delegated proof-of-stake networks. Popular staking coins include Ethereum, Solana, Cardano, and Polkadot.

Here's how staking works in simple terms:

1. **You commit your crypto to the network.**
2. **Your funds are used to validate transactions and keep the blockchain secure.**
3. **You get rewarded with more of that crypto in exchange for your contribution.**

Think of it as renting out your crypto's energy to help keep the lights on in the blockchain — and getting paid for it.

Benefits of staking include the following:

>> **Passive income:** Your crypto earns while you hold.

>> **Compound growth:** Many platforms let you automatically restake your rewards.

>> **Network support:** You're helping the ecosystem stay secure and decentralized.

You don't need to run your own validator node to stake. Many exchanges, like Coinbase, Kraken, or Binance, let you stake your crypto with just a few clicks. Also, staking rewards vary, depending on the coin and platform, and some require lock-up periods. Always check the terms before committing your funds.

Staked assets are still exposed to market volatility. If the price of the coin drops, your staked rewards may not make up for the loss. Staking is not risk-free, but it *is* a way to put idle crypto to work.

Non-fungible tokens

Non-fungible tokens (NFTs) are one of the most talked-about applications of blockchain technology. At their core, NFTs are unique digital assets stored on a blockchain that represent ownership of something that is one of a kind. That "something" can be anything: art, music, event tickets, virtual land, digital fashion, or even a tweet.

Unlike cryptocurrencies like Bitcoin or Ethereum, NFTs are not interchangeable. One Bitcoin is always equal to another Bitcoin. But each NFT is different, which is what makes it non-fungible.

The technology behind NFTs has real potential — and it goes way beyond just digital art. Here are a few real-world applications that are already in motion.

>> **Art and collectibles:** Digital artists can now sell and track ownership of their work with authenticity built in.

>> **Gaming:** Players can buy, sell, or trade in-game assets — like characters or weapons — as NFTs.

>> **Memberships and access:** Some NFTs serve as digital keys to communities, events, or perks.

>> **Real estate and identity:** Long-term, NFTs can represent deeds, IDs, or other legal documents.

If you're wondering whether NFTs belong in a triple compounder's portfolio, here's my take: they're *not* must-haves, but they *can* be an interesting part of your strategy if you understand their utility, scarcity, and creator value.

The most valuable NFTs tend to have strong communities, real-world use cases, or connections to influential creators or brands. If you're just buying random images hoping they'll go to the moon (skyrocket), you're gambling, not investing.

NFTs are powered by smart contracts, and most live on blockchains like Ethereum, Solana, or Polygon. If you're already exploring those ecosystems, NFTs may be a natural next step.

The NFT space is still speculative and unregulated. Many projects are driven by hype, and scams are common. Don't invest in an NFT just because someone else made money on it. Invest because you understand the asset and believe in the long-term value.

If you want to dive deeper into crypto investing, visit `www.triplecompounding.com/crypto`.

Forex

Forex — short for foreign exchange — is the largest and most liquid financial market in the world. It's where global currencies are bought, sold, and traded 24 hours a day, five days a week.

In forex, you're not buying physical currency. You're trading currency pairs — like EUR/USD or USD/JPY — speculating on how one currency will move in relation to another.

If you've ever traveled abroad and exchanged money, you've already participated in the forex market on a much smaller scale.

Here's what makes forex unique:

>> It's the most liquid market in the world — trillions of dollars traded daily.

>> It runs 24/5 across global time zones.

>> It uses leverage, meaning you can control a large trade size with a relatively small amount of money.

>> Currency values are influenced by interest rates, inflation, economic reports, and geopolitical events.

Although the potential for profit is real, so is the potential for loss, especially when leverage is involved. That's why most retail traders who jump into forex without a plan end up losing money.

If you're going to explore forex, treat it like a skill — not a slot machine. Study the fundamentals, learn technical analysis, and start small. Forex can be an active, short-term income strategy that complements your long-term portfolio, but only if you have rules and discipline in place.

Leverage can magnify gains, but it also magnifies losses. Don't risk more than you can afford to lose and never trade with money meant for bills or savings.

Even though I no longer trade forex full time, the lessons I learned in that market — about timing, psychology, and risk — still shape how I invest today. That's the beauty of triple compounding: Every experience builds your foundation for smarter investing.

FOREX: IT'S PERSONAL

My first experience with forex wasn't in a finance class or a trading seminar. It was during a global crisis, and I had no idea what I was doing.

I was living in Tokyo, studying electrical engineering, with zero background in finance. When the 2008 recession hit, I kept hearing people say, "The US dollar is getting cheaper against the Japanese yen." I didn't fully understand what that meant in economic terms, but I *felt* it every time I exchanged currency.

As a foreigner in Japan, I regularly exchanged yen for other currencies when I traveled. Sometimes I'd come home with more money, sometimes less, depending on the exchange rate. So, when the dollar kept dropping, I had a thought: *If I ever move to the US, now may be a good time to exchange my yen into dollars since dollars are so cheap!*

So, I began manually converting a little bit of JPY to USD every day. But the dollar kept falling. Every day, I'd kick myself for exchanging too soon, thinking, *If I'd just waited one more day, I'd have gotten a better rate!*

One day, I said out loud to a friend, "I wish I could write a code that tells my bank to exchange my money only when the dollar hits a price I like." He laughed and said, "That already exists. It's called forex trading, and you don't need to build a system, just open a trading account."

That conversation changed my life.

With his help, I opened a forex account and unknowingly started trading with 14X leverage. By sheer luck (and a little bit of beginner's intuition), I made $10,000 in September 2008, right in the middle of a market crash when everyone else was losing money. I was hooked.

A year later, I moved to the US and started working at a forex broker on Wall Street. After I got fired from that job, my passion for forex didn't fade. In fact, it became the foundation of my first book, *Invest Diva's Guide to Making Money in Forex* (McGraw Hill, 2013).

I continued trading for years, until one highly leveraged position wiped out everything. That painful loss reduced my risk tolerance and ultimately shifted my investing approach toward lower-risk, higher-reward strategies. It also led me to develop the IDDA framework so that others could learn from my wins *and* my mistakes.

Options

Options are one of the most misunderstood and misused financial tools out there. When used strategically, they can *protect* your portfolio or *amplify* your returns. But when used recklessly, they can wipe out your account faster than you can say "theta decay."

An option is a contract that gives you the right — but not the obligation — to buy or sell an underlying asset (usually a stock) at a specific price, within a specific time frame.

There are two main types of options.

>> **Call options:** Give you the right to *buy* a stock at a certain price (useful when you think the price will go up).

>> **Put options:** Give you the right to *sell* a stock at a certain price (useful when you think the price will go down).

Options aren't new. My team has created a whole course on using them to *reduce* risk and *boost* passive income inside my Triple Compounding system. It's available at `https://www.triplecompounding.com/options`.

What most people don't realize is this: Options were originally invented as a risk management tool rather than a get-rich-quick strategy.

When used wisely, options can do the following:

>> Generate income through strategies like covered calls

>> Hedge against market drops with protective puts

>> Boost returns with less capital compared to buying full shares

>> Add flexibility to your overall investing approach

The reality is that most beginners dive into options without a strategy and end up chasing short-term gains using high-risk, high-leverage bets like weekly options, zero-DTE plays, or meme-stock hype trades. *Zero-DTE* (zero days to expiration) refers to options contracts that expire on the same day they're traded, making them extremely high-risk and time-sensitive. They're often used by advanced traders for fast, speculative bets.

Options are like power tools: They're amazing in skilled hands and dangerous in untrained ones. Learn the mechanics before placing real money on the line. In my Triple Compounding Live events, we hold our Triple Compounders by the hand and show them how to trade options without taking too much risk. Look for an event near you at www.triplecompounding.com/live.

Options can expire worthless. That means you can lose 100 percent of what you paid for the contract. Always manage your risk and never trade options without understanding the Greeks (like delta, theta, and implied volatility).

When used intentionally, options can be a powerful tool inside your triple-compounding portfolio and give you leverage with control. But when misused, they turn into nothing more than educated gambling.

Index funds

If forex and options are the fast lane of investing, index funds are the scenic route. For many triple compounders, index funds are the *sweet spot* between simplicity, safety, and long-term growth.

Index funds are investment funds — usually structured as ETFs (exchange-traded funds) or mutual funds — that track a specific market index. That means instead of picking individual stocks, you invest in an entire basket of companies that represent a segment of the market.

One of the most well-known examples is the S&P 500 index fund, which includes 500 of the largest publicly traded companies in the US, including Apple, Microsoft, Amazon, and Google.

When you invest in an index fund, you get

>> **Instant diversification:** One fund gives you exposure to hundreds (sometimes thousands) of companies.

>> **Low fees:** Because index funds are passively managed, they're way cheaper than traditional mutual funds.

>> **Minimal effort:** You don't need to research individual companies or time the market. You set it, forget it, and let it grow.

Index funds are especially powerful for

>> Beginner investors

>> Busy professionals who want to automate

> » Long-term wealth builders who value steady, compounding growth over hype

> » Retirement accounts such as IRAs and 401(k)s

TIP

Index funds are one of the few investments even Warren Buffett recommends for everyday investors. He's said that if he could only give one piece of advice to most people, it would be, "Put 90 percent of your money in a low-cost S&P 500 index fund."

REMEMBER

In triple compounding, you don't just chase excitement; you also build stability. Index funds can anchor your portfolio while other assets give you room to grow and explore. You can dive into the world of ETFs with *Exchange-Traded Funds For Dummies* by Russell Wild (Wiley, 2021).

REITS

If you want to invest in real estate without fixing toilets, chasing down tenants, or worrying about broken HVAC systems, then you need to know about Real Estate Investment Trusts (REITs).

A REIT is a company that owns, operates, or finances income-generating real estate, and it's legally required to pay out at least 90 percent of its taxable income to shareholders in the form of dividends. That means you, the investor, get regular cash flow without ever owning or managing a property yourself.

REITs are kind of like real estate mutual funds. You buy shares (often through the stock market), and in return, you get exposure to a portfolio of properties — sometimes hundreds — ranging from apartment buildings and office parks to malls, hospitals, and even cell towers.

There are two main types of REITs:

> » **Publicly traded REITs:** Bought and sold just like stocks or ETFs through your brokerage account. These are the most liquid and beginner-friendly.

> » **Private or non-traded REITs:** Offer access to different kinds of real estate but may have higher fees, less transparency, and longer lock-up periods.

REITs are a powerful fit for your triple-compounding strategy because they offer

> » **Passive income** through consistent dividends

> » **Diversification** across property types and locations

>> **Liquidity** because you can buy or sell shares easily

>> **Low barriers to entry** because you don't need $100,000 or a mortgage to get started

You can invest in REITs with as little as $100. Some popular ones even pay monthly dividends, which is great for automating your passive income stream. However, just because a REIT pays a high dividend doesn't mean it's healthy. Use the same fundamental analysis you would with a stock. Look at occupancy rates, management quality, debt levels, and payout ratios.

REITs are still tied to the real estate market. If commercial property values drop or vacancy rates spike, your investment can lose value. Always diversify your income streams, even within real estate.

Find out more about REITS in *REITs For Dummies* by Brad Thomas (Wiley, 2023).

Chapter **7**

Investing in Offline External Assets

Most people think of investing as something that happens online — buying stocks, crypto, or options with a few taps on a screen. And although those digital markets are powerful tools (which I cover in Chapter 6), they're not the only way to grow your wealth.

There's a whole other category of external assets that live in the physical world — things you can touch, own, or operate in real life. I call these *offline assets*, and for many triple compounders, they create a second layer of security, income, and long-term growth.

This chapter is your guide to the most common offline investment vehicles, including

» Real estate, from flipping to rentals to commercial buildings

» Private equity, including venture capital and growth equity

In this chapter, you find out how to spot the opportunities that make sense for your goals, your time, and your energy — and avoid the ones that tie you down or drain your bandwidth.

Offline assets are often slower to move but more stable in the long term. They can be your portfolio's foundation while your online investments provide speed and flexibility.

The goal isn't to copy what other people are investing in. The goal is to create a personalized, resilient portfolio that supports your entire wealth-building flywheel.

Building Wealth with Real Estate

Real estate is one of the oldest — and most trusted — ways to build wealth. From generational landlords to HGTV-style flippers, people have long turned to property as a way to generate income, hedge against inflation, and create long-term financial security.

I have some good news: You don't have to buy a house to invest in real estate.

Whether you want to roll up your sleeves and flip properties, collect passive rental income, or own a slice of the real estate market through Real Estate Investment Trusts (REITs), which I cover in Chapter 6, there's an option for every risk level, budget, and lifestyle.

Your goal as a triple compounder is not just to own "stuff." It's to create automated, intentional income that grows with time. Real estate can do exactly that, *if you choose the right strategy for your season of life.*

In the next few sections, I break down the following most common ways investors tap into real estate as an external asset:

House flipping: The fast-paced, high-risk way to profit from undervalued properties

>> **Rental properties:** A steady stream of cash flow — and headaches, if you're not careful

>> **REITs:** A hands-off way to invest in real estate without ever touching drywall

>> **Residential real estate:** Properties where people live, from single-family homes to vacation rentals

>> **Commercial real estate:** Larger-scale investments like office buildings, shopping centers, and industrial warehouses

Real estate can build real wealth, but it's not passive by default. You need a strategy that matches your energy, risk tolerance, and time capacity.

You don't need to buy a house to get into real estate. Thanks to modern tools like REITs and crowdfunding platforms, there are more accessible ways to get started than ever before.

House flipping

House flipping may be the most glamorous — and most misunderstood — real estate strategy out there. Thanks to TV shows and influencer reels, it's easy to think that flipping a home is just a quick trip to Home Depot and a few weekends of DIY magic.

But here's the truth: Flipping real estate is a full-time business, not a passive investment. And unless you know what you're doing (or have a team who does), it can cost you far more than you make.

Flipping involves buying a property at a discount, fixing it up, and reselling it for a profit — ideally in a short period of time. It's all about timing, margins, and speed. The longer you hold the property, the more it eats into your potential profits.

Some flippers do all the work themselves. Others outsource everything and manage the project like a business. Either way, success in flipping comes down to one thing: your numbers.

Before you ever swing a hammer (or hire someone who does), you need to know the following:

>> The purchase price

>> Your renovation budget

>> Expected selling price (after repair value, or ARV)

>> All holding costs (loan interest, taxes, insurance, utilities)

>> Closing costs and commissions

>> Your profit margin

Your profit margin is the most important consideration. Many pros aim for at least 20 percent to 30 percent net profit after all expenses.

REMEMBER

Flipping is not triple compounding unless it's systematized. If you treat it like a one-time hustle, you're just buying yourself a part-time job. If you treat it like a business — with teams, checklists, and automation — it can be a powerful wealth-building tool. Also, it works best in hot markets that have low inventory and high buyer demand. But those same markets can also be the riskiest if things turn.

WARNING

Underestimating repair costs is the number one reason flippers lose money. Always estimate high on your budget and build in extra time. Renovation delays are more common than you think.

Rental properties

Rental properties are one of the most popular ways to turn real estate into a recurring income stream. The idea is simple: buy a property, rent it out, and collect monthly payments. Although the income can be passive, the work involved *usually isn't* — especially in the beginning.

When done right, rental properties can offer

>> Monthly cash flow from tenants

>> Long-term appreciation of the property

>> Tax benefits like depreciation and mortgage interest deductions

>> Leverage from controlling a large asset with a relatively small down payment

>> A hedge against inflation because rent prices often rise with inflation

But the truth is that owning rental properties can also mean late-night plumbing emergencies, broken leases, and months with no income if a tenant leaves or stops paying.

That's why successful rental investing requires more than just buying a cute house in a nice neighborhood. It takes the following:

>> Careful location analysis

>> Accurate cash flow projections

>> Smart property management, whether you do it yourself or hire help

>> Legal awareness of tenant rights, leases, and eviction rules

In my own investing journey, I discovered that being a landlord is not the same thing as being a passive investor. If you want rental properties to support your triple-compounding lifestyle, you need to build systems or delegate them.

You don't have to start with a multi-unit building. Some of the best rental portfolios start with one small, cash-flowing, single-family home. Focus on properties that are cash-flow positive from day one — not just "potentially profitable in a few years."

If your mortgage, taxes, and maintenance costs are higher than your rent income, your property is bleeding money rather than building wealth. Never assume appreciation will bail you out.

Residential real estate

Residential real estate includes any property where people live: single-family homes, condos, duplexes, townhouses, and small apartment buildings (typically four units or fewer). This is often the first stop for new real estate investors because it feels more familiar and accessible than commercial properties.

Residential properties tend to be more stable than commercial, especially in uncertain markets. People always need a place to live, regardless of what the economy is doing. And if you pick the right neighborhood, residential rentals can provide steady cash flow, long-term appreciation, and tax advantages.

Here are some common ways that investors earn with residential real estate:

>> **Long-term rentals** (traditional landlord-tenant model)

>> **Short-term rentals** (Airbnb, Vrbo, and so on)

>> **House hacking** (living in one unit and renting out the others)

Residential real estate is typically easier to finance and manage than commercial, and there's a wider pool of buyers if you ever decide to sell.

Start with what you know. If you've lived in a certain type of home or area and understand what renters want there, that insight can give you an edge as an investor.

You're not just investing in a property; you're investing in a community. Pay close attention to school zones, crime rates, job growth, and local amenities.

Buying in the wrong neighborhood — or underestimating property taxes, vacancies, or maintenance — can turn a residential "deal" into a money pit. Run the numbers, and don't get emotional.

Commercial real estate

Commercial real estate includes income-producing properties used for business purposes: office buildings, retail centers, warehouses, apartment buildings with five or more units, hotels, and even storage facilities.

This is where the *big money* is made in real estate, but it often requires more experience, capital, and risk management than residential real estate. Commercial leases tend to be longer, tenants may cover more of the operating costs (known as triple-net leases), and the valuation of these properties is based on income potential, not just comparable sales.

Commercial real estate can be incredibly rewarding when done right, by providing the following:

>> Higher income potential due to multiple units or higher rents

>> Economies of scale (especially with multifamily or mixed-use buildings)

>> More professional tenants because businesses are often more predictable than individual renters

>> Stronger long-term appreciation if the area is growing

But this space also comes with more risk. A vacant storefront or large commercial unit can cost you thousands per month if it sits empty.

If you're interested in commercial real estate but not ready to buy a strip mall, you can get exposure through REITs, crowdfunding platforms, or syndications.

Lenders often require higher down payments (20 percent to 30 percent or more) and stricter approval for commercial loans. Make sure that you understand the numbers and have a solid team in place.

Investing in Private Equity

Private equity is one of the most powerful — but least understood — external asset classes in the investing world. It's where the ultra-wealthy often play: investing in private companies before they go public (if they ever do) and earning returns through business growth, acquisitions, or eventual exits.

Unlike stocks or REITs, private equity investments aren't traded on public exchanges. That means they're less liquid, harder to access, and usually come with higher minimums. But for investors who qualify, private equity can offer higher returns, more control, and a deeper connection to the companies they support.

Private equity can take many forms, including

>> Direct investments in start-ups or growing businesses

>> Venture capital funding early-stage companies with high growth potential in exchange for partial ownership

>> Private equity funds managed by firms that pool money from investors

>> Angel investing in early-stage companies

>> Crowdfunding platforms that allow smaller investors to access private deals

In my own journey, private equity became part of Phase 3 of triple compounding (see Chapter 6)— *after* I had built my own income and systems and only when I had capital I could afford to tie up for years.

In the following sections, I look at three of the most common types of private equity investments you may come across, whether you're a retail investor exploring crowdfunding platforms or an accredited investor ready to dive deeper.

Venture capital

This is private equity at the start-up stage. Venture capital focuses on high-risk, high-reward investments in early-stage companies — usually in tech, biotech, or disruptive industries.

Venture capitalists typically invest in exchange for equity (ownership), and they expect that most of their investments will fail but that one or two big winners will more than make up for the losses.

As an everyday investor, you may not have access to top venture capital funds. However, thanks to platforms like SeedInvest, Republic, and StartEngine, you can now invest small amounts into vetted start-ups and get a front-row seat to innovation.

Venture capital investing is like planting seeds. Some won't grow, some will shoot up fast, and a few may become a forest. Only invest what you can afford to let sit and grow for years.

Growth equity

Think of this as the "teenage" phase of private investing. Growth equity investors fund companies that are past the start-up stage but need capital to expand, enter new markets, or restructure operations.

Unlike with venture capital, the companies they invest in often have proven revenue and are looking to scale — not just survive.

As an investor, growth equity lets you tap into businesses that are less risky than raw start-ups but still offer potential for a big upside. Some crowdfunding platforms, syndicates, and small business funds offer access to these kinds of deals.

Growth equity is ideal for investors who want to support expansion-stage companies with a clear use of funds and a path to profitability.

Buyouts and private acquisitions

This is the heavyweight class of private equity. Buyouts involve purchasing a controlling interest in a company, often using a mix of investor money and debt (called a leveraged buyout or LBO).

Buyout firms typically target mature businesses with steady cash flow, cut costs or boost performance, and sell them later at a profit.

Although this kind of investing is mostly reserved for institutional or accredited investors, some fractional platforms and private equity funds of funds are starting to open the door to smaller investors.

Private equity buyouts aren't about quick flips. They're about improving businesses over time and getting paid well for the patience.

Funds of funds

If you like the idea of private equity but don't want to pick individual companies or deals, a fund of funds may be your entry point. These are professionally managed portfolios that invest in multiple private equity funds — kind of like the private investing version of a mutual fund. Instead of betting on one company or one manager, you get exposure to a broader pool of deals, strategies, and industries.

Some funds of funds are available only to accredited investors, but a few platforms and retirement plans offer access to retail investors through structured products or lower minimums.

Funds of funds are great for diversification, but they often come with extra layers of fees, so make sure that the access is worth the cost.

You may not know exactly which companies are in the portfolio, so always look for transparency around fund strategy, past performance, and lock-up periods.

Getting into private equity without billions

You don't need to be a billionaire to get into private equity anymore. Platforms like AngelList, Republic, and StartEngine have lowered the barrier for both accredited and nonaccredited investors.

Private equity is illiquid, meaning that your money may be tied up for five to ten years. And yes, many private companies fail. Never invest more than you can afford to lose, and always do your due diligence.

Private equity isn't for everyone. But for triple compounders who've built stable income streams, solid investments, and a long-term financial vision, it can be an exciting next-level play.

Investing Old School: Physical Precious Metals

If real estate is the dinner-party flex of offline investing, and crypto is the rebel genius, then physical precious metals are the grandparents. Quiet. Old school. And still incredibly valuable.

For thousands of years, people have stored wealth in gold, silver, and other metals. Why? Because unlike currencies or companies, these elements never go to zero. They don't rely on CEOs or central banks. They just *are*.

In a world of digital everything, holding real, tangible gold in your hand can feel oddly grounding — and strategic.

In the following sections, I uncover what to know before adding shiny things to your triple-compounding portfolio.

Understanding the role of metals in your portfolio

Precious metals aren't designed to skyrocket like stocks or crypto. They're built to hold value when everything else feels shaky. This is why many investors use metals as

>> A hedge against inflation

>> A safe haven during economic downturns or global crises

>> A diversifier that moves differently than the stock market

Gold and silver won't make your net worth explode, but they can help keep it from imploding.

Metals don't produce income. They don't pay dividends. You don't "scale" gold. Their job is to preserve, not multiply. And that's okay.

REMEMBER

Choosing among gold, silver, and other metals

The two most common metals for individual investors are gold and silver:

>> **Gold:** The classic. It is more stable, more expensive, and easier to store large amounts of value in a small space.

>> **Silver:** Cheaper and more volatile. It takes up more space but gives you more flexibility for smaller transactions.

Other options like platinum and palladium exist, but they're more industrial and less common for everyday investors.

If you're just getting started, most people begin with silver (for affordability) or small gold bars and coins (for compact value).

Buying and storing precious metals

When it comes to buying physical metals, you've got a few options:

>> **Bars and coins:** These are the most common. You can buy them online or from local dealers.

>> **Jewelry:** This isn't ideal for investing because the markup is high, and resale is tricky.

>> **Vaulted storage:** Some companies let you buy metals that they store for you in secure vaults (think Brinks or the Royal Canadian Mint).

If you take delivery yourself, store it in a safe or safety deposit box — not under your mattress or next to your cookie jar.

Watch out for collector coins or fancy packaging. Unless you're a collector, stick to bullion-grade metals from reputable dealers with clear pricing.

Avoiding the "shiny object" trap

Precious metals are great for stability, but they can't do the heavy lifting of wealth-building alone. They don't compound, and they don't generate cash flow. They just *sit there and sparkle*.

So, although they absolutely belong in a well-rounded offline asset strategy, they're more like your portfolio's fireproof vault — not your growth engine.

Think of gold as your seatbelt, not your engine. It won't drive your wealth forward, but it'll help keep you safe if things crash.

Using Crypto Hard Wallets: The Offline Side of Your Digital Assets

You may be surprised to see crypto in a chapter on offline external assets. After all, crypto lives online, right?

Yes — but also no.

In Chapter 6 and in my book *Cryptocurrency Investing For Dummies*, I walk you through how to buy, trade, and evaluate digital currencies like Bitcoin, Ethereum, and altcoins. That's the *online* side of crypto investing.

There's another side most beginners overlook, and it's one of the most important things you can do as your crypto portfolio grows: Take your assets offline.

This is where cold wallets, also known as hard wallets, come in.

Hot wallets versus cold wallets

When you first buy crypto, your coins are usually stored in a *hot wallet* — a digital wallet connected to the internet. These are often hosted by exchanges (like Coinbase or Binance) or exist as apps and browser extensions (like MetaMask).

Hot wallets are easy to use, convenient for frequent trading, and ideal for beginners and small balances. But they also come with risk: If someone hacks your exchange, you lose access. If the platform freezes withdrawals (yes, this has happened), your money is stuck. And if you fall for a phishing scam, your assets can be drained in seconds.

Consequently, serious investors eventually move to *cold wallets* — offline tools that keep your private keys completely disconnected from the internet.

Cold wallets may be digital in nature, but their storage, security, and setup are completely offline. That makes them part of your external asset protection strategy, especially once your crypto holdings start to grow.

Cold wallet have the following benefits:

>> Let you be your own bank

>> Add a layer of security most online users never consider

>> Keep your freedom fund safe from tech glitches, platform shutdowns, or centralized control

Cold storage is not about making your crypto do more. It's about keeping what you've already built safe.

If you're building serious wealth in crypto, a hard wallet isn't optional. It's essential.

Popular cold wallets

Here are three of the most trusted and widely used cold wallet options:

>> **Ledger:** One of the most popular hardware wallets, Ledger offers the Nano S Plus and Nano X, both of which support hundreds of coins and tokens. The Nano X even has Bluetooth, so you can manage your assets from your phone.

>> **Trezor:** This is another OG in the crypto space. The Model One and Model T are both easy to use, beginner-friendly, and support major cryptos. The Model T has a touchscreen for extra security and simplicity.

>> **Bitkey:** A newer option from Block (formerly Square), Bitkey is designed to simplify self-custody for everyday users. It includes a hardware device *and* a mobile app, making cold storage more intuitive without compromising on safety.

If you're holding crypto as part of your long-term Phase 3 triple-compounding strategy, at least a portion of your coins should be stored offline.

Protecting your crypto with paper

Surprised to see *paper* in a section about crypto? You're not alone. Most people think crypto belongs in the metaverse — not in a manila envelope.

But despite the high-tech nature of digital currency, one of the oldest, most low-tech tools in the crypto world is still one of the most secure: the paper wallet. A paper wallet is the most low-tech cold storage method. You generate a private and public key, print it out, and keep that paper somewhere safe, like a safe deposit box or fireproof safe.

Pros of a paper wallet include that it's completely offline, so there's no hacking risk. It's also free to create a paper wallet.

Cons of a paper wallet are that it's easy to lose, damage, or misplace. Also, if anyone finds your paper, they have access to your crypto. Of course, there's also the downside that a paper wallet doesn't support modern features like staking or smart contracts.

Paper wallets are best suited for truly long-term holding. Think of them like a physical treasure map. If you go this route, protect it like gold.

If you create a paper wallet, store backup copies in separate, secure locations. Fire, flood, or forgetfulness can wipe out your entire portfolio.

Adding Your Investment Profits to Your Triple-Compounding System

Investing in external assets isn't just about watching your net worth grow. It's about feeding the entire triple-compounding machine. The profits you generate from stocks, crypto, real estate, or private equity don't exist in isolation. When reinvested intentionally, they can fund new skill-building (compound 1X), expand your systems and teams (compound 2X), or roll back into your portfolio for accelerated returns (compound 3X).

Every dollar earned — from a dividend payout, a rental income stream, or an exit from a private deal —becomes fuel. The more you circulate it through your triple-compounding strategy, the faster you create *true financial freedom* — not just bigger numbers on a spreadsheet.

Think of every external asset profit as a decision point: Will this money buy you more time, more leverage, or more long-term growth? Triple compounders choose all three — on purpose. By applying the triple compounding system across all areas of life, my Accelerators and Diamond members have grown their portfolios to seven and even eight figures — often in a fraction of the time it typically takes using conventional methods.

Don't let these assets sit in isolation. If you don't funnel the profits back into your triple-compounding system, they become dead weight.

3
Generating with Your Triple-Compounding System

IN THIS PART . . .

Build the confidence and momentum to follow through on your wealth-building plan.

Discover the principles of running a compounding business that supports your goals.

Use the Invest Diva Diamond Analysis to pick winning investments.

Chapter **8**

Generating Confidence and Momentum

Most people think compounding is just about numbers, but you and I know better. You could have the smartest investment strategy in the world, but if you don't trust yourself to follow through, you'll sabotage it before it has a chance to work.

The real compounder behind all the other compounders is *you*. Not your job. Not your portfolio. Not your business. *You*. Your beliefs. Your energy. Your decisions. Your consistency.

This is the part of the Triple Compounding system that runs under the hood. It's the software update you didn't know you needed. Once you make the internal upgrades I cover in this chapter, the external ones from the other chapters get *way* easier.

You're not here to hustle harder. You're here to become the kind of person who doesn't need to hustle at all because confidence, clarity, and alignment are doing the heavy lifting for you.

Inside this chapter, I guide you through how to rebuild self-trust, reframe limiting beliefs, and replace old fear-based patterns with habits that move you forward. The people who succeed with triple compounding aren't necessarily the smartest or most experienced. They're the ones who discover how to trust themselves *deeply* and keep going even when it's hard.

You can't compound confidence if you're constantly breaking promises to yourself. Small wins matter. Tiny actions matter. You matter.

If you try to outwork your self-doubt, it'll catch up with you. This chapter gives you tools to move past that — for good.

Rebuilding the Lost Trust in Yourself

If you've ever said, "This time I'm serious," and then didn't follow through, welcome to the human club.

Everyone breaks promises to themselves. Started diets. Bought planners. Declared, "This is my year!" on January 1 — only to ghost those goals by February.

And the problem isn't the failure. It's what you *make it mean* about yourself.

Each time you don't follow through, it creates a small crack in your self-trust. Eventually, those cracks add up. Until one day, even when you *want* to go after something new, a voice inside whispers, "Yeah, but you've said that before."

This chapter is about repairing those cracks. Not with hustle or guilt but with small, compounding actions that build your *energetic credibility* back up.

Because when you trust yourself again, *everything* gets easier.

Doing What You Said You're Gonna Do

Imagine that I text you this:

`Let's grab coffee tomorrow at 5pm at that trendy little cafe you love!`

You're excited. You plan your day around it. You show up at 4:58 p.m. (because you're a respectful human). You grab a table. You order a latte. You wait.

5:05. No Kiana.

5:10. Still no Kiana.

At 5:20, I finally call you:

"OMG I'm SO sorry — my daughter got sick, and to top it off, I *ripped my pants* bending over to grab her plushie from under the couch. It was a whole disaster. Can we reschedule for tomorrow?"

You're understanding. You say yes.

Next day, same time. You show up again.

5:00. No Kiana.

5:15. Still no Kiana.

At 5:30, I call:

"Ugh, you won't believe this. My Uber got pulled over because the driver tried to do a TikTok dance *while driving*. And I spilled a turmeric smoothie all over my white blazer. But I swear — *tomorrow* is the day!"

Now, be honest. Are you showing up tomorrow? Probably not. Because at that point, you've lost trust that I actually mean what I say.

So, let me ask you this: Why do you keep doing this to *yourself*?

Every time you say, "I'm going to start budgeting," and don't . . .

Every time you say, "I'm waking up early to work out," but hit snooze instead . . .

Every time you set a new money goal, and then ghost your own plan . . .

. . . you become the person who keeps no-showing on *yourself*. And if you can't trust *you*, how can you expect confidence, momentum, or follow-through?

Self-trust isn't something you feel your way into. It's something you build, one micro commitment at a time. Confidence isn't loud. It's quiet *evidence* you collect every day that says, "I keep my word."

Don't let self-trust erosion be the reason your compounding system stalls. If you can't show up for small promises, you'll never believe yourself when it comes to the big ones.

Identifying and Reframing Limiting Beliefs

If confidence is the engine behind your momentum, your beliefs are the fuel. And unfortunately, most people are unknowingly filling their tank with junk. Stuff like

>> "I'm bad with money."

>> "I'm just not consistent."

>> "People like me don't get rich."

>> "I need to be perfect before I start."

>> "I'm not disciplined enough to change."

Sound familiar?

These aren't facts. They're just *thoughts,* but you've heard them repeated so many times (by your parents, your environment, your own inner monologue) that they *feel* like truth.

Every belief you have is either expanding you or limiting you. There is no neutral belief. If you're not questioning your beliefs regularly, odds are that some of them are keeping you small.

Limiting beliefs don't show up wearing devil horns. They arrive wearing *logic.* They disguise themselves as "being realistic" or "playing it safe." They sound like your mom's voice trying to protect you. They quote statistics and bring charts and say things like this:

>> "Most businesses fail in the first five years. You should wait until you have more experience."

>> "You already have a good job. Don't mess it up."

>> "You tried before and it didn't work. Why would this time be any different?"

These statements seem *reasonable,* but they're not aligned with your freedom.

In a triple-compounding system, beliefs have the power to accelerate or *reverse* your results because your beliefs determine your behavior, and your behavior determines your outcomes.

A belief is just a thought you've repeated long enough that your brain automated it. If you can program it in, you can also *reprogram* it. You don't need to delete every limiting belief overnight. You just need to stop treating it like law and start treating it like *a theory you're willing to challenge.*

If you cling to a belief just because it's "how you've always thought," you're not preserving your identity; you're limiting your potential.

Flipping a limiting belief system

Here's a simple process I use (and teach) to start shifting belief patterns that don't serve you:

1. **Identify the story.**

   What's a sentence that keeps showing up in your inner world?

   - "I never follow through."

   - "I don't deserve to be wealthy."

   - "I'm too [old, young, behind, late, or whatever else] to start now."

2. **Ask, "Who does that belief serve?"**

   Does it protect your comfort? Avoid failure? Keep other people from feeling threatened by your success?

3. **Ask, "Who told you that?"**

   Was it your dad? A teacher in 8th grade? Someone who made a comment in passing that you've been dragging around for 20 years?

4. **Flip the script.**

   What's a new belief that's equally (if not more) true but expansive? Try these:

   - "I'm learning to follow through one small promise at a time."

   - "Wealth doesn't require perfection; it requires intention."

   - "This chapter isn't too late. It's perfectly timed for who I'm becoming."

5. **Practice believing the new thought.**

   Say it out loud. Write it down. Put it on sticky notes. Repeat it until it starts to feel familiar because *familiar is what becomes believable.*

Compounding progress with small wins

When most people think about changing their financial life, they imagine a big leap. A six-figure windfall. A viral business launch. A perfectly executed investing strategy that turns $500 into $5 million overnight.

And sure, that's fun to fantasize about.

But in reality? That kind of quantum leap is *extremely rare.* The real magic is in small, consistent wins that compound over time because confidence doesn't come from *arrival.* It comes from *evidence.*

Every time you follow through on something — no matter how small — you're sending a signal to your brain: "Hey . . . I can count on me." That matters because self-confidence is really just self-trust built through repeated evidence.

Making progress feel addictive

Here's how to use the power of progress to create momentum even when life is chaotic:

1. **Track tiny wins.**

   Keep a "done list" instead of just a to-do list. At the end of the day, jot down *what you actually followed through on* — no matter how small. This keeps your focus on movement, not perfection.

2. **Set ridiculously easy goals.**

   Can't write a whole business plan? Outline the first bullet. Can't review your whole portfolio? Just open the brokerage app and glance. The easier the entry point, the more likely you are to start. Once you start, you tend to keep going.

3. **Attach rewards to action, not results.**

   Don't wait until you "make $10,000" to celebrate. Celebrate the fact that you made your first investment, created your first automation, or finished your first week of your new habit. That's how you build emotional momentum.

4. **Avoid the all-or-nothing trap.**

   Missed a day? Messed up a step? *Welcome to being human.* Don't let one mistake justify a spiral. Just reset and keep moving.

The *faster* you celebrate your progress, the *faster* you build compounding confidence. You don't need permission. You need evidence, and you're already creating it.

Big change isn't one big move. It's a series of small, intentional actions taken again and again, even when no one's watching.

Waiting until you've "earned" celebration keeps you in a loop of self-criticism. If you never feel good about your progress, you'll stop making it. Give yourself some dang credit!

Overcoming Anxiety and Replacing It with Excitement

If you've ever sat down to check your bank account and felt a lump in your throat, you're not alone.

Financial anxiety is real. It doesn't matter how much money you have (or don't have). What matters is how safe — or unsafe — you feel when it comes to your future. What you may not know is that *emotion is more chemical than it is logical.*

Your nervous system doesn't know the difference between being chased by a bear and being chased by a bill collector. That's why even the thought of investing, selling, or setting new financial goals can trigger a full-blown stress response. You're not lazy. You're not broken. You're just wired to survive. Your brain is doing what it thinks it needs to do to protect you.

But what if anxiety isn't the enemy? What if it's energy waiting for new instructions?

In this section, I explain how to flip that wiring.

Understanding the root causes of financial anxiety

Financial anxiety doesn't just come from not having enough money. It often comes from the following

>> **Uncertainty:** Not knowing what will happen if you lose your job, make a bad investment, or fail

>> **Lack of information:** Feeling lost in the noise of financial lingo, market headlines, or conflicting advice

>> **Past experiences:** Maybe someone you loved making a terrible financial decision, or you being punished for wanting more

>> **Learned fear:** From teachers, parents, media, or even culture that told you money is evil, complicated, or "not for people like us"

Anxiety is usually not about the money. It's about *your relationship to the unknown.*

You know what excitement is? Also a response to the unknown.

The physical sensation of anxiety — racing heart, tight chest, butterflies — is *identical* to excitement. The difference? The story you attach to it.

Using visualization and affirmations to change your financial mindset

If your thoughts are the script, then your emotions are the actors, and your nervous system is the stage crew trying to follow along. Want to rewrite the show?

Use the same tools high-performance athletes, visionary entrepreneurs, and world-class artists use: visualization and affirmations. Here's how:

>> **Visualize your desired outcome in detail.** See yourself logging into your accounts and feeling *excited*. Picture the emails from clients saying "yes." Feel the pride of sending money to your future self, without fear.

>> **Speak it into the nervous system:** You have to do it in a way that actually *sticks*.

Most motivational gurus will get you to say things like, "I am building wealth every day," or "I make money with joy and ease." But let's be real: If you say, "I am wealthy," and your subconscious immediately fires back, *No, you're not!* that affirmation is already dead on arrival!

That's why I love using empowering questions instead.

Instead of saying, "I'm building wealth," ask yourself, "Why do I continue to build wealth every day?"

The first statement may trigger resistance. The second sends your brain on a search mission to find reasons it's true. When your subconscious gets curious, it stops arguing and starts upgrading.

Ask yourself questions like these:

>> "Why is it so easy for me to attract opportunities?"

>> "Why does money love me so much?"

>> "Why do I trust myself more every day?"

Then answer them:

>> "Because I've made it through harder things."

>> "Because I show up even when no one's watching."

>> "Because I'm rewiring my identity — not just my income."

These aren't just affirmations — they're identity activators. They do more than make you feel good. They also make your brain *work for you*, instead of against you.

This isn't woo-woo. This is neuroscience. When your thoughts and emotions sync up, your body creates *certainty*, and certainty is the cure for fear.

Creating Habits That Compound

Most personal finance books skip this truth: Your habits are compounding even if your money isn't yet.

Every time you hit snooze, break a promise to yourself, or "forget" to check in with your goals, you're still compounding. You're just compounding *doubt*.

The good news? You can reverse that trend *today* by compounding *trust* instead.

This isn't about hustle or perfection. It's about designing *micro-decisions* that create massive ripple effects over time.

In this section, I show you how to build compounding habits that actually stick.

Starting smaller than you think

If your habit is too big, your brain will try to sabotage it. Start so small it's laughable.

» **Not:** "I'll review my finances for an hour every Sunday."

Try: "Every Sunday, I'll log in and check my accounts for one minute."

» **Not:** "I'll journal for 30 minutes every night."

Try: "Each night, I'll write one sentence, such as 'Today I compounded by ___.'"

When the habit is small, you'll do it. When you do the habit repeatedly, it becomes identity.

Success isn't about doing something once. It's about making it *normal*.

Tying a new habit to something you already do

When you tie a new habit to something you already do, it's called *habit stacking*, and it works like magic.

Here are some examples:

» After I brush my teeth, I review my daily spending.

» After I make my morning coffee, I ask myself one wealth-affirming question.

» Before I open social media, I invest $10.

The action becomes automatic. The identity becomes real.

Celebrating like you mean it

Want a fast way to tell your nervous system, "Yes! Do more of this"? Celebrate immediately — *even the smallest win*.

If you say no to an impulse buy, smile and say, "I'm becoming someone who values their future more than the sale." If you transferred $5 to savings? Throw a little dance party and tell yourself, "This is who I am now."

Your brain will chase whatever gets rewarded, so reward the stuff that leads to freedom.

Discipline isn't about self-punishment. It's about self-prioritization.

Anchoring the momentum

The longer you keep a streak going, the harder it is to break. Use visual cues if needed: a habit tracker, a sticky note on your laptop, a "Triple Compounded Today" journal.

Keep the streak alive. Let it snowball. Watch it compound. Because confidence isn't built in one giant leap; it's built in a hundred quiet moments where you *keep your word.* And momentum isn't magic. It's simply the result of motion multiplied by consistency.

WARNING

If you wait for motivation, you'll lose to someone who acts from momentum. Design the habit. Honor the habit. Let it compound.

You've got this.

TIP

If you need inspiration for developing new habits for yourself, you can grab my personal morning routine at `www.triplecompounding.com/abundance`.

IN THIS CHAPTER

» **Deciding whether business ownership is right for you — and what kind of business to build**

» **Avoiding the wrong customers and choosing a niche that aligns with your values**

» **Designing an irresistible, scalable offer that compounds your income**

» **Reframing sales as service and tapping into your moral obligation to sell**

» **Using your business income to fuel all three phases of triple compounding**

Chapter 9

Generating with a Compounding Business

The second phase of triple compounding includes investing in your income-generating extensions. One of the most powerful ways to do this is by creating your own business.

This can be a business you run on the side of your full-time job to add new revenue streams, a business you buy and take over, or a business you start from scratch.

Starting a business from scratch is not for the faint of heart. I used to think *everyone* should have their own business. But after working with thousands of triple compounders, I've learned that there's a certain personality type that thrives in this kind of adventure.

Becoming a business owner works best for people who

>> Have a high tolerance for ongoing uncertainty.

>> Are absolutely relentless.

>> Embrace change and volatility.

>> Are cool with uncertainty. (Oops, did I say that twice? That's because it's *that* important!)

>> Can handle rejection without taking it personally (like when your bestie "loves your idea" but still doesn't buy).

>> Are willing to make imperfect decisions faster than most people make lunch.

You may not have been born with these traits, but you can absolutely acquire them over time. But I won't sugarcoat it — this path isn't always smooth.

If you decide that business ownership isn't the right move for you right now, no sweat! You can *still* take full advantage of triple compounding. Just flip to Chapter 5, where I explain how to increase your income through your job or other lower-risk extensions.

But if you feel the pull toward building something that's yours — something that can grow and compound with or without your daily effort — then welcome to Phase 2, version B of scaling your income.

Here's what that looks like in action:

>> **Phase 1 — Invest in Yourself:** Take part of your business profits and reinvest them into your growth — skills, coaching, mentorship, certifications, or energy management. Anything that makes *you* more valuable makes your business more powerful.

>> **Phase 2 — Invest in Your Extensions:** Use your business revenue to hire support, upgrade your systems, automate your processes, or delegate the tasks you've outgrown. This is how you buy back your time without slowing down growth.

>> **Phase 3 — Invest in External Assets:** Once your business income becomes consistent, you can start directing overflow into your long-term wealth engine: stocks, crypto, real estate, index funds, or even other businesses. This is where your money starts working for you *while* your business continues to grow.

This is the magic of triple compounding. This chapter is your road map to building a business that aligns with your values, protects your energy, and supports your long-term financial freedom. From legal structure to irresistible offers, I show you how to turn your ideas into income — and your income into something that multiplies.

Deciding You're a Business Owner

Becoming a business owner doesn't start with a bank loan, a fancy logo, or even your first sale.

It starts with a decision. Not a decision to try. Not a decision to dabble. A decision to step into the identity of someone who builds a compounding income machine — even if it's messy at first.

Here's the thing: The IRS (and other tax authorities around the world) don't need you to register anything fancy to consider you a business owner. In fact, as soon as you decide to start offering products or services in exchange for money, congratulations! You're legally a sole proprietor (or a sole trader, if you're outside the US).

Let me break it down:

>> In the United States, the IRS considers you a sole proprietor the moment you begin operating your business — even if you haven't registered a business name. You'll report business income on Schedule C of your personal tax return.

>> In the United Kingdom, you become a sole trader once you start earning from self-employment. You need to register with His Majesty's Revenue & Customs (HMRC), but you don't need a separate legal entity.

>> In Canada, you're a sole proprietor as soon as you start generating revenue. You may need to register with your province, but you don't need to incorporate.

>> In Australia, operating as a sole trader is the simplest structure. You just need an Australian Business Number (ABN) to get started. No need to form a company.

The moment you sell something — even if it's on Etsy, Upwork, or Instagram — you're officially in business. You don't need to wait for a certificate to start behaving like a CEO.

The sweet surprise: Getting tax benefits

Once you step into sole proprietorship, you open the door to a world most employees never get to access: tax write-offs.

As a business owner, you may be able to deduct a long list of ordinary and necessary business expenses, including the following:

>> Your phone and internet (if you use them for business)

>> A portion of your home or rent (if you work from home)

>> Your computer, printer, or office setup

>> Software, subscriptions, and online tools

>> Coaching, courses, or certifications

>> Travel and meals related to business activities

>> Marketing and advertising

>> Contractor or virtual assistant (VA) expenses

>> Even this book

That means the money you were already spending — on your phone, Wi-Fi, Zoom subscription, Canva Pro, or even that coffee shop coworking session — can now lower your taxable income.

The money you save on taxes can now be reallocated into your triple-compounding system. That means you just found more fuel for Phase 1 (investing in yourself), Phase 2 (scaling your income), or Phase 3 (external assets). Congrats! You just created money by making a mindset shift.

I'm not a tax professional, and this book is not intended to provide tax advice. Always consult with a qualified accountant or tax advisor in your country.

Getting the legalities right

Once you've decided that you're a business owner and stepped into sole proprietorship (even unofficially), the next step is to make it legit on paper. No, this doesn't mean you need to hire a lawyer, write a 30-page business plan, or spend months obsessing over your logo font.

It means setting up a few basic legal and financial foundations to protect yourself, stay compliant, and keep your business life separate from your personal life.

Here's what that can look like:

>> **Register your business name.** If you're using a name that's different from your personal name (like "The Compounding Creative" instead of "Jane Smith"), you may need to register a DBA ("doing business as") in your city, state, or province.

>> **Get the appropriate licenses or permits.** Depending on your location and industry, you may need a basic business license, a seller's permit, or professional certifications. Check with your local city hall or government business portal.

>> **Open a business bank account.** Even if you're a sole proprietor, keeping business finances separate from personal is one of the best moves you can make. It keeps your books clean and protects you in case of an audit.

>> **Set up simple bookkeeping.** You don't need fancy software on day one. A spreadsheet works just fine as long as you're tracking every dollar in and out.

>> **Look into business insurance.** If you're offering services, handling sensitive client data, shipping goods, or operating in a risk-prone industry, a simple liability policy can be a lifesaver.

>> **Consider whether to remain a sole proprietor or form an LLC.** A sole proprietorship is the default, but if you want more legal protection or tax flexibility, forming an LLC may be a smart next step.

Start simple but start smart. You don't need to do everything at once, but you should do something to protect your growing business from day one.

This is about building something sustainable, and sustainable businesses have structure, not just passion.

Deciding Who Your Customers Are

Who do you want to help? What problems do they have?

Your answers to these questions are significantly more important than *how* you're going to help them. If you identify your *who*, you can then ask them what problems they want resolved — and find a way to solve those problems for them.

It sounds simple, but most new business owners skip this step. They focus on branding, logos, pricing, and social media strategy without being clear on *who they're even talking to* — or worse, they try to help "everyone." But if you don't know who your customer is, you're building a business in the dark.

In this section, I focus on choosing customers who are a good fit for you and your triple-compounding goals. Because when you choose right, *everything compounds faster.*

Avoiding the wrong type of customers

You need to start by getting honest about who you don't want to work with, because serving the wrong people will drain you, distract you, and destroy your ability to scale.

I first heard this from one of my mentors, Myron Golden, and it has been an absolute game-changer in my own business. I've since been expanding on this at my Triple Compounding Live events to help triple compounders avoid making costly mistakes right out of the gate.

Here are the four types of customers:

>> **Freepeople:** They love your content, share your reels, and ask lots of questions but never buy. They want the transformation, but they don't want to pay for it.

>> **Cheapeople:** These folks only open their wallet for deep discounts, massive bonuses, or limited-time deals. They'll buy — once — but they won't stick around.

>> **Feepeople:** These customers are ready to pay because they value the result. They ask smart questions, take action, and often become repeat buyers.

>> **Prepeople:** These are your dream clients. They don't just pay; they *prepare.* They're eager, invested, and fully bought into the journey before you even pitch.

Now here's the hard truth: You attract what you are. If you were once a freeperson (like I was!), there's no shame in that. I wore new clothes to dates and returned them the next day. I consumed free YouTube videos for years. And I believed people wouldn't pay high prices — because *I* wouldn't. That belief system showed up in my business until I changed it.

If you want feepeople and prepeople in your world, you have to become one first. That means

>> Investing in yourself

>> Acting before you feel ready

>> Valuing results over convenience

You don't have to chase or convince the wrong people. You just need to become the person who attracts the right ones and to build systems that filter the rest.

If you feel bad for freepeople and genuinely want to help them, here's what you do: Go make *tons* of money with customers who are willing and able to pay, and then come back and help freepeople through scholarships, sponsorships, or charitable contributions. You can help them *more* once your business is thriving.

Romanticizing your audience or trying to "save" people who aren't ready will slow your growth and drain your confidence. Focus on those who are prepared and committed.

Selecting the right niche

Once you've filtered out who *not* to serve, the next step is identifying who you *do* want to serve and who's actually ready to receive what you offer.

In *$100M Offers: How to Make Offers So Good People Feel Stupid Saying No* (Acquisition.com Publishing, 2021), Alex Hormozi lays out four key traits of an ideal customer:

>> **Hungry:** They have a real problem they're eager to solve.

>> **Capable:** They have the money to pay.

>> **Committed:** They're emotionally and mentally ready to change.

>> **Accessible:** You can find and reach them easily.

These traits are critical because a niche full of unmotivated, broke, or invisible customers isn't a business. It's a hobby.

But I want to add one more trait that's often left out of the conversation: aligned. Even if someone is hungry, capable, and committed, if you *don't actually like them*, you're going to resent showing up for them. And that's not why you started a business.

Your ideal niche isn't just about market size or profitability. It's about the people you genuinely enjoy serving. The ones you feel excited to help. The ones who align with your values, your energy, and your vision for the future.

This is how you create a niche that's not just profitable; it's *personal*. And when your niche is personal, something magical happens: competition disappears. Because no one else is you.

No one else has your exact preferences, values, or lens on what it looks like to help *those* people solve *that* problem in *that* way.

When your customers feel that, they're not just buying your product; they're buying into *you*. And that's what builds trust, loyalty, and referrals on autopilot.

A true niche sits at the intersection of

>> What the market needs

>> What you're great at

>> Who you genuinely love serving

You don't need a massive audience; you need the right people — people who are hungry for change, able to invest, committed to growth, and *aligned with what you stand for.*

If your niche is profitable but misaligned with your personality or values, it won't compound. You'll burn out, plateau, or sabotage your own momentum. It's not worth it.

Identifying Your Solution

Once you know who you want to serve, the next step is figuring out how you're going to help them. I don't mean in a vague, "I want to inspire people," kind of way. You need to solve a *real, specific, painful* problem for your niche — one they're already trying to fix, thinking about daily, or Googling at 2 a.m.

Here's the good news: You don't have to start with a perfectly packaged offer. In fact, I don't recommend it. Start with the customer. Ask them questions. Find out what they're struggling with. Figure out what they *wish* existed. Then reverse-engineer a solution that's clear, actionable, and valuable.

The best business ideas don't come from inspiration. They come from observation. And when you find that sweet spot between what people need, what they'll pay for, and what you're willing to deliver, you have the makings of a compounding business.

Don't wait to feel "qualified." You're allowed to learn as you go, solve problems creatively, and build offers based on what you can actually deliver now — not some imaginary version of yourself five years from now.

If your offer sounds nice but doesn't solve a specific problem, it will feel vague and hard to sell, no matter how pretty the branding is.

Creating an Irresistible Offer

Once you've nailed down who your ideal customer is and what problem they need solved, it's time to design the thing they can't say no to: your irresistible offer.

Not just something they *want*. Something they feel *compelled* to buy because it speaks directly to the result they desire and makes the path to that result feel clear, doable, and worth every penny.

The following sections walk you through how to

>> Identify the outcome your customer really wants

>> Understand what's stopping them from achieving it

>> Brainstorm solutions that remove those obstacles

>> Create an offer that's easy to sell *and* easy to fulfill

>> Prevent your business from becoming a cheap commodity

Identifying the outcome for your customer

Most business owners focus too much on *features* and not enough on *outcomes*. Your customer doesn't care how many videos are in your course. They don't care how many calls are included. They care about what their life will look like *after* they've worked with you.

That transformation — that clear, desired outcome — is what they're really buying.

Ask yourself these questions:

>> What does my ideal customer want *to be, do, or have* after this offer?

>> How will they feel once they've achieved that result?

>> How will they describe that transformation in their own words?

Get obsessed with your customer's "after." That's the real product you're selling. Everything else is just the delivery system.

Identifying the difficulties in achieving the outcome

If the outcome was obvious and easy, your customer would've done it already. Your job is to uncover the reasons they haven't. These are their roadblocks, and they depend on your niche. Here are some examples:

>> A lack of time

>> Confusion or a sense of being overwhelmed

>> Mistrust in the process or in themselves

>> Past failures

>> A noisy, overcomplicated marketplace

Your offer needs to address these challenges head-on — not just with "motivation," but with real tools, support, and a simplified path.

Every problem you solve inside your offer increases its value. And every roadblock you eliminate makes it more irresistible.

Brainstorming solutions

Now that you know the outcome and the obstacles, you can start crafting your unique method for getting people from A to B. This is where your creativity and intuition get to shine. There's no one right way to deliver your solution. You get to choose based on

>> Your skillset

>> Your customer's lifestyle and preferences

>> Your business model

>> How much support you want to provide

Your "solution" can be

>> A coaching program

>> A done-for-you service

>> A digital product or membership

>> A tool or app

>> A group experience

>> A hybrid offer

Whatever the format, the key is that it solves *their* problem in a way that works for *you*.

When in doubt, start simple. You can add bells and whistles later. A clear, focused solution will always outperform a bloated, complicated one.

Creating the "Easy to Sell, Easy to Fulfill" Offer

This is the secret to scalable compounding. If your offer is hard to sell, you'll spend too much energy on marketing. If it's hard to fulfill, you'll burn out trying to deliver it.

A compounding offer does both:

>> It's easy to sell because it solves a specific, urgent problem for a specific type of person.

>> It's easy to fulfill because it's aligned with your strengths, systems, and energy capacity.

The sweet spot lives where

>> Your customer is eager for the result.

>> You can deliver it efficiently and reliably.

>> The offer doesn't rely on you being available 24/7.

If you're drowning in customizations, it's not scalable. If you're overexplaining it, it's not clear. Simplify.

Preventing the commodity problem

Now that you're a business owner with the intention of making a profit, you need to be in the right type of business if you want to scale without burning out.

There are two types of businesses:

>> A business that sells a service tied directly to your time

>> A business that sells a product that can scale and be automated

If you pick the wrong type of business, you'll limit your income.

If you ever tie your revenue generation to a limited resource, you're capping your earning potential.

If you sell a service, you have to *fulfill* that service after you sell it. And what does that take? Time. Is time something you have an unlimited supply of, or a limited one? Right — limited.

That's why service-based businesses tend to hit income ceilings unless you intentionally break that pattern. Here's how you break the pattern: productize your service. When you sell a product, it doesn't take more time to sell 1,000 units than it does to sell 1. The work is in the system — not in the fulfillment.

I break this down in the following section.

Choosing your million-dollar path

What's your million-dollar path?

There's no one-size-fits-all answer here. There are *many* paths to $1 million and beyond. But every single one of them starts with this: doing the math.

Start with your goal, then reverse-engineer it. Let's say your goal is to make $1,000,000. That can look like any one of these:

» Selling a $20 product to 50,000 people

» Selling a $200 product to 5,000 people

» Selling a $2,000 product to 500 people

» Selling a $10,000 product to 100 people

» Selling a $100,000 product to 10 people

It's basic fifth-grade math, but most business owners skip this part. And it's not because they can't do it. It's because they don't pause to think strategically.

Instead, they spin their wheels, working hard on offers that won't scale, or trying to serve everyone without a focused plan.

If your business isn't moving fast enough, check your math. You may be trying to sell 1,000 of something that's only making you $5 per sale. That's a recipe for burnout, not compounding.

Selling smarter, not harder

Let me show you what this looks like in real life. One of our Accelerators was in the women's empowerment space. But she found it hard to get individual women to pay for empowerment products. So instead, she partnered with a company that already served women. Now *that* business pays her to empower thousands of their female employees.

She didn't have to go find 1,000 women. *They* came to her.

If my goal is to sell 100,000 copies of *Triple Compounding For Dummies,* I'm not going door to door. I'll partner with a company to buy in bulk and gift it to their customers. Same effort. Bigger result.

In my own business, I made my first million dollars by selling a $1,000 product to 1,000 people.

You want a business that sells a product. Don't sell your time for money — unless it's *really* worth your time. That's why I charge $25,000 per hour to work one-on-one and offer my $350,000 Diamond package to only *one* person and *only* if I'm passionate about their mission. Otherwise? Burnout city.

Tapping into Your Moral Obligation to Sell

Let's keep it real: For most new business owners, selling feels gross.

You're not alone if you've ever thought

>> "Selling feels pushy."

>> "I don't want to manipulate anyone."

>> "What would my family think if I became a 'salesperson'?"

I've been there. When my mentor told me I needed to sell from the stage to scale my business, I cried. Like, actually cried. I had so much shame and resistance related to selling. I thought selling was about *doing something to people*, like tricking them into giving me their money.

But here's the truth I want you to hear loud and clear: *Selling is not doing something to people. It's doing something for them.*

Understanding the principles of selling

Think about it: Every joyful purchase you've ever made happened because someone *sold* it to you.

>> That vacation you loved

>> That pillow that finally helped you sleep through the night

>> The birthday gift that made you cry happy tears

>> Even your iPhone, car, or the coffee you sipped this morning

None of that would exist in your life if someone, somewhere, hadn't created it, marketed it, and sold it for a profit.

REMEMBER

Salespeople are the heartbeat of the economy. Without them, nothing moves. Without movement, money stagnates, and everything collapses.

Entrepreneurs are not the problem. They're the solution. By selling, you're helping the economy. You're keeping money in motion. You're creating jobs, opportunity, and *joy.*

So no, you're not a bad person for charging money. You're not manipulative for making an offer. You're not greedy for pricing based on the value you bring.

You're an economy activator. A transformation catalyst. And if you do it right? You're a legacy builder.

Creating the right buying conditions for your customers

Here's the key to ethical, powerful, feel-good selling: Sell your best stuff to people who already want it.

That's it. That's the strategy.

You don't push offers on people who aren't interested. You don't try to convince people who aren't ready. You *find your people,* ask them what they want, and then give it to them at a price that reflects the value.

Selling is simply creating value for a profit by selling to someone who's already looking for a solution. When you think of it this way, you realize that

>> You're not pressuring people.

>> You're helping them access a result they already want.

>> You're honoring them by offering something that can change their life.

And you're doing it in a way that *also* builds your triple-compounding system.

Here's another powerful truth: People who pay, pay attention. If you give something away for free, people treat it like it's worthless. But when they invest — even just a little — they show up differently. They value it. They apply it. They get results.

So, when you charge for your best work, you're not just honoring your time; you're honoring their transformation.

Want to serve more people? Start by serving the ones who are ready, willing, and excited to go all in. You're not here to convince people. You're here to call in the right ones and create the conditions for them to say yes to their future.

Don't buy into the lie that selling is selfish. The real harm is keeping your solution to yourself while people stay stuck. If you *know* you can help, it's your responsibility to offer that help — for a price that reflects its value.

Adding Your Business Income to Your Triple-Compounding System

Let's not forget why we're here. The goal of building a compounding business isn't just to say, "Look, I'm an entrepreneur!" The goal is to generate income that multiplies across your entire financial ecosystem.

Business income — when treated right — is one of the most powerful forms of fuel in your triple-compounding engine.

The three phases of triple compounding are

>> **Phase 1 — Invest in Yourself**

>> **Phase 2 — Invest in Your Extensions**

>> **Phase 3 — Invest in External Assets**

Most people stop at "make more money." But triple compounders know that earning is just the beginning. The real power is in what you *do* with the money once it hits your account.

If you've ever felt guilty about making money or feared becoming too successful, this is your reframe: The more income you generate, the more you can automate, reinvest, and accelerate your freedom. Then you can go ahead and give more to charity and people you want to help out!

Money is not the end goal. Money is the tool. The more of it you direct through this system, the faster your time, energy, and freedom compound.

WARNING

If you treat your business income like spending money instead of seed money, you'll stay stuck in survival. Treat every dollar like it has a job and assign it to the phase where it can grow the fastest.

Grab your spot now for the next available event at `www.triplecompounding.com/live`.

Chapter 10

Generating with Invest Diva Diamond Analysis

What do you do when you lose your job, get dumped, and your mom's biggest wish is for you to "just get married already"? You give yourself a diamond.

That's exactly what I did.

In the same week, I was fired from my job on Wall Street and dumped by my boyfriend (you truly can't make this up), so I decided it was time to stop waiting for someone else to secure my future. No man. No boss. No luck.

I was approaching 30, and my family had *opinions:* "You should be married by now." "Don't wait too long." "Just pick someone!"

But I had a different plan. Instead of saying yes to a date, I said yes to a deadline: No dates until my first book was published.

So, while everyone else was swiping right, I was writing chapters, studying markets, and building what would later become my financial empire. I spent months diving deep into every investing strategy I could get my hands on — stocks, forex, and more. I watched what worked. I tested what didn't. And I realized that the most profitable investing decisions all had five things in common.

That's when I created the framework I now teach to investors all over the world: Invest Diva Diamond Analysis, or IDDA for short.

Five points. One shape. Built to shine under pressure.

I didn't get an engagement ring that year, but I gave myself something better: a diamond-shaped decision-making system that changed my life.

IDDA is the GPS that helps you generate profits from your external assets — like stocks, crypto, forex, and options — without getting lost in hype, headlines, or emotional chaos.

Following the IDDA framework isn't about becoming a Wall Street whiz or watching candlestick charts all day. It's about having a personalized process that makes your investing decisions feel clear, empowering, and repeatable. When you use the IDDA system, you're not just guessing. You're generating.

In the rest of this chapter, I show you how to use the five points of IDDA to

>> Pick the right assets for your unique goals

>> Invest confidently — even when the market gets loud

>> Know exactly when to buy, hold, or exit

>> Generate results that align with your triple-compounding journey

Overviewing the Five Points of the Diamond

Before I dive into each point of the Invest Diva Diamond Analysis, here's a quick look at how the five points come together to help you form a clear, confident investing decision.

Just like how a diamond sparkles brightest when all its facets are aligned, the IDDA framework helps you make high-quality investment choices by looking at the following key angles (see Figure 10-1):

» **Capital analysis:** Your financial fuel — how much you can afford to invest confidently

» **Intentional analysis:** Your *why* and your timeline — what you want from this investment, and when

» **Fundamental analysis:** The asset's DNA — what it is, how it works, and whether it has real value

» **Sentimental analysis:** Reading the room — what other investors are feeling and doing right now

» **Technical analysis:** Timing your move — what the price chart is saying about ideal entry and exit

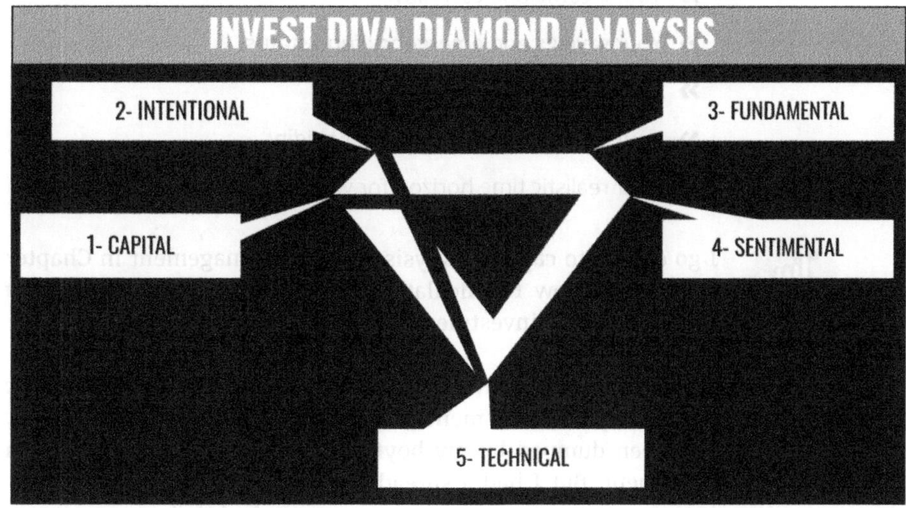

FIGURE 10-1: Invest Diva Diamond Analysis.

Source: investdiva.com

Each point helps reduce risk, increase clarity, and align your strategy with your triple-compounding goals.

Points 1 and 2 are about your personal situation and goals. Points 3, 4, and 5 are about the external asset you're investing in.

REMEMBER

Assessing Your Capital: Knowing Where You Stand Financially

Every smart investing decision starts with one thing: clarity.

Before you look at the market, before you analyze charts, before you pick the next "hot" stock — you need to know *your numbers*. That's why capital is the first point of the Invest Diva Diamond Analysis framework. Because without a solid understanding of where you stand financially, everything else becomes shaky.

This isn't just about how much money you have. It's about how much you can confidently commit to your investments without putting your financial stability (or sleep) at risk.

Your financial standing includes

>> Your income and cash flow

>> Your savings and emergency fund status

>> Your debt obligations

>> Your current investments and liquidity

>> Your realistic time horizon for when you may need the money

I go deep into capital analysis and risk management in Chapter 3, where I show you exactly how to calculate your ability, willingness, and confidence when it comes to taking investment risks.

When I first began investing, I didn't have a six-figure income or a trust fund. In fact, as I previously mentioned, I had just been fired from my Wall Street job, had been dumped by my boyfriend, and was living alone in a tiny Manhattan apartment. But I had a spreadsheet. I knew exactly how much I could afford to invest — *without touching my rent money*. And that gave me power.

Even if you're starting with just $100, what matters most is that your capital is clear, committed, and clean. No guessing. No gambling. Just facts.

Don't pretend you have more than you do. Overestimating your capital leads to overexposure and emotional investing. Start from truth, and you'll build real traction.

Setting Intentions: Knowing Exactly Why You're Investing

Most people jump into investing with one blurry goal: "make more money." But as a triple compounder, you're not here to wing it. You're building a system that accelerates your freedom, and that requires clarity.

This is where intentional analysis comes in. It's the second point of the IDDA, and it's all about answering one powerful question: What is the purpose of this investment in your life?

Are you aiming for long-term wealth? Passive income? A safety net? A legacy for your kids? Different assets serve different purposes, and if you don't define yours, you'll default to what the internet tells you is "hot."

Think of intentional investing like using GPS. If you don't set your destination, every turn looks like a detour.

You can have different goals for different parts of your portfolio. Here are a few examples of what intentional investing may look like:

>> This portion is to generate monthly income while I step back from my 9 to 5.

>> This crypto portfolio is a long-term play for legacy and sovereignty.

>> This dividend stock strategy is to cover my kids' future college costs.

>> This REIT exposure is to supplement my retirement income.

>> This high-growth allocation is my wealth acceleration bucket.

Even if you invest in the *same* asset as someone else — say, the S&P 500 — your strategy, holding period, and allocation may be totally different based on your intention.

Without clear intention, you risk panicking when the market drops or selling too soon when it rises. A strong intention is your anchor.

Connecting Intentional Analysis to Your Triple Compounding System

Phase 3 of triple compounding is all about making your money work for you. But your money doesn't know what to do unless you tell it. That's what intentional analysis does. It tells every dollar, "You have a job to do. Here's your role in my financial freedom."

Once you clarify your intention, every investment decision becomes easier:

>> You know how long to hold.

>> You know whether to reinvest or take profits.

>> You know when something no longer fits your plan.

And here's the best part: When your investments align with your intentions, they don't just grow your money. They grow your *confidence.*

Author Napoleon Hill says, "A goal is a dream with a deadline." I say, "A goal is a *measurable* dream with a deadline."

Here are some examples of measurable dreams with planned deadlines:

>> I want to grow a $1 million portfolio by April 9, 2035.

>> I want to generate $100,000 per year in passive income by my forty-fifth birthday.

>> I want to make it possible for my spouse to retire in the next seven years through real estate and dividend stocks.

Vague dreams don't create compounding results. Specific goals do.

Conducting Fundamental Analysis: Spotting Value Beyond the Hype

Fundamental analysis is how you look under the hood of a company to see what it's really worth. It's like swiping past the marketing filter and asking, "Is this business built to last — or just trending for now?"

For long-term investors, especially triple compounders, this type of analysis is the heartbeat of confident decision-making. It's how you determine if a stock is a true asset or a liability in disguise.

I'll start with the legends. Warren Buffett famously says he only invests in companies he'd be happy to own if the market shut down for ten years. Peter Lynch reminds us to invest in what we know and use. Both of them built their wealth by focusing on value. Not hype. Not next-quarter earnings. But intrinsic, real-world value.

I've taken those principles and added a modern twist. Instead of chasing the trend of the day, I look for what I call Category Kings and Category Queens brands. I got this idea from the book *Play Bigger: How Pirates, Dreamers, and Innovators Create and Dominate Markets* (Harper Business, 2016), which teaches how businesses that dominate their niche don't just win but *own* the category.

Now, *technically*, the book calls them only Category Kings. But as a female investor who's played a role in shifting the old boys' club of Wall Street, I like to include the Queens, too.

I applied that lens to my investment strategy, and let me tell you, it's played out beautifully. My portfolio has now hit eight figures. #humblebrag

So, what does it mean to spot a Category King or Queen? These are the brands that instantly pop into your head when someone mentions an industry. Want to play a quick round?

>> If I say *search engine*, you say . . . *Google*.

>> If I say *convenient online retail*, you say . . . *Amazon*.

>> If I say *social media* . . . well, that depends on your age, but probably *Facebook, Instagram, TikTok,* or *Snapchat.*

>> If I say *easy online design tools*, you say . . . *Canva*.

>> If I say *dating app where women make the first move*, you say . . . *Bumble*.

>> If I say *consumer AI* . . . you probably say *ChatGPT*.

>> If I say luxury sneakers with high heels, you say . . . *Sneex*.

See? These brands don't just have market share; they have *mindshare*. That's what I look for as a long-term investor. Not just cash flow and price-to-earnings (P/E) ratios (although those matter, too), but also cultural dominance and staying power.

Getting your fundamental data

To analyze a company's financial health, I use tools like the following:

>> **Morningstar:** For financials, moat ratings, and fair value estimates

>> **Yahoo Finance:** For earnings, P/E ratios, and historical data

>> **Seeking Alpha:** For investor commentary, dividend updates, and growth metrics

You can also join the Invest Diva Premium Investing Group, which is where I share and crowdsource high-level insights with the members. Visit `www.Triple Compounding.com` to see how you can join us.

These platforms help me track key indicators like

>> Revenue growth

>> Profit margins

>> Earnings consistency

>> Debt levels

>> Free cash flow

>> Dividend health (if applicable)

But numbers are only part of the story.

Digging deeper: Analyzing the company itself

Here's what I do when I'm seriously considering adding a stock to my portfolio:

>> **Go to the company's website.** What's its mission? Is it solving a real problem or just generating buzz?

>> **Research the leadership team.** I look them up on LinkedIn to check their experience, qualifications, and track record.

>> **Check the company's partnerships.** Who is it aligned with? Is the company collaborating with reputable organizations?

>> **Read Glassdoor reviews.** Are employees happy? A toxic internal culture often shows up in long-term performance.

>> **Look at the company's hiring patterns.** Is it scaling up? Rapid hiring often signals confidence in future growth.

>> **Observe its positioning.** Is the company first to market? Does it dominate a niche? Do customers rave about it?

And most importantly, you should ask yourself, "Would I be a loyal customer?"

One of my biggest filters for investment is personal. I start with companies I love and brands I'm already obsessed with. If I'm willing to continue buying from them even during bad PR, a downturn, or a temporary dip, this tells me something powerful. It tells me the business has *stickiness*.

When you're a superfan of a product or service, you already have insider knowledge that Wall Street analysts don't. You see customer experience in action. You feel the brand loyalty. And you know what makes it work — or not.

Fundamental analysis isn't just numbers. It's logic and loyalty. Start with what you know, then go deeper. You're not investing in stock symbols. You're investing in businesses, people, missions, and systems.

If you skip this step of deeper analysis and rely solely on trending charts or influencer picks, you're not investing; you're speculating. And speculation doesn't forward-compound. It may *reverse*-compound, though, which costs you money. (Turn to Chapter 5 for more information about reverse compounding.)

Understanding Market Sentiment: Going against the Crowd

When it comes to evaluating an investment, most people stop at financials. But as a triple compounder, you already know that markets aren't driven by math alone. They're driven by humans, and humans are emotional.

This is where sentimental analysis comes in. It's the art of reading the mood of the market — the hype, the fear, the media narrative — and using that awareness to make smarter, calmer decisions.

Let me take you back to one of the most emotional market moments in recent history. Think about March 2020. COVID-19 lockdowns. Wall Street in free fall. Everyone panicking. Toilet paper shortages.

Financial experts were screaming, "Recession!" and cashing out. CNBC ran fear-driven headline after headline. Reddit and Twitter were ablaze with predictions of doom. One influencer told their entire audience, "Sell everything. The markets are dead."

Meanwhile, what was I doing? Buying.

Why?

Because I wasn't just looking at the panic; I was *analyzing* it. I pulled up the Fear and Greed Index, a tool that gauges investor sentiment based on factors like volatility and market momentum, and saw it flashing *Extreme Fear.* I knew that historically, moments of maximum fear are actually the best times to invest.

So, I went in on some of my favorite long-term stocks — ones I'd already done the fundamental and intentional analysis for. They were on sale. And because I trusted the process, I didn't hesitate.

That decision alone grew my portfolio exponentially over the next 18 months.

Sentimental analysis doesn't mean ignoring the news. It means *decoding* it. Your job is to figure out what the crowd is feeling and decide whether they're right.

Recognizing What the Markets Truly Are

Back when I was still trying to find my way through the maze of investing, I had this idea: *If I just copy what the big guys on Wall Street are doing, I should be fine, right?* I was working at the New York Stock Exchange, surrounded by all these "quants" — the rocket scientists of Wall Street. They were supposed to be the smartest of the smart. Some had PhDs from MIT. I figured they must be doing something that always works. So, I copied them.

And I lost my entire savings.

That's when I started asking questions. I hit up one of the most intimidating quants I knew — basically a walking Wall Street stereotype. When I said, "Be real with me. How much of your math PhD do you *actually* use when investing?" he laughed and said, "It's all for show. We don't actually use math. We build relationships, get clients drunk, and sign them up to hand over their money."

Yup. The math? Just for the resume. The markets? They move based on one thing: emotion.

I realized then that the stock market isn't about logic. It's about psychology. Prices go up and down not because of some neat little formula but because people get scared. Or greedy. Or hyped. Or panicked. That crowd psychology creates waves that most people chase. But not triple compounders.

We don't just study sentiment. We go against the crowd.

When the headlines are full of doom and gloom and your uncle is pulling his money out of the market, you look closer. When the talking heads on CNBC scream, "Buy, buy, buy," you pause.

Here's how to practice recognizing what's going on with the markets.

>> **The Fear and Greed Index:** Is the market emotionally overextended?

>> **News headlines and media tone:** Is the press fueling extreme emotions, such as panic or euphoria?

>> **Google Trends, Twitter/X, TikTok:** What's catching fire in the investor conversation?

>> **Retail trader activity:** What are the masses chasing or avoiding?

>> **Community temperature check:** What's the Invest Diva community feeling right now?

Triple compounders don't dismiss emotions. We study them. And then we go against the crowd. We regularly share our findings with our own community inside the Premium Investing Group.

We take the pulse of the market — not just the numbers — and use that to spot opportunities *where everyone else is running away.*

I have an example. In 2017, Chipotle had a foodborne illness outbreak. Headlines were brutal. People were scared. The stock tanked. But I knew I loved Chipotle. I knew they weren't going anywhere long term. So, I set a buy limit order using the price projections from my Diamond system. When the market hit panic mode, I bought at the bottom. A little over a year later, that investment returned more than 200 percent.

Nvidia is another example. In 2022, it crashed 66 percent, but the fear in the market didn't shake me. I looked at the fundamentals, saw it was still a Category King in AI, and trusted my system. Eighteen months later, it had rebounded nearly 800 percent.

Most people create long-term disasters trying to solve short-term problems. When you're able to pause and analyze *why* people are making moves instead of only analyzing what moves they're making, you position yourself for serious gains.

Sentimental analysis helps you become a leader who *anticipates* instead of a follower who reacts. And that's how you accelerate your compounding journey.

Analyzing the Charts: Using Technicals to Price Your Entry and Exit

If sentimental analysis is reading the mood of the market, technical analysis is reading its *behavior* — specifically, where price levels are likely to attract buyers or sellers.

It's not about predicting *when* something will happen; it's about identifying *where* a decision should be made. It's how you price your entry and exit points, set your buy and sell limit orders, and let the market come to you instead of chasing it.

You've probably heard the phrase, "History doesn't repeat itself, but it rhymes." That's the soul of technical analysis. It's the art of studying market history — price action, chart patterns, and past behavior — to anticipate what's *likely* to happen next.

I didn't always speak chart. Back in my early days on Wall Street, I was surrounded by loud, fast-talking men — people I now lovingly refer to as the Wall Street bros. I didn't have a finance degree, I didn't trade options in college, and I definitely didn't have a Bloomberg terminal at home. But I *did* have a deep desire to figure it out.

I'll never forget the moment everything clicked.

I was working at a forex brokerage. One of the chart analysts — an old-school, kind of crusty-but-brilliant guy — was drawing lines and patterns like a stock market psychic. I asked him what he was doing, and he said, "The market leaves clues. These charts are like footprints. Find out how to spot them, and you'll know where it's headed."

That's when I realized something: This isn't about being right 100 percent of the time. It's about recognizing patterns that repeat.

I went all in. I studied candlestick patterns, support and resistance, moving averages, momentum indicators, Fibonacci retracements (my favorite!), and more. I even traveled the world teaching technical analysis while writing *Invest Diva's Guide to Making Money in Forex* (McGraw Hill, 2013) and teaching at top universities like Baruch College in New York.

And yes, I still use these tools today, inside my Triple Compounding system.

Using the Power of Charts to Triple-Compound

Whether you're investing long-term or swing trading for extra cash flow, technical analysis helps you make decisions *based on behavior, not feelings.* Technical analysis helps you

>> Buy and sell based on your unique risk tolerance

>> Enter at low-risk, high-reward zones

>> Avoid emotional trades driven by hype or panic

>> Spot trends and reversals before the crowd

>> Set up your automated systems for buy and sell triggers (more on that in Chapter 13)

This is especially helpful for those of us who don't want to sit around watching charts all day. I use technical zones to set buy limit and sell limit orders, so I'm not glued to the screen, and my system runs on autopilot.

When your investing moves are backed by data and pattern recognition rather than emotion, you gain confidence, clarity, and control.

In Chapter 16, I walk you through the most effective chart patterns, timing strategies, and technical indicators and show you how to automate them for smarter investing.

Automating Your Triple-Compounding System

IN THIS PART . . .

Identify where you are in your financial impact journey and how to build a system that grows your wealth without constant oversight.

Automate your business income generation with scalable offers and systems.

Set up automation for your external asset investments using tools like limit orders, DRIP, and recurring transfers.

IN THIS CHAPTER

» **Shifting from hustle to harmony through the Four Levels of Financial Impact**

» **Letting go of micromanagement and trusting your systems**

» **Activating the energy of ease so you can scale without burnout**

Chapter **11**

Automating Your Path to Financial Freedom

When most people hear the word "automation," they think of software. Timers. Funnels. Maybe even robots. But triple compounders know better. Automation isn't just about tools. It's about trust. It's about creating systems that run even when life demands that *you* pause.

For me, that moment came when I got pregnant with my daughter. At the time, I didn't have a team. Not a single assistant. No marketing department. No one running ops behind the scenes. I was a one-woman show: writing emails, running webinars, managing my investments, and building my brand single-handedly.

However, I had something powerful: a system.

I had evergreened my webinar. (Flip to Chapter 12 to find out how you can do the same.) I had automated my investments (using a method I reveal in Chapter 13). And I had set things up so the business could keep growing even if I wasn't on live camera, posting on Instagram, or checking my email.

That was the plan, at least . . . until two weeks into maternity leave, when I got a call from Wiley: "Would you like to write *Cryptocurrency Investing For Dummies?*"

Cue the plot twist.

Suddenly I was breastfeeding, sleep-deprived, and writing a book at the same time. But the systems I'd already put in place made all this plate-spinning possible.

My evergreen webinar continued bringing in leads and sales without me. My buy and sell limit orders kept compounding in the background. I wasn't tied to the screen. I was tied to my vision.

I wrote that book during 15-minute pumping breaks, during my daughter's naps, and in the rare, precious moments between mom duty and mission.

That's the kind of automation I want *you* to have.

This chapter isn't just about automating your income (that's Chapter 12) or your investments (see Chapter 13). This is about automating your *path* so you can live freer.

In the following sections, I show you how to

>> Recognize the Four Levels of Financial Impact — and where you are now

>> Shift from the hustle-heavy *grinder* phase into the liberated *automator* phase

>> Rewire your beliefs about time, work, and control

>> Embody the accelerator identity so deeply that freedom isn't just a goal — it's your normal

Find out what I mean by "accelerator identity" later in this chapter in the section, "Level 3: Accelerating."

Identifying Your Financial Impact Level: From Grinding to Automating and Accelerating

After studying some of the most financially impactful people in the world, I've come to realize that there are four levels of financial impact you can make.

Most people think the way to increase their financial impact is to *work harder*. If that were true, the hardest-working people would be the richest, and that's not the case. Many hard-working people still haven't generated enough wealth to be truly financially free or work-optional, even after retirement.

What I've discovered is this: self-made wealthy people operate at higher levels of financial impact. In the following sections, I reveal what those four levels are (see Figure 11-1) and how you can evolve through each one.

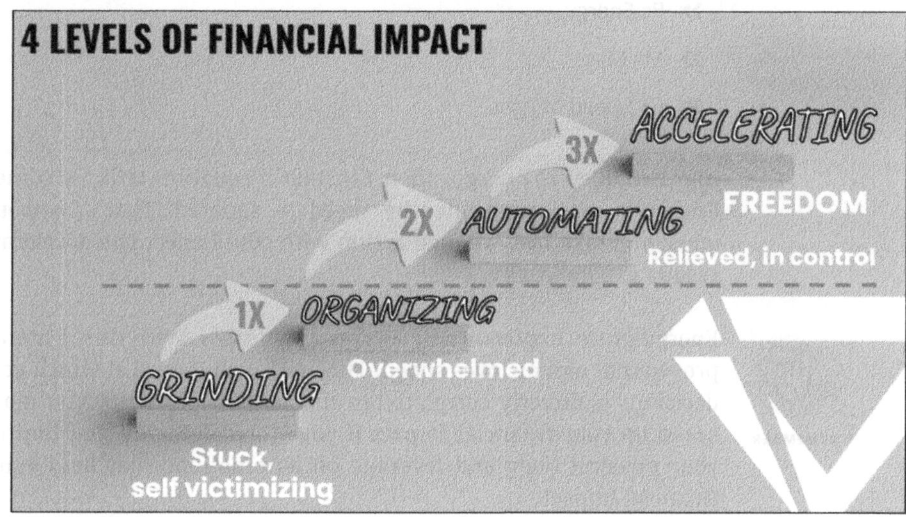

FIGURE 11-1: Four levels of financial impact.

Understanding why money is energy

Money isn't valuable because of what it's made of. It's valuable because of the confidence and energy people place in it. A penny may be made of more valuable raw materials than a $100 bill, but no one would trade the two. That's because the $100 bill represents far more financial impact. Its power comes from impact, not the paper.

This is true across all assets — stocks, crypto, real estate, even cash. Their value rises or falls based on sentiment, which I explore in greater detail in Chapter 10. The collective energy investors pour into them. That's why tools like the Fear and Greed Index exist: to measure the emotional energy in the market.

At its core, money is not material; it's energetic. It transfers value, stores potential, and responds to confidence. Just like a calorie is a unit of physical energy, a dollar is a unit of financial energy.

When I was studying electrical engineering, I spent two years studying energy. In fact, my master's degree thesis in Japan was on Einstein's famous theory of relativity: E = mc², where

>> E= Energy

>> M= Mass

>> C= Speed of light

And if money is energy, then Einstein's equation tells us something powerful: Energy is mass multiplied by speed — squared. That's *compounding speed*. So, when you take fast, aligned action with confidence, you accelerate your financial results exponentially.

Energy grows exponentially as speed increases. With this, I literally scientifically proved that money loves speed. This means the speed at which you make financial decisions is directly correlated to the amount of money you make. You can only speed up your financial impact if you stop relying on just limited resources like your physical body and leverage on automations that help you accelerate your financial impact.

Level 1: Grinding

The grinder does it all — and does it the hard way. This is the person who shows up, punches the clock, and powers through every shift.

The *hardest*-working people in a hotel are the housekeeping staff. Why do they often earn the least? Because they're using a physical resource (their muscles) over a limited resource (time) to produce an energetic result called money. They can't make more because both their time and energy are capped.

In other words,

>> Muscles are limited in strength.

>> Time is limited in supply.

So, the income you generate on this level will always be limited.

If grinding is your only method of making money, you're hurting yourself and your family's financial future.

Even if you pay your bills every month, at this level

>> You'll struggle to handle emergencies.

>> You'll struggle to give generously.

>> You'll feel stuck, keep feeling sorry for yourself, and get in the habit of self-victimizing and blaming others.

>> You'll struggle to be present for your family in a meaningful way.

The income range at this level is minimum wage to $700,000 per year. (Yes, even a general surgeon who earns $300,000 to $700,000 can still be a grinder because they're still trading time and physical labor for income.)

And guess what? Most of the surgeons I used to date (before I got married!) ended up getting sued and losing a large chunk of their wealth anyway.

When you're stuck in the grinder level, your financial impact is low.

Level 2: Organizing

The organizer starts to build breathing room. This person doesn't *do* the thing. They manage the *people* who do the thing.

The resource now is not just time. It's resourcefulness. If you're at this level, you're leveraging others. You're managing energy, people, and processes instead of doing all the labor yourself.

At this level, you shouldn't be asking, "How can I do this?" You need to ask, "Who can do this for me?"

The ultimate version of this level is a corporate CEO, and the income range **is** $40,000 to $1.8 million per year (from a shift manager at Taco Bell to the CEO of Lockheed Martin).

Even at this level, income is capped and

>> You're still trading time and control for a salary.

>> You answer to a board.

>> You're probably traveling constantly.

>> You likely have no work-life balance. (And yes, the divorce rate among CEOs is sky high.)

>> You feel overwhelmed.

If organizing is your only financial engine, your impact and lifestyle still have a hard ceiling.

Level 3: Automating

This is where the game changes. The automators uses systems, not sweat. This person has automated their savings, set buy and sell limit orders, and created one-to-many income streams through business or portfolio growth.

At this level

>> You're not chasing shiny objects.

>> You trust the process.

>> You know that your wealth is growing — even when you sleep.

Your money is no longer something you *earn*. It's something you *grow*.

Here's a low-end example: You invest $50 per month into an index fund like VOO. In 40 years, that becomes $100,000. Or maybe you get a side hustle, you write a book that generates book sales revenue on auto, and you set buy and sell limit orders so you're not glued to your screen all day.

In a high-end example, you invest every extra dollar (after expenses), optimize your portfolio using the Invest Diva Diamond Analysis (IDDA) framework, and hit your financial freedom number of $1.5 million in five years. By retirement, you may cross $20 million. You have embodied the habits of financially impactful people, so you make fast decisions on autopilot. You have systems in place that generate real income automatically — like my own automated webinar, which brings in up to a million dollars per month. With these automations in place, you feel relieved and in control, and your financial impact is higher than that of grinders and organizers.

Level 4: Accelerating

This fourth level is where triple compounders live. The accelerator doesn't just have wealth; they have freedom, and more importantly, the highest level of impact.

Your income comes from systems that compound, not just effort. You make decisions based on frameworks, not just feelings. And you use your time to enjoy life rather than chase money.

At this level you

>> Take the systems you've already set up in generating and automating.

>> Layer on additional resources, skills, and leverage (often from other people or from reinvested profits).

>> Create a multiplier effect so your results grow much faster than if you only used your own time, effort, and capital.

>> No longer hustle for security. You live from abundance.

Accelerating is compounding multiple automated systems, other people's skills, reinvestments, and time with your own. The low-end income for an accelerator is $1 million per year. The high end **is** billions of dollars.

These are the people who

>> Generate income

>> Invest income

>> Automate the entire process

>> Repeat the formula over and over again

This is the pinnacle of financial evolution, and it's where the Triple Compounding system is anchored. You are now free to make real impact in the world, instead of waiting for the government or other billionaires whose values you may or may not share.

What does *Generate → Automate → Accelerate* remind you of? That's right: triple compounding.

Every time you upgrade your level of financial impact, you collapse time and expand possibility. Don't settle for grinding when your future self is ready to accelerate.

Identifying Where You Are in the Journey

Whether you're currently grinding away at your 9 to 5, organizing systems at your job or business, investing part of your income, or fully living the compounding lifestyle, you're somewhere on the path. Knowing exactly where you are is the first step to automating your next level.

This section helps you identify your current phase and gives you a road map to rise with intention.

Moving from grinder to organizer

If you're currently doing *everything* yourself, you're in the *grinding phase.* You may be overworking, underearning, or simply trading time for money. The shift to organizing begins with one powerful reframe:

TIP

Ask, "Who can help me do this?" instead of "*How* can I do this?"

You move into the organizer phase when you start

>> Delegating tasks — even if you start with just one

>> Documenting what you do, so others can replicate it

>> Hiring part-time help or using automation tools

>> Prioritizing *leverage* over *labor*

REMEMBER

Even a solopreneur can be an organizer. The moment you stop doing everything manually, you begin shifting your impact.

Moving from organizer to investor

Once you've created breathing room by managing systems, people, or workflows, it's time to let your *money* do the heavy lifting.

You move into the investor phase when you

>> Start saving with intention (not just "leftovers")

>> Create automated contributions to your brokerage or retirement accounts

>> Set up buy/sell limit orders, as I show in Chapter 16

>> Reinvest your profits and dividends

>> Begin thinking in *multiples* — not just *more*

Use the IDDA framework that I introduce in Chapter 10 to vet each investment with confidence. You don't need a degree in finance; you just need a system that aligns with your goals.

Moving from investor to automator

This is the most powerful shift, and it's where triple compounders shine. The automator doesn't just earn and invest. They've created systems and partnerships that scale themselves. At this level

>> Income is mostly passive or semi-passive

>> Investments are set-it-and-forget-it with long-term targets

>> Business systems and your partners sell while you sleep

>> Your calendar is spacious, and your peace is rich

You can finally

>> Take on passion projects without stressing about money

>> Say "no" to opportunities that don't excite you

>> Spend more time with your family without sacrificing income

>> Have a bigger financial impact

You don't reach this level by accident. You reach it by design. It starts with a clear intention and builds with strategic action.

Once you automate one part of your life, you get addicted to the freedom it brings. Your finances become a machine, and your mind gets to breathe.

Drawing Inspiration from Impactful Financial Leaders

One of the best ways to gain confidence in your financial journey is to see what's possible. The truth is, the most financially impactful people on the planet don't just hustle; they generate, automate, and accelerate their wealth using the exact principles of triple compounding.

That includes me and nearly every one of my mentors. From Guy Spier, who trained under Warren Buffett, to David Parke, one of my first business mentors (and a veteran), to Myron Golden, Marie Forleo, Eileen Wilder, Russell Brunson, Leila and Alex Hormozi, and Tony Robbins — every one of them operates across all four levels of financial impact.

What's more, they do it in alignment with their values while building meaningful lives, relationships, and communities.

Everyone's triple-compounding system looks different depending on their stage of life, experience, personality type, and what they enjoy doing. But what are the principles that drive financial impact? Those are universal.

Transforming a life through financial impact: The Tony Robbins example

Today, Tony Robbins is a globally recognized powerhouse with

>> A nine-figure net worth

>> More than 80 businesses invested in or owned

>> More than a billion meals donated to charity

>> A deeply fulfilling marriage with his wife Sage, who's also been a mentor to me and helped me save my marriage

But it wasn't always that way. In his early forties, Tony was at rock bottom:

>> Going through a highly public divorce

>> Estranged from his adopted children

>> Nearly broke — financially and emotionally

That's when he stopped grinding and began applying the higher levels of financial impact:

>> **Organizing** his business into systems

>> **Investing** with intention

>> **Automating** through scale and recurring models

Today, he lives in alignment with his values, prioritizing contribution, peace, and purpose over hustle.

Be careful who you learn from. Don't chase Instagram "success." Follow people who've built real wealth, healthy relationships, and meaningful lives.

Following your unique journey while applying a proven blueprint

Whether you're a grinder working long hours, an organizer leading a team, an investor growing your portfolio, or an automator living with financial peace, your journey is valid. And it's just beginning.

What matters most is that you focus on one level at a time, master it, and then move to the next. That's how real wealth is built — without burnout.

You don't have to automate everything at once. Focus on the level you're at today, give it your all, and build momentum.

Each level unlocks new freedoms:

>> More time

>> More flexibility

>> More energy for your family, your goals, and your impact

And remember: *If you're not growing, you're dying.* That applies to you — and to your money.

The most successful triple compounders don't stop when they reach their goals. They reinvest, reinvigorate, and repeat on all four levels of financial impact.

If you're ready to automate your path but want guidance and clarity on where to begin, I created Triple Compounding Live for people like you. It's the event where I personally help you map out your next move — whether you're a grinder looking to rise or an investor ready to become an accelerator. Go to `https:www.triple compounding.com/live` to see if a live session is coming up.

IN THIS CHAPTER

» Creating scalable, one-to-many offers that free you from trading time for money

» Turning one-time buyers into lifelong customers through continuity programs

» Building partnerships that expand your reach and income — without extra effort

Chapter **12**

Automating Your Business Income Generation

f you're doing *everything* in your business — and if taking even one day off means things collapse — you don't have a business. You have a job.

Triple compounders understand that the only way to scale is to remove themselves from the day-to-day grind and build systems that run (and grow) without them. Your business isn't supposed to be your boss. It's supposed to be your extension — one that works *for* you, not *because* of you.

I found this out the hard way. Five years into my business, I believed the only path to growth was to hustle harder. So, I did. Late nights. Weekend webinars. DMs. Emails. Networking events. Blog posts. Sales calls. You name it — I was doing it. And I was stuck.

I hustled myself straight into burnout. Then I decided to take a much-needed vacation to Mexico, hoping to finally rest and reset. But instead of peace, I got panic.

Sales stopped. Customer emails piled up. Refund requests and disputes rolled in. By the time I came back, I actually wished I hadn't left. That trip cost me more than just mojito money.

And hiring a full-time sales team? Out of the question. I couldn't afford it. I felt like I was trapped in the very business that I'd built to escape the 9 to 5.

That's when I saw an ad from my now friend and mentor, Russell Brunson. It said something like, "How to continue selling while you sleep — without managing an annoying sales team." It was like he'd read my mind.

That ad led me down a rabbit hole of systems, funnels, webinars, and automation strategies that helped me rapidly scale to $100,000 per month on auto.

In this chapter, I explain how you can

>> Build one-to-many offers so your income doesn't rely on 1:1 time

>> Use automated webinars, live events, and e-commerce platforms to scale your reach

>> Launch continuity programs that grow month after month — without extra effort

>> Set up partnerships that work for you even while you're off the grid

After these systems are in place, your business becomes a compounding asset — just like your stock portfolio or rental property.

Creating One-to-Many Offers That Compound

Your time is limited. So, if your offer depends on you being present every time someone buys, delivers, or asks a question, your business will eventually hit a wall.

Triple compounders break free by creating one-to-many offers: packages that solve big problems for many people at the same time without needing your one-on-one time. This structure is the backbone of scalable income. In this section, I describe the four steps to creating a framework that works on autopilot.

Step 1: Solving a hair-on-fire problem

Your offer needs to fix a problem that feels *urgent* and *painful* — like the customers' hair is literally on fire. If your audience feels like they can "deal with it later," your offer won't convert, no matter how good it is.

So how do you find the right problem? Simple: Ask them.

First, get crystal clear on who you want to serve. Then figure out what their big goal is. Is it to lose weight? Get out of debt? Build a six-figure side hustle?

Once you know their desired outcome, go straight to the source. Text them. Email them. Post on social. Use this simple template to get the gold:

Hey [Target Audience]! What's the biggest challenge keeping you from achieving your [GOAL]?

At Invest Diva, we call this "The Ask Campaign." I run it every time I'm creating a new offer or when I feel out of sync with my audience. The responses are always eye-opening — and often result in the exact copy we use in our marketing.

This step isn't just market research. It's your first clue to a high-converting offer.

Business isn't about convincing. It's about *serving*. Sell them what they want. Give them what they need. Read Chapter 9 for more on identifying your solution for the right type of customers.

Step 2: Packaging your process into a repeatable framework

Once you've identified the problem your audience urgently wants solved, it's time to show them how you're going to solve it — with a clear, step-by-step framework.

Here's why this matters: If your process feels random, complicated, or like it only works when you are personally involved, you'll stay stuck in the one-on-one grind. But if you create a system that's repeatable, scalable, and teachable, it becomes a product that you can sell over and over again. That's where your unique framework comes in.

A great framework has the following characteristics:

>> It has a name your audience can remember.

>> It breaks the transformation down into clear steps.

>> It feels structured, not overwhelming.

To create the framework, consider what the three to five steps are that your ideal client needs to take to go from where they are right now to where they want to be. Here are some examples:

>> A three-part weight-loss formula

>> A five-phase relationship reset system

>> A "diamond" method for analyzing stocks (sound familiar?)

The turning point for me came when I stopped trying to explain all of investing in one go and instead taught my students the Invest Diva Diamond Analysis. See Chapter 10 to see how it's structured. The Invest Diva Diamond Analysis gave structure to my method, made it easier for others to follow, and gave me a way to deliver the same result without having to be live every time. That shift was the foundation of my first scalable offer.

Don't worry. Your framework doesn't have to be fancy. You don't need to invent quantum physics. You just need to organize your existing knowledge into a pathway people can walk through — and succeed with.

A framework isn't just for educational products. You can use frameworks to automate even your e-commerce business.

Let's say you run an e-commerce store selling luxury candles. You may think, *I'm just* selling *a product. What kind of framework do I need?* Well, people don't just buy candles. They buy a *feeling.* A *vibe.* A *mood.* So, instead of just selling wax in a jar, you could create a three-step ritual framework to position your offer like this:

The Evening Reset Ritual

>> Step 1: Light the unwind candle to cue relaxation.

>> Step 2: Play the curated playlist we include with your order.

>> Step 3: Use our guided journal prompt to release the day.

Now, you're not just selling a candle; you're selling a *lifestyle upgrade*. You've taken a one-time product and wrapped it in a repeatable, branded experience people can come back to again and again.

And best of all? This makes your marketing, upsells, and email automations way easier to build around.

Physical products get more powerful when they're paired with a process your customer can follow.

Confused customers don't buy. A framework gives them confidence — and gives you freedom.

Step 3: Making the offer so good they can't say no

Once you package your process into a repeatable framework, it's time to wrap that framework in an *irresistible offer* — one so good, your audience feels silly saying no, as I explore in Chapter 9.

I've had many offers that completely flopped. Here's the formula I now use to create "can't-look-away" offers:

>> **Be crystal clear on the result.** Tell them exactly what they'll get — *in their words*, not yours. Avoid vague promises like "level up your finances" and say something like, "Grow your portfolio to six figures — even if you're starting from scratch."

>> **Add speed.** The faster the result, the higher the perceived value. "Get control of your money in 30 days" sounds way more exciting than "Someday you'll figure this out."

>> **Reduce risk.** Offer guarantees, trial periods, or "can't fail" elements. Even if someone never asks for a refund, just knowing it's there builds trust.

>> **Stack irresistible bonuses.** Think of the top excuses your audience has and then give them bonuses that solve those exact objections.

When I launched my Triple Compounding system, I didn't just sell a course. I sold a transformation: from stuck and stressed to confidently building wealth. Then I sweetened the deal with real tools, like my Risk Management Toolkit, Premium Investing Group (PIG) coaching, accountability partners, Diva Money Coach certification, Recession Proofing Hack, and the "Zero to $10M Roadmap."

I even included a bonus just for watching the free masterclass. Why? Because I know people procrastinate. That one bonus alone pushed hundreds of people to take action fast.

The goal here is simple: Make your offer feel like a steal compared to the value. The rule of thumb is the value should be 10X the price they pay. So, if your price is $5,000, it should feel like they're getting $50,000+ in transformation, tools, support, and speed.

People don't compare your price to your competitor; they compare it to the *cost of staying stuck.*

Solve their top three objections in your bonuses and you'll boost conversions *without* sounding salesy.

Step 4: Using a one-to-many delivery vehicle

When I first started, every sale had to happen one on one. I was hopping on calls, answering DMs, writing custom emails — whatever it took to close. It was draining and unsustainable.

So, I switched to running live webinars. That helped me sell to more people at once, but I was still repeating myself week after week, fielding the same questions live, and staying glued to my screen for hours. I traded one kind of burnout for another.

The real shift came when I finally recorded my highest-converting webinar, plugged it into an evergreen funnel, and hired a team to handle questions, tech issues, and customer onboarding. That's when things truly became automated — and scalable. Now, I wake up to payment notifications from people who sign up, watch, and buy. And I never need to show up live.

This is what I mean by a one-to-many delivery vehicle. It's kinda like a dishwasher. You could wash each plate by hand — scrubbing, rinsing, drying one by one — but why would you when you can just load them all in the dishwasher, press a button, and walk away while the machine does the work?

Triple compounders use one-to-many delivery vehicles to compound time-saving and income.

Here are a few delivery models that compound:

>> **Self-paced online course:** Your framework — recorded once, and delivered through videos, worksheets, and a login portal — works while you sleep.

>> **Group coaching program:** You show up to lead a live call once a week, while hundreds go through the same material together. It's high-leverage, high-touch.

>> **Paid challenge or live workshop:** Five days. One result. One upsell at the end. This is the fast path to both transformation *and* conversions.

>> **Evergreen webinar:** Record once, automate forever. You can use these webinars to sell courses, memberships, or even high-ticket coaching without ever needing to "jump on a quick call."

One-to-many delivery isn't about what you sell. It's about *how* you deliver it.

Discovering the Power of Continuity Compounding

Continuity is what one of my business mentors, Russell Brunson, calls "the other compounding." For a while, I was doing it without even realizing it. In this section, I walk you through how continuity offers quietly build stability in your business, the three types of continuity programs that triple compounders rely on, and how to design one that keeps customers coming back month after month.

Creating continuity programs that compound automatically

When I first launched my Make Your Money Work For You PowerCourse, I thought it would be helpful to offer course buyers a weekly check-in call — for a small monthly fee — to make sure they stayed on track. I called it the Premium Investing Group (PIG). To my surprise, 100 percent of people who bought the course opted into the membership — and 79 percent of them stayed for *years*.

A couple of years later, my business started facing headwinds. More and more "finance gurus" were popping up on every platform. Investing courses were becoming mainstream. I wasn't unique anymore, and my front-end sales started to slow down.

But unlike businesses that relied *only* on course sales, mine stayed afloat. That's when one of my mentors said something that hit me like a bolt of lightning: "If you only sell upfront offers, you don't have a business — you have a promotion."

And it clicked. That continuity offer I created as an afterthought was the *safety net* that kept my business thriving.

A *continuity program* is any product or service your customers subscribe to and *keep paying for over time* because it continues to deliver value. Instead of chasing new sales every day, you build a base of recurring revenue that stacks, compounds, and supports your long-term growth. It's the *other* compounding that you can add to your Triple Compounding system.

There are three main types of continuity programs that triple compounders use across different industries.

>> **Membership programs:** Subscriptions that give people access to exclusive content, tools, community, or coaching.

   Example: A fitness coach offers $49-per-month access to live online workouts, a meal plan library, and a private accountability group.

>> **Subscription boxes/product refills:** Physical products that are delivered regularly, often tied to a lifestyle ritual.

   Example: A skincare brand delivers monthly refills of personalized serums and a bonus seasonal face mask. Customers never run out — and never want to.

>> **Ongoing access to support/tools:** This can be software, digital tools, templates, or a community.

   Example: A real estate expert charges $97 per month for weekly market breakdowns, scripts, and deal calculators used by agents across the country.

Turning sign-ups into superfans

Real business stability comes from recurring revenue. But how can you ensure that people don't cancel? Hint: When people stop paying, your recurring income stops compounding.

Here are some ways to keep people hooked (in a healthy way), ensure that people happily stick with you forever, and make recurring revenue actually . . . recur!

>> **Solve a persistent problem.** If the problem goes away after one use, people will cancel. Choose something your audience *wants to stay plugged into* — like accountability, up-to-date insights, or exclusive perks.

>> **Keep delivering fresh or ongoing value.** This doesn't mean you need to create brand-new stuff constantly. You can rotate content, spotlight community wins, or build a content library they can explore at their own pace.

>> **Make the first experience amazing.** One of the biggest reasons people cancel a membership has nothing to do with the membership but everything to do with onboarding. Your onboarding flow matters more than you think. Give people a *quick win* in the first week. That early momentum dramatically increases retention.

Continuity programs compound income the same way automated investments compound interest. They stack over time and grow quietly in the background.

Confused people don't pay. If people can't tell what they're paying for — or don't see results quickly — they'll cancel. Clarity + momentum = retention.

WARNING

Building Partnerships That Compound

When I first got started, I had major trust issues. I didn't believe anyone could do things the right way, so I thought I had to do everything myself. It wasn't until I partnered with someone I once saw as a competitor that I realized the value of collaboration over competition.

You don't have to build your business alone.

As a triple compounder, I now know that partnerships are one of the fastest ways to expand your reach, boost your credibility, and multiply your income without multiplying your workload.

But not all partnerships are created equal. If you've ever been burned by a flaky affiliate, a one-sided collab, or a joint venture that felt more like a job than a win-win, you're not alone.

In this section, I walk you through how to create *smart, scalable partnerships* that actually compound.

Understanding compounding partnerships

When you think of "partnerships," don't just think about business co-founders. In the world of scalable income, *partnerships* can mean the following things:

>> **Affiliate partners:** These people promote your offer in exchange for a commission.

>> **Cross-promotional collaborations:** You promote their product to your list, and they promote yours to theirs.

>> **Joint ventures:** These can include a one-time campaign, webinar, or offer that you create and run together.

>> **Strategic introductions:** Someone connects you to a new audience or niche.

>> **Platform partnerships:** You align with a marketplace, software tool, or community to gain traffic and trust.

Partnerships that compound don't just add exposure. They *multiply* it.

One of the fastest ways to grow your business is by partnering with other businesses whose *audience* overlaps with yours, even if their *product* doesn't. A productivity coach may be a great partner for a finance course. A fertility expert may be a great fit for a hormone-friendly food subscription.

The process of building lasting partnerships is similar to building superfan customers. You must make it a win-win. Here are some methods I've used to build partnerships that actually compound:

>> **Make it easy for them to say yes.** No one wants more work. Provide swipe copy, graphics, clear instructions, and plug-and-play assets. The easier you make it, the more likely they are to promote.

>> **Offer irresistible incentives.** This can be commissions, referral bonuses, exclusive content, or co-branded offers. Your partner should feel like they're getting a win just by saying yes.

>> **Focus on long-term relationships.** Don't treat it like a one-off transaction. Follow up. Ask how their audience responded. Offer to return the favor. Compounding partnerships are *nurtured*, not just activated.

Want to grow faster without ad spend? Build a mini affiliate army. Even just ten people sharing your offer consistently can rival the results of a paid campaign.

If your only strategy is, "Hey, promote my thing," you'll burn bridges fast. Focus on value exchange and shared results.

Compounding legacy through partnerships

One of the most exciting outcomes of becoming a financially impactful triple compounder is watching how that personal transformation creates a ripple effect. As I built my system and results, the knowledge I shared evolved into long-term, scalable impact — not just for me, but for the high-level professionals I mentor and the communities they go on to serve. That's exactly what happened when three of my Diamond members — a PhD-level corporate executive, a former CPA, and a private equity principal — met through my Accelerator program. By getting in the room with other serious triple compounders, they found aligned values, complementary strengths, and a shared vision and decided to take their compounding to the next level by launching a venture together focused on wealth empowerment for physicians and high-earning moms.

Their mission is to help clients reduce taxes legally, protect their income, and build multigenerational wealth — without burnout, overwhelm, or guesswork. And they don't just teach it; they systematize it.

At the heart of their business is what they call the *Legacy Waterfall* — a framework that automates financial decision-making through tax strategy, layered investing, and long-term protection.

It starts with tax efficiency, using tools like in-kind charitable giving. Instead of donating cash, clients give appreciated assets like stocks, crypto, or art directly to qualified charities. Because the donation is deducted at fair market value, this strategy not only avoids capital gains tax but also maximizes the deduction — freeing up capital.

In-kind charitable giving allows you to donate assets you've held for over a year — like stocks or crypto — without triggering capital gains tax. The charity gets the full value, and you get a bigger deduction.

This can raise a red flag with the tax authorities if you do things incorrectly. Make sure to consult with a CPA before taking action, and read Chapter 18 for more on strategic tax planning.

From there, the "waterfall" flows into a layered investment structure designed for compounding at every level:

- **Top layer**: High-upside opportunities like private equity (see Chapter 7)

- **Middle layer**: Growth-focused assets such as ETFs and equities (see Chapter 6)

- **Base layer**: Stable, income-generating investments like real estate or structured insurance (see Chapters 7 and 17)

This intentional stack helps preserve and multiply wealth across generations while automating much of the decision-making through tax-smart strategies and diversified vehicles.

It's a real-life example of triple compounding in action: strategic tax savings + intentional portfolio design + automated legacy planning.

And more importantly, it shows what's possible when you stop grinding, start systemizing, and step into your identity as a triple compounder.

If you're a physician or high-earning mom ready to build wealth with clarity and confidence, explore their work at www.onepercentplaybook.net. You'll see the exact principles I teach brought to life by students who've mastered Level 3: Automating.

Chapter **13**

Automating Compounding of Your External Asset Investments

When I first started investing, I had all the time in the world to analyze the markets. I was reporting trends for big-name financial companies and spending hours glued to my screens every day.

But then I had a baby.

My daughter took up 90 percent of my waking hours. And the other 10 percent? I was exhausted. If you've ever had a newborn, you know exactly what I mean. Sleep? Nonexistent. Time to analyze candlestick patterns and economic data? Not happening.

That's when everything changed for me. I couldn't invest like I used to. So, instead of obsessively checking the markets, I cut it down to looking *once a day* — during one of my 15-minute pumping sessions while my daughter slept. Eventually, I got it down to *just once per week*.

And the wild part? I actually started getting *better* results. Why? Because I removed the emotion. I replaced manual micromanagement with *automation*.

This is the heart of how I triple-compound with external assets like stocks, especially now that I don't have hours to waste. In this chapter, I show you how to do it, too.

Reviewing the Triple-Compounding Formula

Triple compounding isn't just about building a portfolio. It's about building a system that builds *you*. Most people think investing starts with stocks. But real wealth creation begins with how you invest your time, energy, and attention *before* you ever buy an asset.

When you become a triple compounder, you're not just investing in financial assets. You're investing in three core categories of your life:

>> Yourself (as I cover in Chapter 4)

>> Your extensions (like your business, brand, systems, and team, as I describe in Chapter 5)

>> Your external assets (like stocks, crypto, and real estate, as I explain in Chapter 6)

Within each of these three investments, you have to follow the same sequence of actions:

1. Generate

2. Automate

3. Accelerate

And it has to happen in this exact order.

Once you've invested in yourself and built your extensions, it's time to make those dollars *compound*. You start by generating your first profit. That could be through a strategy like my Invest Diva Diamond Analysis, which I dive deep into in Chapter 10.

Then you automate your strategy using the tools I show you in the following segments and let your system take over.

And finally, you accelerate by stacking more external assets — crypto, options, real estate, private equity — based on your risk tolerance and lifestyle goals that I cover in Chapter 3.

When you follow this order — generate, automate, accelerate — you build a flywheel that feeds itself. Your growth becomes inevitable.

Selecting Your Investment Time Frames

Before you start automating your investments, you need to know what kind of investor you want to be. Not all investing strategies are created equal, and the time frame you choose determines how often you check your portfolio, how you set your automations, and how involved you need to be.

The good news? There's no right or wrong here. What matters is what works best for your goals, lifestyle, and risk tolerance.

Following are the three main investment time frames and how triple compounders approach each one.

Long-term investing (years)

This is the triple compounder's home base. If you're someone who wants to grow your wealth steadily while living your life and without obsessing over every market move, this one's for you.

Long-term investors

>> Buy high-quality assets and hold them for years

>> Focus on big-picture trends, not short-term noise

>> Rely on automations like dollar-cost averaging, dividend reinvestment plans (DRIPs), and interest compounding

>> Check their portfolios once a month (or even less!)

The longer your time horizon, the less likely short-term volatility will hurt you.

This approach works beautifully if you're working a full-time job, raising a family, or building a business on the side. It's how I built my eight-figure portfolio 15 minutes at a time.

Swing trading (weeks to months)

Swing trading sits between long-term investing and day trading. You're not watching the charts all day, but you *are* looking for medium-term trends to profit from.

This method is exactly how one of my triple compounders reached a million-dollar portfolio in just three years, and it can work for you if

>> You enjoy market analysis.

>> You can dedicate one to two hours per week to checking your trades.

>> You want to lock in profits more frequently than long-term holders.

Swing trading gives you a nice balance: more action than long-term investing without the stress of day trading.

Day trading (minutes to hours)

This is the high-stakes, high-intensity version of investing. Unless you've made it your full-time job, I recommend staying far away.

When I first got started working as a reporter at the New York Stock Exchange, I was ready to dive into the markets and make my money work for me, just like you may be right now. I didn't have much experience, and I definitely wasn't confident in my choices yet, but what I *did* have going for me was that I was surrounded by some of the best traders in the world. So, I thought, "I'll see what they're doing and just copy their moves!"

I went all in with my savings of $15,000 (which was *a lot* of money for me at the time), convinced I was about to become a millionaire overnight by following the Wall Street finance bros.

Can you guess what happened? I lost the whole $15,000. Gone. My entire savings — wiped out. I remember thinking, *Girl, how could you mess this up? All these finance bros are making millions, you're copying them, and you lose everything?!*

So, I did what any reasonable person would do: I posted about it on LinkedIn. To my surprise, Guy Spier, bestselling author of *The Education of a Value Investor* (St. Martin's Press, 2014) and a student of Warren Buffett, slid into my DMs.

He offered to send me his book and told me I was approaching the markets all wrong. At first, I didn't understand — after all, I was following the same strategies I'd seen used on Wall Street. But then he explained his perspective, and it completely shifted how I viewed investing. Instead of reacting to every headline and market fluctuation, he emphasized the power of blocking out the noise and building a long-term strategy.

That's when it clicked. I realized what I had been doing — what caused me to lose $15,000 — was day trading following the market noise. I was trying to guess where the market was going next in order to make a quick profit. But it was too risky, and it wiped me out.

REMEMBER

Wall Street traders who day-trade aren't using their own money. They're managing other people's funds with zero emotional attachment. And it's not $15,000. They're trading *millions* or *billions* of dollars. Here's the kicker: Some of the most successful hedge funds only have to be right 51 percent of the time to earn massive profits because they make money off commissions, not consistent accuracy!

WARNING

If you try to use a Wall Street day-trading strategy on your personal account, especially if it's less than $100,000, you're putting yourself at serious risk. You'd be trying to guess the market's next move every day, hour, or even minute. Without institutional tools or deep pockets to back you up, you can lose everything before ever seeing a profit.

When your investing moves are backed by data and pattern recognition, not emotion, you gain confidence, clarity, and control.

Automating Your Investment Contributions

Most people invest when they *feel like it* — after the bills are paid, after a bonus comes in, or when they get hyped up from a financial podcast. But triple compounders don't leave their future up to feelings. They invest on autopilot.

Why? Because automation is how you make sure that investing happens consistently, no matter what's going on in your life, the economy, or your emotions. Regardless of whether you're having a rough week, a busy season, or just forgot to check your accounts, your money keeps moving toward freedom.

In this section, I walk you through how to set up this foundational part of your triple-compounding system.

Deciding on the amount of your unique contribution

The very first step is the most important financial decision you'll ever make:

> What percentage of your income are you committing to take off the table — for you, your future, and your freedom?

This is your *freedom fund*. It's money that gets automatically directed to your investment account before you ever have the chance to spend it.

There's no perfect number, but here's a solid rule of thumb:

>> Start with at least 10 percent of your income.

>> Aim for 15 percent to really build momentum.

>> Go up to 20 percent or more as your income grows.

And yes, it's okay if you start small. What matters most is consistency.

If you've committed to increasing your income by investing in yourself (see Chapter 4) and your extensions (as I discuss in Chapter 5), your contribution percentage can — and should — increase over time.

When you automate your contributions to your investment portfolio, you're not gonna miss it. You're not gonna spend it on liabilities that aren't going to make you money. You are going to automatically compound it.

REMEMBER

Make a quick decision right now. Don't delay this. What percent of your income are you committed to taking out and setting aside for your freedom fund, ongoing, no matter what?

TIP

Finding the right broker to automate your investments

You may be thinking, *Okay, Kiana, but where do I go to invest in external assets? Where is my contribution automation even going? Is there a website?*

To invest in online financial assets, you need access to the markets. As an individual investor, you can't just knock on the door of the New York Stock Exchange and ask if you can buy stocks. You need a go-between to facilitate these purchases.

The "go-between" people are called *brokers*, and they're very similar to real estate brokers, except instead of a person, you can do work with a broker online through their platforms, which makes the whole process easy. All you have to do is create an account with the broker's online platform, and you instantly gain access to the markets.

There are online brokers in almost all countries, so you should be able to invest regardless of where you are. However, make sure you're selecting a credible one. Figure 13-1 shows some good brokers for stocks in the US, UK, Eurozone, Australia, and Canada. My favorite app in the US is Robinhood, which is super user-friendly at the time of this writing.

FIGURE 13-1: List of online financial brokers in the US, UK, Eurozone, Australia, and Canada.

TripleCompounding.com/Invest Diva

My largest stock account is with Charles Schwab because it lets me borrow against my portfolio to invest in other assets to accelerate my earnings.

TIP

Here's what to look for in a broker that fits your triple-compounder lifestyle:

>> No or low fees on trades and account maintenance

>> Recurring deposit features from your bank

>> Automatic investment tools like DRIPs (see the section, "Using dividend reinvestment plans," later in this chapter)

>> User-friendly interface (especially mobile, if you're on the go)

>> Customer service that actually picks up the phone

Creating an automation from your bank to your broker

Once you've chosen your contribution percentage *and* your broker, it's time to make the magic happen. Here's your step-by-step plan:

1. **Log in to your bank.**

   Set up a *recurring transfer* from your checking account to your brokerage account. You can choose weekly, bi-weekly, or monthly — whatever lines up with your income flow.

2. **Pick a consistent date.**

   For example, if you get paid on the 1st and 15th, schedule transfers for the 2nd and 16th to give time for funds to clear.

3. **Set it and forget it.**

   Treat this like a bill, except this bill pays *you*. Once it's scheduled, leave it alone. Let your freedom fund do its thing.

4. **Avoid the temptation to pause.**

   Even if money feels tight one month, *don't* cancel the automation. Lower the amount if you need to but keep the habit alive.

Turning off your investment automation is like skipping brushing your teeth for a week. It may not hurt right away, but over time, the damage adds up.

Automating Your Investment Profits

Most people stop at "I invested," but triple compounders ask:

>> How can I make this investment reinvest itself?

>> How can I lock in profits without micromanaging the market?

That's where the six automation tools I reveal in this section come in. They help you compound your profits with minimal effort, so you don't have to live on your trading app or stress over every move.

Getting ahead of the crowd sentiment

Everyone wants to buy low and sell high. That's the goal, right? But here's the thing: Buying low and selling high becomes risky when you're following the crowd. Why? Because by the time the general public (and the headlines) start talking about an asset, you're already late.

Wall Street knows this. In fact, they depend on it.

The good news? You can beat them at their own game — without guessing, gambling, or checking CNBC 20 times a day. Back when I was consulting for a Wall Street firm that specialized in *high-frequency trading,* I was invited to help expand their services into Japan. During one of those trips, I ended up chatting about market psychology at a corporate afterparty with a client. He shared something that completely shifted the way I approached market timing.

His firm used a Japanese market sentiment indicator, a tool designed to help them anticipate Wall Street's behavior *before* the big moves happened. It showed them how institutions were feeling and positioned them to *go against the herd* at just the right time. I explain exactly how this tool works in my book, *Ichimoku Secrets* (CreateSpace, 2016), and my Triple Compounding Masterclass at www.TripleCompounding.com.

When I saw how it worked, I knew it had to become part of my Triple Compounding system. Here's how it works:

Say that you've identified your risk tolerance (low, medium, or high). Based on that, my system gives you a clear signal. It's similar to the trail signs on ski slopes:

>> Green circle for beginners

>> Blue square for intermediate

>> Black diamond for advanced

My system works exactly the same way:

>> If you have low risk tolerance, you enter on signal 1 (green circle).

>> If you have medium risk tolerance, you wait for signal 2 (blue square).

>> If you have high risk tolerance, you enter on signal 3 (black diamond).

Anticipating, not reacting

Tony Robbins says, "Leaders anticipate. Losers react." That's exactly what this part of the Triple Compounding system helps you do: anticipate market sentiment, then plan your entries based on your unique risk tolerance.

No more blindly following the crowd. No more panic-selling because a headline scared you.

When you lead with strategy rather than emotion, you give your money the best chance to multiply while you focus on living your life.

And yes, even *I*, a girl who openly admits she sucks at math, used this system to retire *my husband* — a literal rocket scientist — from his stressful corporate job.

If I can do it, so can you.

Using buy and sell limit orders

This is one of my favorite strategies and the one that saved my sanity after becoming a mom. In case you're unfamiliar with buy and sell limit orders, here's a brief definition of each:

>> A *buy limit order* lets you tell your broker, "Buy this stock if it drops to this price."

>> A *sell limit order* says, "Sell this stock if it rises to this price."

Instead of staring at charts or trying to time the market perfectly, you create rules ahead of time based on your analysis (like the Invest Diva Diamond system; see Chapter 10) and let your broker do the rest.

Limit orders are like a slow cooker for your investments: Set it, forget it, come back later to find a fully cooked profit. And this isn't just theory. I've used it with real investments, as I describe in the sidebar.

CASE STUDY: TESLA

Here's an example on how I use buy and sell limit orders to automate portfolio income.

Back in August 2018 — well before Tesla's stock split and all the political buzz — my system identified a technical signal suggesting Tesla's price may decline. On August 15, the price broke below the green Ichimoku cloud, which indicated a potential drop toward the $262 range.

Now, instead of watching the markets every day or trying to guess the timing, I simply opened my broker's app and placed a buy limit order at $262. That means I instructed the system to buy shares *only if* the price dropped to that level. It took less than a minute to set up. Then I moved on with my day.

Sure enough, the order executed. I received a notification that I'd bought Tesla shares at my target price — no screen time or second-guessing required.

The next step? Using the same system to identify a smart sell target based on my medium-risk strategy. I'm not a day trader, so I don't need to rush. I review my system once a month.

On October 25, the data showed a strong resistance level around $327. I placed a sell limit order at that price and let the automation take over again.

When Tesla reached $327, the shares sold — locking in a $65 per-share profit in just over two months.

If you had bought 100 shares, that's $6,500 in automated profit. And because setting up both the buy and sell orders took about five minutes total, that works out to more than $1,000 per minute of decision-making.

But the real magic isn't in one trade.

(continued)

(continued)

From 2017 to 2025, this system identified multiple opportunities to buy Tesla low and sell it high — on autopilot. My members and I didn't have to guess. We didn't have to time the market. And we didn't have to stay glued to our screens. As a result, we collectively achieved over 3,000 percent in compounded gains — far exceeding what a simple buy-and-hold investor would have captured during that same period.

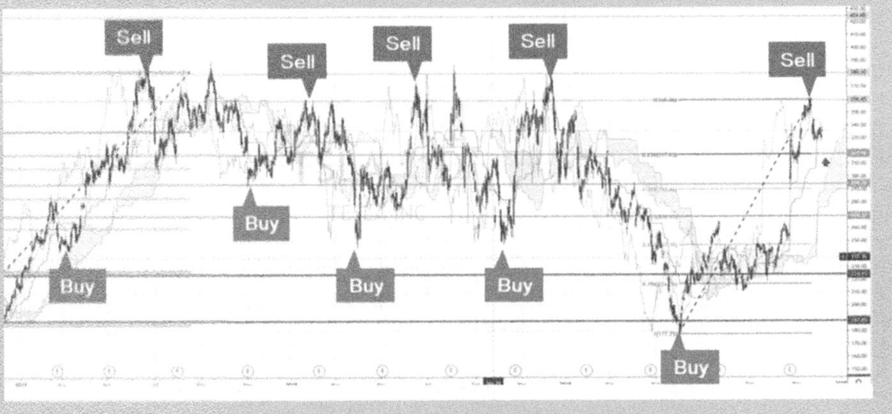

Using dividend reinvestment plans

If your investments pay dividends and you're not automatically reinvesting them, you're leaving free compounding on the table. A dividend reinvestment plan (DRIP) is a feature that lets you automatically buy more shares with the dividends you earn. It's a small but mighty form of compounding.

For example

>> You own 100 shares of a dividend-paying stock.

>> That company pays you $50 in dividends.

>> DRIP reinvests that $50 into more shares automatically.

Over time, this snowballs. Your share count increases, which means your dividend payouts increase, which means *even more* gets reinvested.

Most brokers offer DRIP for free — just toggle it on. Even if the dividends seem small at first, they add up fast over time.

REMEMBER

Automating your dollar-cost averaging

Dollar-cost averaging is a strategy in which you invest a fixed amount at regular intervals no matter what the market is doing. This helps you avoid buying at the "wrong" time and reduces emotional investing. Some months you buy high, some months you buy low. Over time, it averages out.

You can automate dollar-cost averaging by doing the following:

1. **Set a recurring deposit from your bank to your broker.**

2. **Choose recurring investments into the same asset (for example, $200 into VTI every Friday).**

3. **Let the system do the rest — rain or shine, bull or bear.**

Dollar-cost averaging is a favorite among long-term investors because it builds discipline and protects against bad timing.

Using market notifications

Although limit orders and DRIP work automatically, sometimes you want to stay *aware* without staying glued to your screen. That's where market notifications come in. These alerts help you

>> Track price moves on assets in your watchlist

>> Know when your limit orders are triggered

>> Get reminders when it's time to review your positions

Most brokers (and apps like TradingView or Yahoo Finance) let you set price alerts, percentage-change alerts, or even moving average crossovers.

Think of market notifications as your virtual assistant tapping you on the shoulder when it's time to pay attention — without interrupting your life.

You don't need to *react* to every alert. These are just reminders to recheck your strategy, not emotional triggers.

Using interest-paying investments

This is where your idle cash gets to pull its weight. Instead of letting uninvested cash sit in a zero-interest account, park it in an account that compounds on its own.

Here are a few interest-paying options to consider.

>> **Money market accounts (MMAs):** Slightly higher interest than savings accounts

>> **Certificates of deposit (CDs):** Lock your money in for a fixed term at a guaranteed rate

>> **High-yield savings accounts:** Perfect for your emergency fund or short-term goals

>> **Bonds and treasury securities:** Pay fixed interest over time

>> **Dividend-paying stocks:** Not technically interest, but a reliable stream of cash flow

>> **Peer-to-peer lending platforms:** Higher yield, higher risk

>> **Real estate notes, or REITs:** Tied to rental or mortgage income

Make sure your money isn't just sitting. Every dollar should be earning more dollars through market gains, dividends, or interest.

Most people believe investing takes time, stress, and constant decision-making. But triple compounders do it differently.

5

Accelerating Your Triple-Compounding System

IN THIS PART . . .

Leverage influence, social media, and personal branding to grow your income faster.

Scale your business with systems, continuity programs, and irresistible offers.

Apply technical analysis to accelerate your investments and capture more opportunities.

Chapter **14**

Compounding Your Influence

I paid Alex Hormozi $135,000 for one meeting to hear his thoughts on how I can scale my business from $25 million to $100 million. The gist of his response was simple: Focus on building a personal brand. You may be thinking, *Well, duh! You didn't have to pay him $135,000 to tell you that! I could have told you that! What a waste of money!*

True. It's not like I didn't know becoming famous can lead to wealth. But the truth is, knowing something intellectually and actually committing to it at a strategic, scalable level are two very different things.

So why did I happily make this investment? Why do I not view this investment in myself as a waste? And more importantly, why did I take the advice seriously and restructure my business around it?

Because it came from someone whose personal brand I trust. Alex didn't just *say* he knew how to scale. He showed it, proved it, embodied it. And that's the power of influence.

And here's something else you may not know: Alex was first a student (like I was) of Russell Brunson, cofounder of ClickFunnels and author of *Expert Secrets*. Over the years, I've invested more than $350,000 into Russell's programs, master-minds, and coaching — not just for the tactics but because of the magnetic pull of his personal brand. Russell didn't just create ClickFunnels. He created a community, a movement, and a gravitational field strong enough to attract the top players in the world — including me.

This is the compounding ripple effect of building influence. It doesn't just build trust. It multiplies authority, attracts the right rooms, and becomes a long-term asset you can bank on.

In the age of AI, personal brands and human-centered communities are becoming *more* valuable, not less. In fact, they are fast becoming one of the most valuable assets in your triple-compounding system. That's why, in this chapter, I show you how you can accelerate your triple-compounding system by building a solid personal brand and compounding your influence.

Understanding Influence

Influence is not about impressing people. It's about impacting them. Better yet, it's about serving people. People who hold real influence

>> Come up in conversation in rooms they're not even in

>> Seem to have opportunities "find" them

>> Are invited to speak, collaborate, lead, and sell without begging for attention

>> Tend to earn more — a lot more.

Influence is not about driving a Lamborghini, staging photoshoots in Bali, or faking your lifestyle to get attention. That's not influence. That's illusion. What I mean by influence is impact.

When you try to impress, which is something I have done in the past, too, you suppress who you really are because you assume people won't like that version of you, and you pretend to be someone you really aren't because you assume people will like that person better.

But my business skyrocketed when I finally stopped pretending to be someone else and tapped into who I really am. Now, every time I get stuck, I realize it's because I was trying to be someone else or fulfill someone else's dream and forgot who I am and my real, deep purpose.

As my understanding of why I do what I do deepens, so does the level of my influence and impact on others. Does everyone on the internet like it? No. But does it help me impact and inspire those who need my help the most and who, in some way, relate to my weirdness? You bet.

You don't need a million followers. You just need a message that matters and the courage to share it consistently. Real influence doesn't come from impressing people; it comes from serving them at the highest level. In the following section, I explain how you can authentically do that without turning into a paparazzi magnet.

Turning Your Mess into Your Message

Les Brown is known for the phrase, "Turn your mess into your message." One of the most powerful mindset shifts you can make as a triple compounder is this:

Stop waiting for someone else to save you. Start seeing yourself as the solution.

We live in a time in which it's easier than ever to outsource blame. The economy. The government. Your parents. Your partner. Your boss. Your past. But none of those things are responsible for building your future.

Responsibility doesn't mean shame or guilt. It means *response-ability*. You have the power to respond with skill, creativity, and action.

Your greatest setbacks, struggles, and even embarrassments can become your most powerful assets — *if* you learn to own them and share them. That's what turning your mess into your message means.

You don't need to be perfect to build influence. In fact, people trust you *more* when you're real. Vulnerability — when paired with growth — is magnetic. It shows your audience what's possible. It gives them a road map. It makes your story relatable.

Your mess doesn't disqualify you. It *qualifies* you because when you solve your own problem, you gain the wisdom and the authority to help others solve theirs, too.

Here's a simple framework to make this real:

1. **Identify your mess.**

   What challenge, failure, or painful moment shaped who you are today? Maybe it was drowning in debt, hitting burnout, losing confidence, or making bad investment choices.

   Start with the moment that made you say, "Never again." That's your turning point.

2. **Extract the lesson.**

   What did this experience teach you? What perspective, skill, or belief changed as a result? This is the seed of your message.

3. **Share the journey (not just the win).**

   Don't just talk about where you are now. Show the path. Share the hard parts, the small wins, and the aha moments. People need to see the *process*, not just the highlight reel.

4. **Connect the situation to your mission.**

   Tie your story to your audience's pain. Why does your journey matter to them? How does your experience help them solve their own problems faster, easier, or with more confidence?

5. **Reinforce it with repetition.**

   You don't need 100 different stories. You need *one story*, told 100 different ways. Use your mess-to-message moment as a throughline in your content, emails, presentations, and even offers.

Repetition builds familiarity. Familiarity builds trust. Trust builds income. Compounded income accelerates your triple-compounding system.

Building an Audience of Your People

One of the highest-return activities you can take on as a triple compounder is building an audience, not just of any people, but of your people. These are the people who already resonate with your philosophy, feel a connection to your story, and genuinely want what you have to offer. When you do this well, your audience becomes a source of aligned clients, business partners, students, and even top-tier team members.

Nearly all of my most dedicated team members and partners have come from within my audience. I didn't need to convince them to join; they were already passionate about what I stand for. That alignment alone has created hundreds of high-quality applications from people who see our work and think, "This is where I'm meant to be." That level of enthusiasm and cultural fit can't be manufactured through a typical hiring process.

The best time to start building your audience was 20 years ago. The second-best time is today.

When you have an audience of people who already trust you and want what you offer, everything becomes easier. You can introduce new programs, test products, or pivot directions without needing to start from scratch. The audience compounds.

SHIFTING FROM CONSUMER TO CREATOR

Marketing expert Gary Vaynerchuk encourages entrepreneurs to create content rather than passively consume it. This isn't just about making videos or going viral. It's about using your voice and perspective to provide value consistently over time. Your content becomes a magnet for your ideal audience — and a filter for those who aren't a fit.

If you're spending hours scrolling social media without a clear purpose, you're leaking energy. Instead, set time aside each week to create. Reflect on what you've discovered, document your journey, and teach what you know. Even if your audience is small in the beginning, your content builds authority. Over time, it compounds into influence.

Rather than waiting for an invitation or permission, show up as a leader. Whether you're selling cupcakes or coaching clients, influence is about becoming a significant part of your audience's lives. That significance isn't achieved through perfection — it's achieved through consistency, authenticity, and service.

Once you've built trust with your audience, they'll often want to buy everything you offer. Not because you're pushing them into it, but because you've already helped them, inspired them, and created transformation. And they want more.

Exploring Influence in Real Life

One of the most powerful ways to understand influence is to see it in action. Not in theory. Not in a perfectly curated social media reel. But in real life — through real people who chose to show up, share their story, and let others witness their growth. The following story isn't about becoming internet-famous or building a massive following overnight. It's about what happens when someone commits to living the triple-compounding method with authenticity, service, and consistency.

Creating ripple effects by living the message

Influence doesn't always spread through a loudspeaker. Sometimes it moves quietly — through consistent action, lived example, and personal transformation. That's what I call a ripple effect: When your growth inspires others to rise with you, without needing to push or persuade.

Here's a real-life example.

When Mandie Jo of Free Nurses first discovered triple compounding, she was a full-time behavioral health nurse, deeply committed to her patients but overwhelmed by financial stress and professional burnout. She had recently gone through a divorce, was managing a 40-bed inpatient psychiatric unit during the height of the COVID-19 pandemic, and had even endured a violent assault from a patient. At the time, she felt depleted — physically, emotionally, and financially.

Everything began to shift when she applied the triple-compounding principles in real time: generating income, automating wealth-building strategies, and accelerating her financial growth. Bit by bit, Mandie used those steps to reclaim her life.

Today, Mandie has built a six-figure dividend portfolio and reached a net worth of $1.4 million. She's made it possible for her parents to retire, helped her partner transition into more fulfilling work, and launched a mission-driven platform and movement, *Free Nurses,* to help healthcare professionals break free from the cycles of overwork and underearning.

Mandie didn't stop there. She's a multiyear member of Invest Diva's Accelerator program. As a true triple compounder, once she hit seven figures in her overall net worth, she circled back to Phase 1 of the method and reinvested in herself — this time at the highest level — by becoming a Diamond member. (Read Chapter 4 for more about Phase 1.) That decision wasn't just financial. It was intentional because she knew her next level of impact would require a new level of mentorship, strategy, and support.

As Mandie began discussing financial freedom with her peers, they were initially curious but cautious. "We're trained to ask for evidence, outcomes, and red flags," she told me. So, instead of trying to convince anyone, Mandie simply lived by the method. She kept investing. She shared her wins, her lessons, and even her losses online. And she let people witness the transformation without pressure.

Two years later, those same skeptical coworkers have become students, supporters, and success stories of their own. What started as passing conversations in the hospital breakroom has turned into full-blown investing Q&As.

Coworkers now approach Mandie with questions and comments like

>> What's the difference between Roth and traditional again?

>> I finally logged into my 401(k). How much should I contribute?

>> I bought my first stock because of your post on Instagram!

Some have even attended my online event, Triple Compounding Live, after hearing about it through Mandie. Others follow her content online to learn and to cheer her on. But the ripple effect doesn't stop at investing. Many of her fellow nurses are now building wealth in creative ways — managing Airbnb rentals, selling insurance on the side, or launching their own brands and platforms.

What Mandie has sparked is more than a portfolio; it's a cultural shift — a new conversation in healthcare in which nurses feel safe to talk about money without fear, shame, or scarcity — just the possibility of becoming a free nurse. She has launched the *Free Nurses* movement, helping burned-out nurses become financially free. That's the power of influence and compounding at work.

As Mandie puts it, "The beauty of triple compounding is that it works even if you're busy, skeptical, or starting from zero. It's not just a method — it's a mindset shift that nurses desperately need."

You can follow Mandie's journey on Instagram at @freenursemandie and download her *Free 5 Step Guide to Loving Your Nursing Career Again* at www.freenurses.co. And it all started with one nurse who decided to go first.

Owning my financial failures to build connection and credibility

When I first started building my portfolio, I made just about every mistake you're warned about. I chased hype. I bought based on emotion. I panicked during dips and tried to time the market. I overtraded. I didn't have a system. I got burned. Repeatedly.

But that "mess" eventually became the foundation of my message. Instead of hiding my missteps, I began to share them. I documented what I'd discovered. I showed how I corrected the course. And I built my first Invest Diva business on the idea that women — especially stay-at-home moms — can take back control of their money and become their own financial managers. The methodology I developed through that experience became what I now call the Diamond system, which I walk you through in Chapter 10.

And once I stopped pretending to be perfect, everything shifted. My audience didn't connect to the polished version of me. They connected to the real version — the one who had made mistakes, learned from them, and then turned those lessons into something useful for others.

That's when my business grew. That's when I started getting DMs and emails from women saying, "I finally feel like I can do this, too." My credibility didn't come from getting it all right. It came from being honest about what I got wrong — and showing people the path to doing it better.

When you build your brand from lived experience, you give people something more valuable than expertise. You give them proof that transformation is possible.

REMEMBER

Debunking Myths about Influence

As you begin to build an audience and grow your influence, it's natural to run into doubts — both internal and external. Many of these doubts stem from outdated beliefs or misinformation about what influence really is and how it works in today's world. In this section, I walk you through five of the most common myths I've encountered while coaching entrepreneurs, creators, and investors. You may recognize a few of these yourself.

If you have a million followers, you'll become a millionaire

This is one of the most common assumptions people make about influence — and one of the most misleading. Just because someone has a large following doesn't mean they're generating real income or impact. In fact, many influencers with millions of followers struggle financially because they've built an audience without building an ecosystem.

When I made my first million dollars, I had only around 5,000 followers on Facebook. My mentors, Eileen and Myron, earned their first million dollars with fewer than 1,000 followers. The truth is, it's not about the number of people following you. It's about the quality of those relationships and the clarity of your message.

Focus on building trust, not just followers. Influence compounds when it's built on a genuine connection.

Your product matters more than your influence

Although a great product is important, it's your influence that brings people to it and keeps them coming back. Influence is about being a meaningful presence in someone's life. It's the reason customers stick around, even when a competitor offers something cheaper or newer.

Do you know how many brilliant inventions are collecting dust in someone's garage right now? Not because the product was bad, but because the inventor believed that if the product was good enough, people would magically line up to buy it. Newsflash — they won't.

You need visibility. You need trust. You need a voice. That's what influence gives you.

Influence is cultivated through storytelling, vulnerability, and shared values. It turns customers into advocates and transactions into loyalty. And in my Triple Compounding system, this is exactly what "compounding your extensions" means. Influence is what transforms your business, brand, or side hustle from a one-time income stream into an expanding flywheel of trust and demand.

A great product is only half the equation. The other half is people knowing, liking, and trusting you enough to buy it — and that's what starts the compounding engine of your influence-driven income.

Influence only works if you're in the education business

Influence isn't limited to coaches, authors, or course creators. Any business — whether it's a restaurant, dental clinic, or cupcake shop — can leverage influence. The key is not just what you offer, but *how* you share it.

Walt Disney wasn't just selling entertainment. Rihanna isn't just selling makeup — and neither is Selena Gomez. Both women have used their personal brands to shape culture, build loyalty, and drive massive growth. Rihanna turned Fenty Beauty into a billion-dollar brand by championing inclusivity and redefining beauty standards. Selena Gomez built Rare Beauty on the foundation of mental health advocacy and self-acceptance, using her platform to spark conversations that matter. Their influence didn't just sell products — it built movements. The same applies to small business owners who choose to lead with purpose. One of my Accelerators, Sofia Vettori, is a violin maker who used the triple compounding method to transform her craft into a mission-driven brand. Her goal is to bring more beauty into the world through music. Today, she's not just handcrafting instruments; she's building a movement. Sofia donates violins to underprivileged musicians so that they can perform at major concerts. She's cultivated a devoted global following, and her waitlist is filled with collectors and performers ready to pay six and even seven figures for her instruments — while she's still alive. Her influence didn't just elevate her business. It turned her art into a legacy.

You have to be perfect

Perfection is not required. In fact, perfection often repels people. It's your humanness — your imperfections, lessons, and growth — that people connect with most. Especially now, in the age of AI-generated content and filtered feeds, authenticity is your advantage.

Start before you're ready. Share as you grow. Influence is a byproduct of showing up with intention, not showing up flawlessly.

If you wait until you feel "ready," you may never start. Growth happens in the doing.

It will take too much time

One of the most common objections I hear about building a brand is, "I just don't have time." And on the surface, that seems valid. Between work, family, and everything else on your plate, the idea of adding content creation or audience-building may feel overwhelming.

But here's the question you have to ask yourself: Do you want to stay stuck in a cycle of always needing more time, or do you want to build something that eventually gives your time back?

That's the magic of brand-building. It may take time upfront, yes. But once it's built, your brand starts doing the work *for you.*

Most people spend their days doing low-leverage work. They answer emails, respond to messages, jump on calls, chase leads, and solve problems as they pop up. All of that takes time, and all of it needs to be done again tomorrow. That's time *spent.*

But when you build a brand, you're investing your time. You're creating assets — content, positioning, trust, visibility — that continue to work for you even when you're asleep. That's time *compounding.*

You can create leverage that saves you hundreds of hours down the line if you spend five to ten hours per week building a brand that does the following things:

» Brings in new leads automatically

» Attracts better-fit clients

» Converts buyers without hard selling

» Draws top talent to your team and

» Elevates your credibility across platforms

In triple compounding, this falls under the "accelerate" phase of your income-generating extensions. It's not just about creating something once; it's about building a system that scales. Your brand becomes a magnet. The more you nurture it, the more it pays you back.

Time spent building a brand is time that starts earning you compound influence. Influence, when paired with the right offer, is the most scalable income source you'll ever have.

So next time you catch yourself thinking, *This takes too much time,* reframe it as, *This is how I buy my future freedom.*

That's time well spent.

IN THIS CHAPTER

» **Designing scalable systems and recurring revenue models that grow with you**

» **Building a team and tech stack that multiplies your time and results**

» **Creating premium offers that accelerate cash flow and deepen transformation**

» **Evolving your identity as a leader to support long-term, sustainable growth**

Chapter **15**

Accelerating Your Business

thought that the moment I hit $7 million I would magically transform into a hammock-loving, beach-bound retiree who never wanted to look at a spreadsheet again. That was the number I'd decided meant "enough." When it happened, I gave myself permission to do something big: I took the whole family to Hawaii to test out what retirement might look like.

The first two weeks were pure bliss. No Zoom calls. No launch planning. No market analysis. Just sand, surf, and shave ice. By the third week, I was getting restless. By the sixth week, I was ready to scream if I had to sit on that beach doing *nothing* one more day.

Here's what I realized: Growth is in my DNA. And if you're reading this book, it's probably in yours, too.

Triple compounders understand that money is never the end goal. It's just the fuel. The goal is evolution — in your identity, in your impact, and in your income streams. So, scaling isn't a one-time milestone. It's a mindset. If you're not growing, you're dying. And that applies to your business and your money, too.

This chapter is about taking your compounding business from steady to scalable. Whether you're just getting your first customers or you're already generating consistent income, this is where you shift gears — from building *something that works* to creating *something that grows without you.* In other words, you stop trading effort for income and start compounding your time, talents, and tools.

Scaling doesn't mean growing bigger just for the sake of it. It means growing smarter so that your business works harder than you do.

If your business isn't growing, it's not just stuck — it's slipping. Inflation, competition, and customer expectations are always evolving. You have to evolve, too.

Building a Scalable Foundation: From Small Steps to Big Wins

Scaling your business isn't about doing more. It's about doing less, *better.* It's the shift from being the driver of your business to being the designer of the machine.

In the early days, you wear all the hats: CEO, salesperson, social media manager, customer service rep, and even late-night janitor. But at some point, you hit a wall. You can't grow beyond your capacity unless you start thinking in terms of *systems.*

That's why scalable businesses don't just hustle; they compound. They build assets that grow over time, not tasks that need repeating. Whether it's a course that sells every day without you being live, a software that solves the same problem over and over, or a team member who brings in results without needing constant direction, scaling starts by planting the right seeds.

Think of the following as business compounding:

>> You invest once in something that keeps giving.

>> You build a system that handles what you used to do manually.

>> You automate a process that once required your brainpower.

These small shifts don't always look sexy on the outside. But behind every "overnight success" is someone who spent months (or years) building the foundation that could handle growth when it came.

In the rest of this section, you explore

>> **Compounding systems:** How to turn your daily to-dos into scalable processes

>> **Compounding continuity:** How recurring revenue gives your business financial breathing room

>> **Compounding talent:** How to hire and train others to take ownership

>> **Compounding AI:** How to use technology to buy back your time and increase your output

Your business will only grow to the extent that your foundation can support it. If the ground is shaky, your growth will collapse under its own weight.

More revenue with broken systems doesn't create freedom. It creates chaos — and eventually, burnout.

Compounding systems: Creating processes that scale

Imagine trying to bake 100 cakes a day from scratch — measuring each ingredient by hand, eyeballing the temperature, and hoping that every one turns out perfect. Now imagine having a recipe, a mixer, a conveyor oven, and a team trained to follow the exact system. That's the difference between a business that hustles and a business that *compounds*.

Systems are how you scale without cloning yourself. At the start, everything in your business runs on your brain. You know the password. You know the pitch. You know how to handle the fire when it shows up. But that's not a system. That's a bottleneck in disguise.

A compounding system is anything that captures your know-how and replicates it with *consistency*. It can be

>> A written SOP (standard operating procedure)

>> A plug-and-play template

>> An automated onboarding sequence

>> A checklist that ensures that nothing slips through the cracks

Each system you create is a little time machine. You invest time once to save yourself hours (and headaches) forever. Over time, these little machines stack. That's the power of compounding.

Here's where to start:

1. **Document what works.**

   If you've done something more than twice, write it down. What steps did you follow? What made it successful?

2. **Automate what repeats.**

   Use tools like Zapier, WebinarJam, ClickUp, or AI integrations like Manychat to handle low-value tasks like scheduling, reminders, or lead follow-ups.

3. **Delegate what drains you.**

   Once a system works, hand it off. If someone else can do it 80 percent as well, that's good enough to grow.

4. **Optimize what breaks.**

   Systems evolve. Expect friction. But every problem you solve makes your machine stronger.

Even if you're still solo, you're not too early for systems. In fact, this is the best time to build them — before chaos forces your hand. The less your business relies on you, the more valuable and scalable it becomes.

If you're constantly reinventing the wheel, you're not scaling. You're stalling.

Compounding continuity: Recurring revenue models

Want to know the real flex in business? Waking up on the first of the month and already knowing your bills are covered because your revenue is *predictable*.

That's what recurring revenue does. It takes the pressure off the endless chase for new customers and gives you breathing room to think long term, hire help, and *compound* with confidence.

I first heard this from one of my mentors-turned-friends, cofounder of ClickFunnels and the author of *Expert Secrets: The Underground Playbook for Converting Your Online Visitors into Lifelong Customers* (Hay House Publishing, 2020), Russell Brunson. He looked at me, knowing that I'm all about compounding in the stock market, and said, "This is the *other* compounding."

Recurring revenue means customers pay you regularly — monthly, quarterly, or annually — for continued access to your product, service, or experience. It shifts your income from one-time bursts to reliable, rolling momentum.

Triple compounders love this because it aligns perfectly with the whole framework:

>> You **generate** a sale once.

>> You **automate** the delivery through a subscription or membership.

>> You **accelerate** your growth by stacking predictable cash flow month over month.

Here are some popular recurring models.

>> **Memberships and subscriptions:** Newsletters, coaching communities, or resource libraries

>> **Retainers:** Service providers offering ongoing work (like marketing, copywriting, or advisory services)

>> **Software-as-a-service (SaaS):** Tools that solve a problem users keep paying to solve (like Canva or Kajabi)

>> **Consumables with auto-ship:** Physical products people need regularly (think vitamins, skincare, dog food)

The key? *Ongoing value.* If someone's going to keep paying, they need to keep receiving something worth paying for. That may mean new content, upgraded access, consistent results, or a transformation that unfolds over time.

And when it's done right? The revenue compounds while your effort stays the same or even decreases. Flip to Chapter 12 to dive deeper into how to build recurring income into your business.

Don't build continuity without a delivery system. If you overpromise and underdeliver, recurring income quickly turns into recurring refunds.

Compounding talent: Hiring and training for growth

At a certain point, your biggest bottleneck isn't your tech or your marketing. It's *you* — your time, your energy, your brainpower. That's when it's time to do what all great investors do: diversify.

But instead of diversifying your portfolio, you start diversifying your *people*. Building a compounding business means building a team — not just a group of helpers, but a carefully selected squad of A-players who extend your vision, multiply your output, and bring skills to the table that you don't have (or don't want to develop).

I'll be honest: This was one of the hardest growth moments for me. I used to have such a hard time trusting that anyone could do as good a job as I do. (Maybe I still do . . . a little bit, lol.) I got *burnt* by my first hires — people who came in, messed up my systems, or worse and took up my time and energy while I trained them, only to ghost the second things got serious. It was painful. Frustrating. It made me want to retreat and go back to doing everything myself.

But that was my signal. That was the moment I realized this wasn't just about delegation. This was about leadership — and more importantly, trust.

So, I stepped into both. I clarified our vision. I reworked our systems. And I decided that I would *trust again* — not blindly, but intentionally. Now? I have a team that's excited to push our movement forward. They take ownership. They take accountability. They take pride in their work. And that gives me space to lead with love instead of control — and scale with *compounding trust.*

Don't wait until you're burnt out to ask for help. That's not a hiring strategy; it's a rescue mission.

Also, this doesn't always mean hiring full-time employees. You can start with the following:

>> **Virtual assistants** for repeatable tasks

>> **Freelancers** for projects like design, copy, or coding

>> **Contractors** for specialized expertise

>> **Agencies** for services you don't want to manage in-house

>> **AI tools** trained to handle common processes (more on that in the next section)

Your first hire doesn't need to be a unicorn. They just need to take something off your plate consistently.

Here's how to compound your talent wisely:

1. Start with a time audit.

Track how you spend your week. Highlight anything repeatable, drainable, or beneath your pay grade.

2. **Systemize before you hire.**

   Don't bring someone into chaos. Get your processes clear first so that they can plug in and thrive.

3. **Hire for attitude; train for skill.**

   The right person with a growth mindset is more valuable than a rockstar who resists change.

4. **Invest in onboarding.**

   Your new hire's success is *your* responsibility. Create training materials. Give feedback. Build trust.

You're not building a business to manage people. You're building a team to manage the business.

Compounding artificial intelligence: Leveraging tech for efficiency

Let's be real. AI isn't coming; it's already here. And the entrepreneurs who embrace it early aren't just getting ahead; they're getting *compounded* results with half the effort.

In triple compounding, the goal isn't to *replace* humans with machines. It's to *free up humans* to do their highest, most creative, most valuable work. That includes you.

AI allows you to multiply your time, reduce your labor costs, and remove bottlenecks that would normally slow your business down.

Think of it like hiring a full team of specialists:

>> A copywriter who drafts your email campaigns

>> A researcher who summarizes trends and data

>> A customer service rep who answers FAQs 24/7

>> A project manager who keeps things moving on schedule

>> A junior analyst who helps identify opportunities in your business

Only this "team" works instantly, never sleeps, and doesn't need a 401(k).

Here are just a few ways you can use AI right now to accelerate your business:

- **Content creation:** Tools like ChatGPT, Claude, or Jasper can help you write emails, social captions, sales pages, and even course outlines in minutes.

- **Customer service:** AI chatbots can handle common questions, process refunds, and escalate issues only when needed.

- **Data analysis:** AI dashboards can spot trends in your revenue, engagement, or customer behavior that would take you hours to find.

- **Automation assistants:** Combine AI with tools like Zapier, Manychat, Airtable, or Notion to create workflows that run your backend without manual input.

- **Personalization at scale:** AI can dynamically adjust offers, messages, and content based on customer behavior or data — something that used to take entire marketing teams.

This doesn't mean that AI replaces your team. It means your team becomes *exponentially more powerful.* You reduce human error. You scale creativity. You move faster than your competitors — and often, with less overhead.

But here's the key: Don't just plug in a bunch of tools because they're shiny. Start with a friction point in your business and ask: *How can AI support or simplify this?*

Get into the habit of asking yourself, "How can I use AI today?"

Creating Premium Packages That Fund and Fuel Your Growth

For many entrepreneurs, the idea of charging premium prices can feel intimidating or even indulgent, but premium packages aren't just about prestige or luxury. They're a strategic tool that can stabilize your cash flow, deepen your client impact, and build the financial runway you need to scale. In a compounding business, these offers serve as both fuel and feedback. They bring in the resources that allow you to grow faster and the insight that helps you build better.

A premium offer doesn't need to be complex. It just needs to be clear, valuable, and designed for transformation.

When I first started scaling my business, my focus was on automation. I had built a $997 online course, paired it with an automated webinar funnel, and watched as it quietly brought in sales around the clock. After selling it to 1,000 people, I had officially made my first million, and I didn't have to be "on" all the time to do it. But when I hired a mentor, they looked at my funnel and asked a question that completely shifted my perspective: *What would it take to double the price to $1,997?* I hesitated. Could I really charge that? Would people still buy? But instead of dismissing it, I took the challenge seriously and began improving the offer — refining the curriculum, adding coaching elements, and increasing the transformation my students experienced.

With that one change, I went from needing 1,000 customers to make a million to only 500. That's when I saw the real power of premium: fewer customers, deeper relationships, and more leverage. As I continued evolving, I launched our most popular program: the Accelerator, a $50,000-per-year experience for high-level professionals ready to scale their portfolios and generational wealth.

Later, I created my highest-value offer yet: the Diamond program, where I work one-on-one with a private client to grow their triple-compounding system to seven or eight figures for $350,000. These were transformational containers for my clients, but also for me. They gave me the capital to reinvest in my team, in technology, and in reach. They also created a natural ascension path, where clients who got results at one level naturally wanted more and became my biggest success stories in the process.

Premium pricing isn't about charging more for the sake of it. It's about creating the kind of container that allows your clients to experience deeper transformation while giving you the freedom to grow without burning out.

Unlocking cash flow for strategic growth

One of the most immediate and powerful benefits of premium pricing is the cash infusion it brings into your business. As it is often said in the entrepreneurship world, "Whoever can spend the most to acquire a customer wins," and you create that ability through margin, earned by charging appropriately for the value you deliver. With each premium package you sell, you're not just earning revenue; you're buying leverage. You get the cash to reinvest in ads, team members, better tools, and better customer experiences. And that not only keeps your business alive but also accelerates its growth.

In contrast, many entrepreneurs get stuck in what one of my mentors, Myron Golden, author of *B.O.S.S. Moves: Business Optimization Success Secrets from a Million Dollar Round Table* (Transcendent, 2021), calls the *low-ticket hustle*. You're hustling to make a million dollars selling $20 products — T-shirts, templates, digital downloads, and e-books — hoping they all add before you burn out. But the numbers tell a different story.

If you're selling a $20 product, you need to sell 50,000 units to earn $1 million. That's a whole lot of customers, a massive audience, and likely a serious advertising bill. This is why premium pricing isn't about ego. It's about *efficiency.*

Now imagine you multiply the price by ten. You go from a $20 product to a $200 product — maybe a mini course, a bundle, or a mid-ticket affiliate offer. Suddenly, you only need 5,000 sales to make the same million. You just saved yourself 45,000 customer interactions.

Then you go further. A $2,000 course — your signature home study program — only needs 500 buyers to hit that same million-dollar mark. That's less than two sales a day. Sell just two $2,000 programs per day, and you're a millionaire.

Now let's say you offer a $20,000 mastermind — something like our Accelerator program. You only need 50 clients per year to make a million. That's one sale per week. One.

Accelerator Rowell Ramos created his first $20,000 offer and sold four of them in one week. That's $80,000 in seven days, earning back everything he invested in the Accelerator program. And he's repeated the process over and over ever since, reinvesting that money into his Triple Compounder System without ever having to pay me a single cent in commissions. None of my Accelerators do. That's because we're not set up like the rest of Wall Street, as I explain in Chapter 1.

I've had people slide into my DMs saying, "Kiana, I want to do one-on-one mentorship with you. How much is it?" I tell them, "Well, I charge $25,000 per hour. Want to spend a full day with me? It's $250,000." And I'm not just throwing numbers out for fun. That day includes strategy, compounding design, and wealth acceleration that can collapse decades into a single year, and more importantly, creates results. You can see exactly how my value ladder works, from the bottom all the way to the top, by visiting www.TripleCompounding.com

When you're operating at a high level, you start to understand: Time is infinitely more valuable than money. If someone can help you go from $1 million to $10 million in one year instead of ten, that's not an expense: It's a *shortcut.*

This isn't theory. I've done this at every level — from selling automated $997 webinars to running $250,000 Diamond Days. And I'm not the only one. There are hundreds of people in $200,000 masterminds every year, and thousands more ready to buy if you're ready to lead them.

Which of the following should you sell:

>> 50,000 of a $20 product?

>> 5,000 of a $200 offer?

>> 500 of a $2,000 course?

>> 50 of the $20,000 mastermind?

>> Or 5 of a $200,000 VIP experience?

The answer? All of the above.

This is how you create multiple revenue streams that work together: stacked, strategic, and scalable. You meet your audience where they are, offer the level of transformation they're ready for, and guide them up the ladder over time.

Once you've generated that revenue, don't waste it on liabilities or lifestyle creep. Reinvest it — into yourself, your systems, and your external assets.

Unlike broke entrepreneurs who make millions but have nothing to show for it, triple compounders know how to turn business income into long-term wealth.

Creating more impact with fewer clients

When someone invests at a premium level, they're more committed. They show up. They implement. They value your insights more. That means you're not only earning more revenue per client, you're also likely to see stronger testimonials, better referrals, and deeper transformations. This naturally compounds your reputation and customer lifetime value. Serving fewer clients at a deeper level can actually create more influence and trust than a broad, shallow audience.

You don't need to reach everyone. You just need to deeply serve the right ones and let their results speak for you.

Building a natural value ladder

Premium offers also help you clarify your overall business ecosystem. Once you have a higher-tier offer, it becomes easier to position your lower-cost options as on-ramps. Each product or service feeds into the next, allowing your clients to ascend based on need, readiness, and results. That's how you move from a collection of disconnected products to a *value ladder* that makes sense for both you and your audience. This also makes marketing easier, since satisfied customers already trust your process and are more likely to say "yes" to the next step.

A well-structured value ladder doesn't overwhelm — it guides. Every offer becomes a natural invitation to what's next.

Confused businesses confuse customers. A clear path of transformation makes it easier for the right people to stay, grow, and invest again.

Transforming Your Identity as a Leader

Perhaps the most powerful shift that happens when you create premium packages isn't logistical; it's internal. You start seeing your work differently. You take full ownership of the results you deliver. You stop underpricing yourself just to be accessible and start pricing in alignment with the value you bring. And the best part? Your clients rise to meet you. The people who once hesitated suddenly lean in. They want to be led. They want results. And now, you've created a container that makes that transformation possible.

Raising your prices is often less about the market and more about your mindset. Your income expands when your identity does.

IN THIS CHAPTER

» **Understanding the idea behind technical analysis and why triple compounders use it**

» **Identifying key support and resistance levels on a chart**

» **Introducing popular chart patterns in bearish and bullish markets**

» **Getting a grip on basic and sophisticated moving averages**

Chapter **16**

Using Technical Analysis to Accelerate Your Investments

O ver decades of observing and investing in many different markets, I have seen history repeating itself in the markets — or at least rhyming with itself. The markets move as a result of a combination of the three top points of the Invest Diva Diamond Analysis (IDDA):

» Fundamental analysis

» Market sentiment analysis

» Technical analysis

Flip to Chapter 10 for the basics of fundamental and market sentiment analysis. In this chapter, I show you how technical analysis can help you identify the best buy and sell price levels whether you're a long-term investor or an active trader.

Many investment brokers offer charting services to make it easier for you to trade directly from their platform. Some of these charts are sophisticated, and some aren't. I like using TradingView (`https://tradingview.com`) for all my technical analysis, from foreign exchange (forex) to stocks and cryptocurrencies. You can use its free service for almost all assets, or you can choose to upgrade to its paid services to access charts without ads and to get some other perks.

Beginning with the Basics of Technical Analysis

In short, *technical analysis* is the art of studying the history of an asset's price action to predict its future. The reason it often works is the result of a bunch of factors, including the following:

>> **Investor behavior:** Research in behavioral finance shows that investors make decisions based on a number of psychological biases that repeat themselves.

>> **Crowd psychology:** Many market participants use the same technical analysis methods, therefore strengthening the key price levels.

When the price movement patterns repeat themselves, investors who spot them early can get an edge in their strategy development and get better-than-average returns. The following sections give you the basics on chart types, time frames, and psychological factors.

Past performance doesn't guarantee future results. Technical analysis only helps to stack the odds in your favor and doesn't guarantee a profit. Therefore, you must conduct proper risk management, as I discuss in Chapter 3.

Technical analysis is a skill that needs a lot of practice. I try my best to explain all my moves here. But imagine what would happen if you decided to take on skiing as a new sport and committed to becoming a professional skier like me. (Fun fact: I'm a ski fanatic.)

So, you pick up Ron LeMaster's *Ultimate Skiing* (Human Kinetics, 2009) and read it word by word from beginning to end. Filled with confidence, you go to the nearest mountain and ask where the most difficult Double Black Diamond route is. You go all the way to the top, reminding yourself of all the techniques you discovered in the book. You get off the gondola, put your skis on for the very first time, and . . .

You may be able to guess what happens if you've only read a book about skiing. You need a coach to hold your hand, show you the way, and give you feedback as you put your knowledge into practice. The same goes for technical analysis.

For triple compounders, these basics are not just for manual trading; they're the foundation for automating smart buy and sell orders that align with your long-term strategy. By understanding chart behavior, you can set limit orders that execute while you sleep, play, or focus on other parts of your triple-compounding system.

I hold my triple compounders' hands and show them how to become investing and technical analysis pros in my *Triple Compounding system*. Many people have become Triple Compounder Certified, which enables them to get side jobs in the ecosystem to earn money while they manage their own portfolio. Find out more about it by attending Triple Compounding Masterclass at `https://triple compounding.com`.

Getting to love the chart art

So, you want to get down and dirty with the historical price movements of your favorite financial asset. As technical as this type of analysis sounds, you often find yourself using the creative side of your brain when you do it; the chart is your canvas. You can use different types of charts to plot the behavior of online financial assets.

Technical analysts love charts because they can visually track an otherwise number-oriented activity. Charts have evolved in the past decades as an increasing number of investors have used them to develop their strategies across different markets, including the stock, foreign exchange (forex), stocks, and crypto-currency markets.

Some charts are simple and track only the price at the end of a session. Other charts are more complex and track every price movement during the session. Some of the most popular charts include the following:

>> **Line charts:** A line chart displays only the closing prices of the market. That means for any given time period, you can know only what the asset's price is at the *end* of that time period and not what adventures and movements it's had *during* that time period. A line is drawn from one closing price to the next closing price, and you can see the general movement of an asset over a period of time. Figure 16-1 shows an example, featuring the price changes of a stock called Nvidia between the months of April and May on a daily time frame.

- » **Bar charts:** No, this option isn't a list of the local drinking establishments. A *bar chart* shows you the opening market price for a given time frame, the price action during that time frame, and the closing price, as you can see in Figure 16-2. The little horizontal line to the *left* shows the price at which the market opened. The little horizontal line to the *right* is the closing point of the time period. I have a fun video in which I explain bar charts at `https://triplecompounding.com/training`.

- » **Candlestick charts:** Candlestick charts look like bar charts, but the area between the open and close prices is colored to show you the general movement of the market during that time period. (See Figure 16-3.) If the market generally moves up during the time period (known as *bullish* market sentiment), the area is normally colored green. If the market goes down (*bearish* market sentiment), the area is normally colored red. Of course, you can choose any colors you like; I normally like to use green for a bullish market movement and purple for a bearish market movement. A candlestick chart also shows the low and high price of the asset during the time period.

This type of chart is my favorite, not only because it's the most visually appealing, but also because it was developed by a Japanese rice trader. I lived in Japan for seven years, so I love anything that has Japanese roots or sounds Japanese.

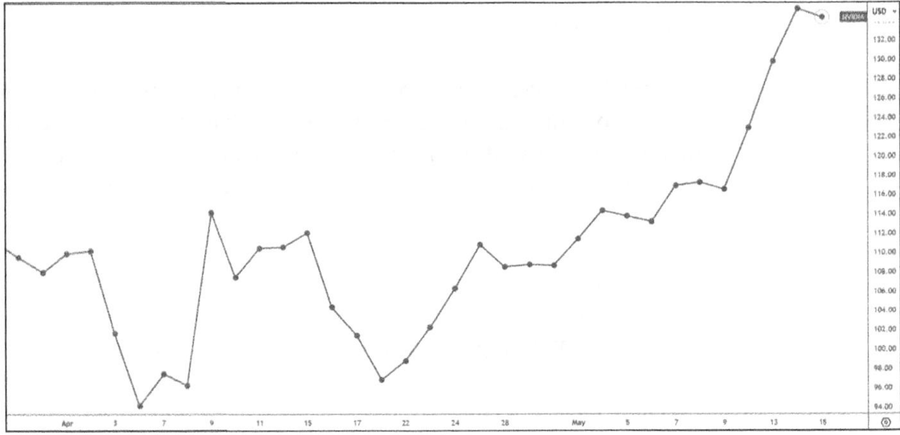

FIGURE 16-1:
Daily line chart of Nvidia stock.

Source: tradingview.com

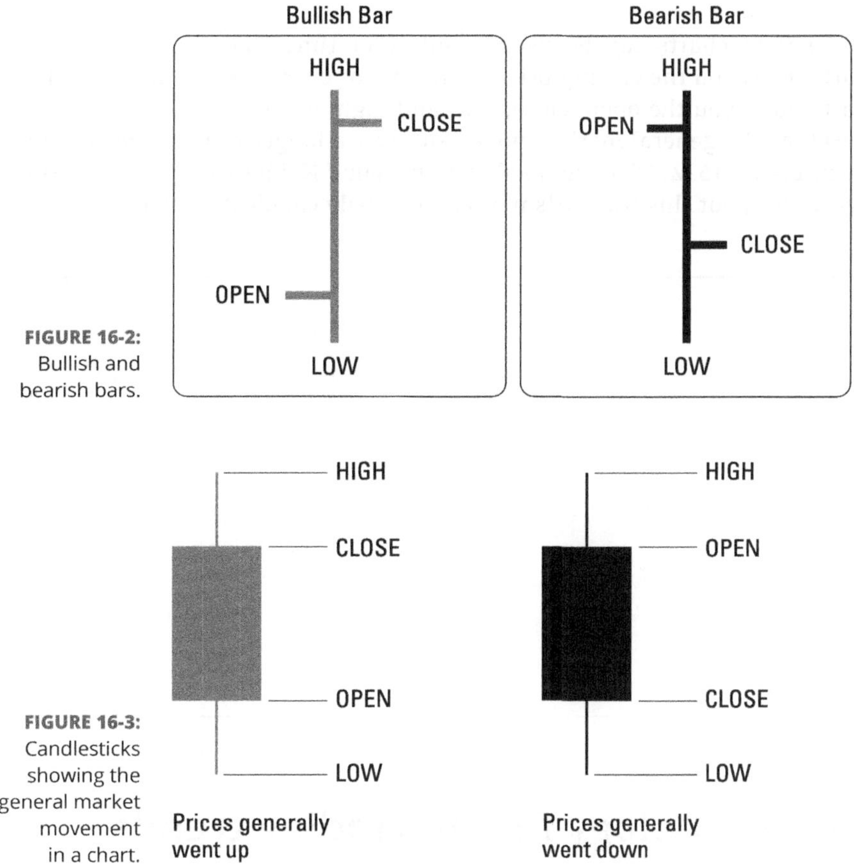

FIGURE 16-2: Bullish and bearish bars.

FIGURE 16-3: Candlesticks showing the general market movement in a chart.

Choosing the time factor

Depending on the type of investor you are, you can choose different time frames to conduct technical analysis. For example, if you're a day trader and want to take advantage of the markets' fluctuations, you can study the market prices in the past 30 minutes, hour, or four hours. On the other hand, if you're a long-term investor and want to let the markets find their way toward your buy/sell limit orders, then you can analyze the price actions in the past days or months to find repetitive patterns and key psychological price levels. (Hint: That's how I develop my strategies.)

This is especially powerful in automating your triple-compounding system. You're no longer tied to screen-watching or emotional reactions.

All types of charts can be used in different time frames. A one-hour line chart shows you the closing price at the end of every hour. A daily candlestick chart shows you the open, close, low, and high prices during one-day periods as well as the general market movement over a longer time frame, as you can see in Figure 16-4. That figure shows the same Nvidia stock's price action as Figure 16-1, but this time, it's plotted on a daily candlestick chart.

FIGURE 16-4:
Daily candlestick chart of Nvidia stock.

Source: tradingview.com

The psychology factor: Finding trends

As you study market movements, you may start finding patterns and prices that keep showing their faces on the chart. A lot of this repetition has to do with market psychology and the crowd's general feeling about an online financial asset.

One of the most eye-catching formations on a chart is a trend. A trend on a chart has nothing to do with trends on social media or in the fashion world, but the idea behind it is similar. When you notice that a stock's price keeps going up on a chart, that movement means the market participants are feeling good about the stock. They keep buying it and therefore push its price higher. You may even say that the stock is trending.

You may have heard the famous investing phrase, "the trend is your friend." If you spot the trend early enough, you may be able to take advantage of the rising prices and make some money. Same goes for when the stock's price is moving down or is on a *downtrend.* If you spot a downtrend early enough, you may be able to either sell your stock or set something called a limit order to buy more at a lower price.

A *limit order* is an instruction you give your brokerage to buy or sell an asset only at a specific price or better.

Here's how it works:

>> A **buy limit order** sets the *maximum* price you're willing to pay. The order executes only if the market drops to your limit price or lower.

>> A **sell limit order** sets the *minimum* price you're willing to accept. The order executes only if the market rises to your limit price or higher.

For example, let's say you want to buy a stock, but only if it falls to $100. You place a buy limit order at $100. If the stock is trading at $110, nothing happens — yet. But the moment the price dips to $100 or less, your order can be filled.

Spotting the Key Levels

The whole point of technical analysis is to identify the best prices at which to buy and sell. Ideally, you want to buy at the lowest price the stock can drop to in the foreseeable future. And you want to hold on to it and sell at the highest price it can reach within your preferred time frame. In well-established markets with a ton of historical data, you can identify these prices by spotting key price levels that have created some sort of restriction for the market movements in the past. In the following sections, I break down some of these important levels.

Marking out support levels

A *support level* is a barrier that prevents the prices from going lower. It's always less than the current market price on your chart. Market participants who spot the support generally wait at that level to buy the stock. One of the popular ways to spot a support level is to study the stock's past performance on the chart. If a price level keeps "supporting" the stock's value from dropping lower, you can mark it as a support level.

As you can see in Figure 16-5, one of the Nvidia stock's key support levels is around $90. Nvidia's stock price tested around this psychological level in 2024 and 2025. But each time, the support level prevented Nvidia's stock price from dropping lower.

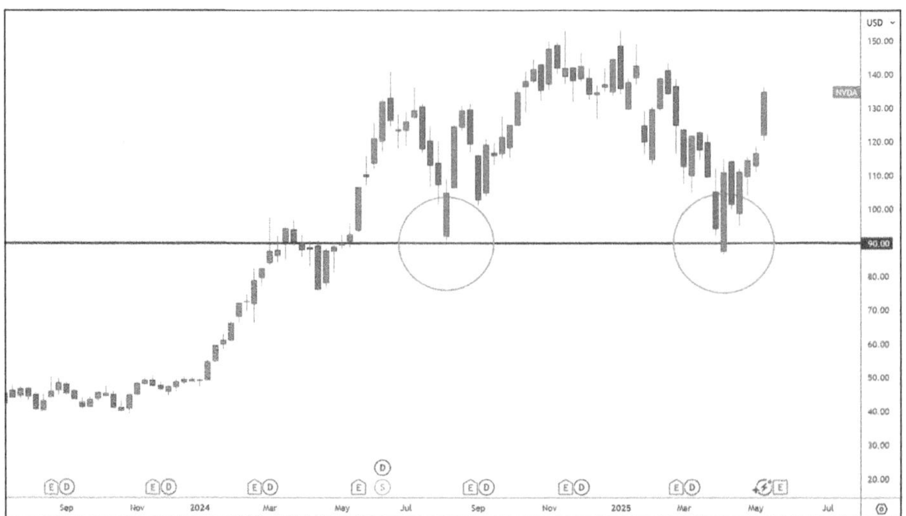

FIGURE 16-5:
Nvidia stock's key support level at around $90.

Source: *tradingview.com*

REMEMBER

Notice I say "around." Support levels aren't always a concrete number. Even though most news outlets say things like "Nvidia dropped below the $90 psychological level," key supports are often a zone rather than a round number.

TIP

The support level becomes stronger the more it's tested. And sometimes, old resistance levels (see the next section) can turn into support levels. For example, the $90 level was in fact acting as a resistance at the beginning of 2024. After the price broke above it, it turned into a support level.

Identifying resistance levels

REMEMBER

Resistance is a barrier that prevents the prices from going higher. It must be more than the current price on your chart, and you can use it as a point to sell your stocks or other online financial assets. You can identify a resistance level with your naked eye by looking for *peaks* on the chart. Every peak can be considered a resistance level as long as it's more than the current market value.

Check out Figure 16-6 for Nvidia's two resistance levels at around $130 and $150. At the time of this image, Nvidia's stock price is *testing* to break above (go higher than) the $130 level. If it does, then the next immediate resistance level is at $150.

TECHNICAL STUFF

I prefer to use a tool called Fibonacci retracement levels to identify support and resistance levels.

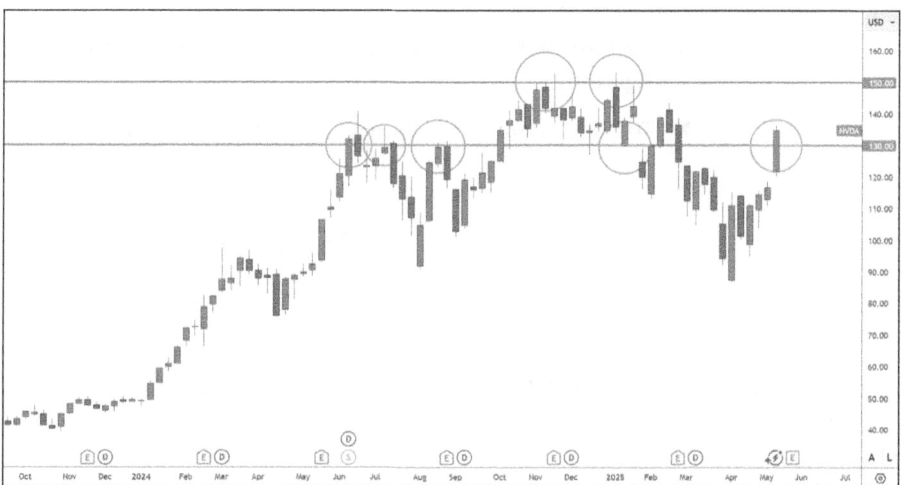

FIGURE 16-6: Nvidia's key resistance levels in May 2025.

Source: *tradingview.com*

Fibonacci retracement levels are horizontal lines on a chart that help investors identify potential support and resistance zones based on the mathematical relationships found in the Fibonacci sequence. In technical analysis, these levels are used to predict *where* the price of an asset may pause, reverse, or continue its trend after a move up or down.

By applying Fibonacci retracement to a past trend, you can immediately see a number of support and resistance levels without having to apply them one by one on your own. Of course, Fibonacci levels aren't always completely accurate, and you may need to play around with your application a bit to get it right.

Drawing trend lines and channels

Earlier in this chapter, I explain how trends can be formed based on market psychology. Some trends are very easy to spot. For example, the period between January 2023 and March 2024 showed an extreme *uptrend* in Nvidia stock when its price just kept going up. Of course, this strong uptrend caught the attention of many people, investors and others, which led to the stock's bubble, which came crashing down in the beginning of 2025. But spotting trends isn't always as easy.

Drawing trend lines is an art. And just as with any other type of art, everyone has a unique opinion of them. Here are two basic methods to draw an uptrend and a downtrend:

>> To draw an uptrend line, when you've casually identified a bullish momentum on the chart, simply click on the trend line instrument on your trading

platform and connect two or more major valleys (bottoms), as shown in Figure 16-7.

>> To draw a downtrend, connect two or more major peaks (tops).

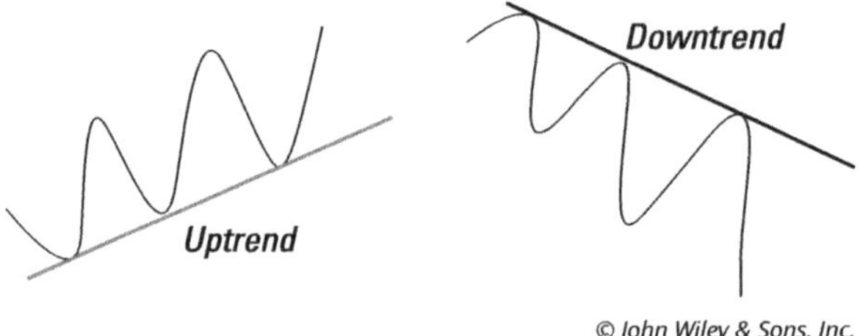

FIGURE 16-7: How to draw uptrends and downtrends.

© John Wiley & Sons, Inc.

If the trend lines are above the current price, you can also consider them *angled* resistance levels. If the line is below the current price, you can use it as a support level.

TIP

Check out this fun, short video where I explain the art of drawing trend lines: `https://triplecompounding.com/training`.

What if the market is moving between two parallel support and resistance levels? Technical chartists call this formation a *channel*. You can use lengthy channels for short-term trading strategies, which I talk about in Chapter 13. For example, a common strategy is buying at the lower band of the channel and selling at the upper band. Figure 16-8 shows basic channels you can identify on your chart.

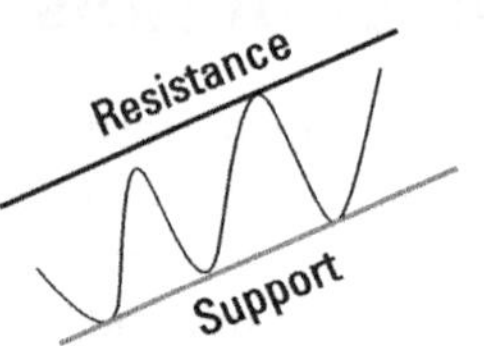

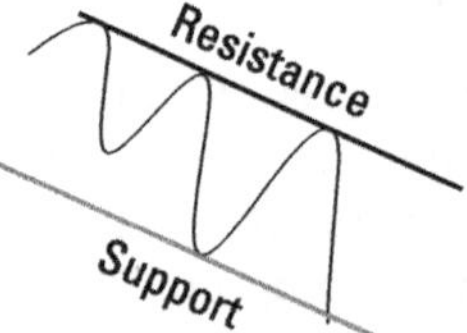

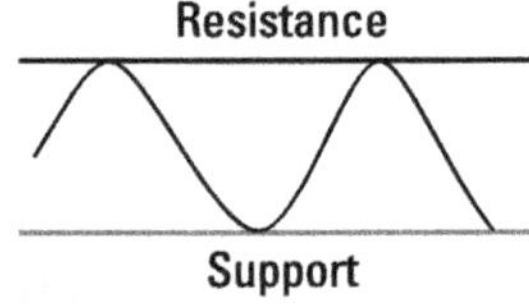

FIGURE 16-8: Basic forms of channels.

© John Wiley & Sons, Inc.

Knowing when the trend is no longer your friend

Unfortunately, trends don't continue forever. All good things must come to an end. What goes up must come down. And many other clichés. Identifying the exact time a trend ends is one of the hardest jobs for technical analysts. Often, the market just teases the crowd with a sudden but short-lived change of direction. Many investors panic. But then the price gets back on track with the long-term trend.

Though key support and resistance levels can help you predict when a trend may end, you must back up your discoveries with fundamental and market sentiment analysis, as I explore in Chapter 10.

Picking Out Patterns on a Chart

Technical analysts are constantly looking for ways to identify key support and resistance levels. This is no easy task, but chart formations can help you with your observations. Becoming an expert technical chartist can take time, and many analysts go through years of studying to gain credentials, such as the Charted Market Technician (CMT). But for now, here's the gist of some important chart patterns.

Bullish reversal patterns

When a *bullish reversal* formation is confirmed, it normally indicates that the trend of the market price will reverse from a downtrend into an uptrend. It reverses the market into a bullish position. Some well-known bullish reversal chart patterns (shown in Figure 16-9) include the *double bottom* (when the price tests a key support level twice, creating two valley shapes at the support level), *the head and shoulders bottom* (when the price tests approximately the same support level three times), and the *saucer bottom* (when the price gradually reaches a key support level and then gradually moves up, forming the shape of a bowl).

FIGURE 16-9: Examples of bullish reversal chart patterns.

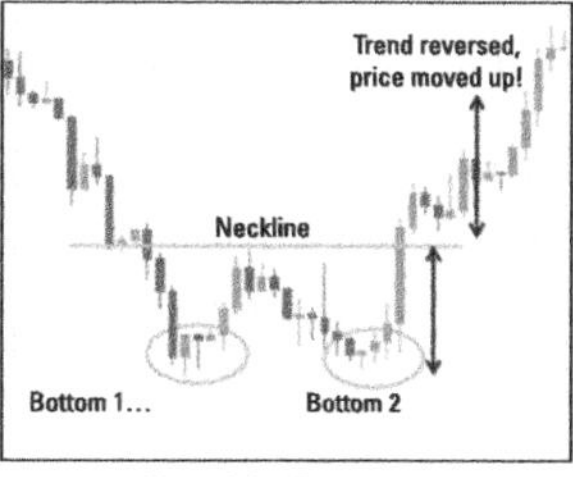

Double Bottom

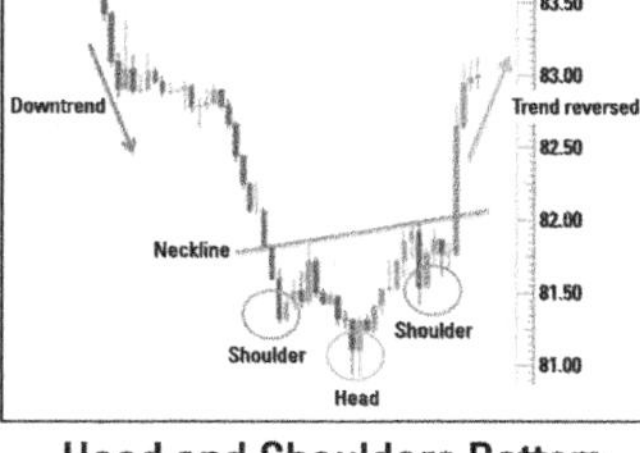

Head and Shoulders Bottom

Saucer Bottom

© John Wiley & Sons, Inc.

A popular trading strategy that uses bullish reversal patterns is to buy when you identify the pattern at its so-called *neckline* (which is a key resistance level) and sell at the next key resistance level.

Bearish reversal patterns

As its name suggests, a *bearish reversal* formation is the exact opposite of a bullish one (see the preceding section). With a bearish reversal, the prices normally hit a resistance during an uptrend and can't go any higher. Therefore, they're forced to reverse into a bear market. Some famous bearish reversal patterns (shown in Figure 16-10) include the *double top* (a formation of two mountain-like shapes on the chart as the price tests a key resistance level), the *head and shoulders* (when the price tests approximately the same resistance level three times, but the second time it goes a bit higher, making it look like a peaking head), and the *saucer top* (when the price gradually reaches a key resistance level and then gradually moves back down).

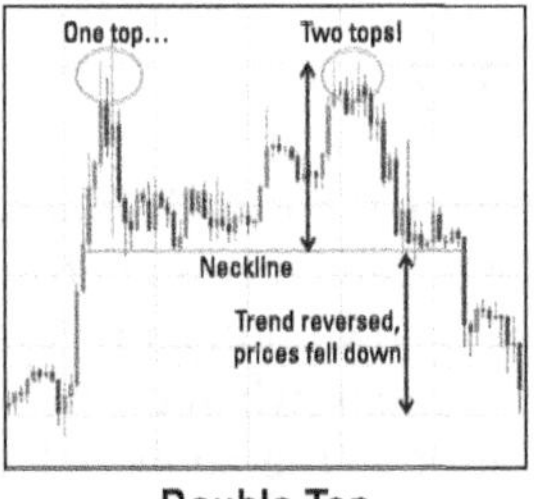

Double Top

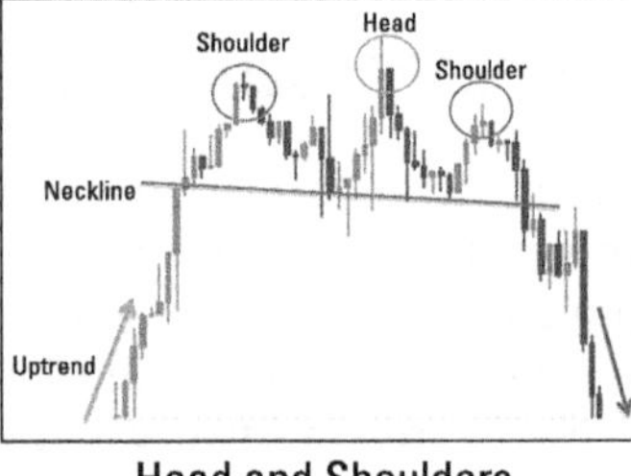

Head and Shoulders

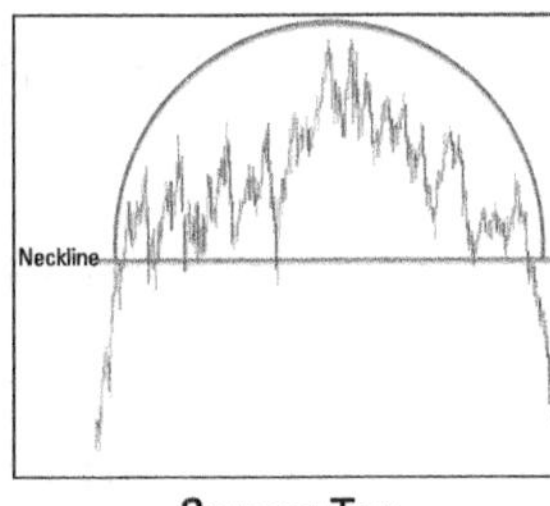

Saucer Top

FIGURE 16-10: Examples of bearish reversal chart patterns.

© *John Wiley & Sons, Inc.*

Some typical strategies using bearish reversals include the following:

>> Taking profit of assets you've been holding after you identify the pattern.

>> Short-selling at the neckline and taking profit at the next support levels. Short-selling is when an investor borrows a stock, sells it at the current price, and hopes to buy it back later at a lower price to return it, pocketing the difference.

Smoothing Charts Out with Moving Averages

If you find price charts and all the information they contain too complicated, you're not alone! Likeminded investors and chartists often turn to tools categorized as moving averages (MAs) to identify those trends more easily.

By definition, a *moving average* is a mathematical procedure that records the average value of a series of prices over time. You have a ton of ways to calculate moving averages and use them based on your trading needs. Some are basic, and some are more sophisticated. Personally, I like to mix and match MAs with technical chart patterns and, of course, Fibonacci retracement levels. The following sections have more on MAs.

You may have gotten used to the idea that trading signals and indicators are often just full of it. The stock market often acts in an arbitrary fashion, ignoring all the supposed rules. That's why you should never rely on only one method of analysis and should *always* confirm your decisions with other tools and points of the Invest Diva Diamond Analysis (IDDA) that I discuss in Chapter 10. On top of that, you should never invest money you can't afford to lose.

Picking basic moving averages

On your trading chart, you can find basic moving averages that smooth out the prices ranging from 10 to 200 time periods. For example, if you look at a daily chart, you can select a short-term MA that calculates a series of 15 data points. This figure is called a *15-day moving average,* or a *fast MA.* If you want to see a longer-term average movement, you can use a longer period, such as 200 days, and call it a *slow MA.*

Longer-term MAs do a better job at picking up the major trends. On the other hand, shorter-term MAs are more sensitive to recent price actions. Technical analysts often use a combination of MAs and study their positioning versus one another.

Using sophisticated moving averages

Geeky technical analysts like me often take their MA practice to the next level, using more complex combinations of moving averages to understand the market sentiment better. Here are some of the most widely used sophisticated MAs:

>> **Moving average convergence divergence (MACD):** This is an indicator that shows the difference between a short-term MA and a long-term MA. Find out more information at `https://triplecompounding.com/training`.

>> **Bollinger Bands:** Created by John Bollinger in the 1980s, this indicator includes two bands above and below the market price. Visit `https://triplecompounding.com/training` for more information.

>> **Relative strength index (RSI):** This is a momentum indicator, or oscillator, that measures the relative internal strength of the stock's price against itself. Read more at `https://triplecompounding.com/training`.

>> **Ichimoku Kinko Hyo:** This option is my personal favorite; it consists of five different MAs all on top of each other. It gives you all you need to know all at once (hence its name, which means "a glance at the chart in balance").

6 Protecting Your Triple-Compounding System

IN THIS PART . . .

Protect your wealth, give your money multiple jobs, and secure your legacy with the right mix of insurance policies that are best for you.

Explore tax strategies wealthy families use to protect and grow their money legally and efficiently.

IN THIS CHAPTER

» **Understanding why insurance is essential for protecting your compounding strategy**

» **Clearing up common myths and misconceptions about insurance**

» **Exploring your core coverage needs: health, life, and disability**

» **Using advanced insurance strategies like IULs, policy loans, and umbrella coverage**

» **Discovering how to give your money multiple jobs**

Chapter **17**

Insuring Your Triple-Compounding System

For a long time — starting when I moved to the United States — I believed that insurance was mostly a scam. After landing my first job on Wall Street, I was frequently approached by insurance companies trying to recruit me as an agent. I'll admit, I was curious. But every time I looked into their tactics, something didn't sit right. Their scripts felt rehearsed. Their incentives seemed confusing. Their promises always sounded just a little too good to be true. And so, like many people, I dismissed the entire industry.

It wasn't until years later, after building my Triple Compounding system, that I was encouraged — repeatedly — by my friends Hanna and Brett to take a closer look. They weren't trying to sell me anything. They genuinely believed I was missing a key part of the financial puzzle: insurance, not just as protection, but as a growth tool. They kept nudging me until I finally gave in and decided to investigate it for myself.

When I dive into something, I don't do it halfway. I studied to become a licensed insurance agent — not because I needed another income stream, but because I wanted to understand what this $1.4 trillion industry was really about. I wanted to separate hype from substance, tactics from truth. Most of all, I wanted to help my members make informed, strategic decisions instead of writing off an entire category that plays a critical role in wealth protection.

What I discovered surprised me. The industry is real. It's also kind of like high school. Agents compete. Some talk behind each other's backs. Everyone claims they have the "best" product. But under the surface, most of them operate from the same set of core principles — regardless of whether they admit it. The key isn't to find the *flashiest* product or smoothest salesperson; it's to understand the principles for yourself so that you can spot the difference between a useful policy and an unnecessary expense.

That's exactly why I include this chapter. Because once you understand how insurance works — and how it fits into your triple-compounding framework — you gain a superpower most investors overlook.

REMEMBER

When you're building a triple-compounding system that multiplies your wealth from multiple angles, it's not just about growing your money; it's also about protecting it. Think of your triple-compounding system like a high-performance car. If you're going to push the pedal to the metal, you'd better have good brakes and insurance. This chapter is about those financial brakes and bumpers: the tools that keep your system intact when life throws you a curveball.

Protecting the Engine Behind Your Wealth

Insurance is often seen as a necessary evil — or worse, a waste of money. But when you're building a triple-compounding system, it isn't just about growing your wealth. It's about making sure you don't lose the momentum you've built. One unexpected event — a medical emergency, lawsuit, or injury — can bring even the strongest financial system to a halt if you don't have the proper safeguards in place.

Think of your compounding strategy like a high-performance car. You can soup it up with the best parts and the fastest engine, but without brakes and bumpers, you won't make it very far. Insurance functions like those essential safety systems: the mechanisms that protect your financial vehicle so that it can keep accelerating, even when life throws a sharp curve in your path.

Now, you may be thinking, "But insurance doesn't make me money." That's technically true. You don't get dividends or market returns from most insurance premiums. But that doesn't mean that it's not a wealth-building tool. The *value* of insurance lies in the protection it offers. It shields you from having to liquidate investments, go into debt, or derail your goals when something goes wrong.

Consider the case of a young entrepreneur who built a thriving e-commerce business. They were on the path to financial freedom until one emergency surgery wiped out their entire savings. They didn't have health insurance, and as a result, they had to pause everything, drain their cash reserves, and put their growth plans on hold. Had they included insurance as part of their wealth strategy, their triple-compounding engine could have kept running without interruption.

A comprehensive financial plan doesn't just focus on growth. It also includes intentional protection for your income, your health, your assets, and your legacy. From foundational policies like health and disability coverage to more advanced tools such as umbrella liability and asset protection trusts, insurance gives you the peace of mind you need to keep compounding without fear of collapse.

Compounding only works if you get to stay in the game. Insurance is what keeps you from having to press pause — or worse, start over.

REMEMBER

Busting the Most Common Insurance Myths

Let's face it — insurance doesn't always inspire confidence. It can feel complex, boring, or even like a trap. But when you peel back the jargon and look at the core purpose of insurance — to protect your ability to compound wealth — it becomes clear that skipping it is far riskier than having it. The challenge is that so many people make decisions based on myths rather than facts.

Here are a few of the most common insurance myths — and why believing them can put your triple-compounding system at risk:

>> **Myth #1: I'm young and healthy, so I don't need insurance.**

This is one of the most common assumptions, especially among people in their twenties and thirties. But health surprises don't check your age. A healthy 28-year-old that I knew was diagnosed with a rare autoimmune disease that led to more than $100,000 in treatment costs. Luckily, they had a solid health plan. Without it, their savings — and their compounding journey — would have been wiped out. The best time to get insurance is *before* you need it.

>> Myth #2: My employer provides enough coverage.

Employer plans are a great starting point, but they're rarely enough on their own. Life insurance through work often covers just one year's salary — nowhere near what a family would need to replace your income or pay off debts. Worse, most employer plans don't follow you when you leave the company, which means you can lose coverage at a vulnerable time. If your financial foundation depends on your ability to earn, you need independent coverage.

>> Myth #3: Insurance is a waste of money if I never use it.

This mindset treats insurance like an investment instead of what it really is: protection. You don't measure insurance by how often you use it. You measure it by the disaster it prevents. Not using your policy isn't a waste. It's a sign that you had a safe year. That's a win.

>> Myth #4: Disability insurance is only for people in dangerous jobs.

Contrary to popular belief, most long-term disability claims are caused by illness — not accidents. A software engineer diagnosed with multiple sclerosis or a teacher struggling with chronic fatigue syndrome can be out of work for months or even years. If your lifestyle depends on your paycheck, disability insurance isn't optional. It's essential.

>> Myth #5: Life insurance is only for people with kids.

Yes, children are a compelling reason to have life insurance, but they aren't the only reason. Life insurance can help cover business loans, mortgages, burial costs, or outstanding debts. It can also be used as a wealth-building vehicle through certain permanent policies. Even if you're child-free, you can still put life insurance to work for your financial strategy.

>> Myth #6: I'll buy insurance later — when I actually need it.

This may sound logical, but it's a dangerous game. By the time you need insurance, it may be too late. You could be uninsurable or face sky-high premiums. A healthy 30-year-old pays far less than a 45-year-old with hypertension or a history of cancer. Insurance rewards *proactive* planning — not reactive scrambling.

>> Myth #7: All insurance is a scam.

It's true that some agents push overpriced or misaligned policies. But the concept of insurance — risk pooling to protect against financial devastation — is sound. The key is to work with someone who educates you, not who pressures you. When structured correctly, insurance can be one of the smartest tools in your compounding strategy.

Buying into these myths may save you a few dollars today — but it can cost you years of progress in the future. Insurance isn't about paranoia. It's about peace of mind that keeps your triple-compounding system safe and steady.

Covering the Essentials: Health, Life, and Disability

No matter how advanced your investment strategy becomes, three types of insurance — health, life, and disability — remain fundamental. They don't just protect your assets; they protect *you*, your income, and the people who rely on you. In this section, I take a closer look at each one.

Protecting your health with medical coverage

Health insurance is often the first line of defense in your financial plan — and for good reason. Medical expenses are one of the top causes of bankruptcy in the United States, and the average hospital stay now exceeds $11,000. That doesn't include surgeries, medications, or ongoing treatments.

Even if you're young and healthy, one unexpected diagnosis or accident can force you to deplete your savings, liquidate investments, or go into debt. This kind of disruption can bring your compounding momentum to a screeching halt.

For many triple compounders, a high-deductible health plan paired with a Health Savings Account (HSA) offers a balance between protection and affordability. HSAs come with unique tax benefits: Contributions are tax-deductible, growth is tax-free, and withdrawals for qualified expenses are also tax-free. That's a triple advantage worth leveraging.

If you're optimizing every dollar, consider your HSA an investment account for future healthcare, not just a rainy-day fund. See more on this in Chapter 17.

Securing your legacy with life insurance

Life insurance is about more than covering final expenses. It's about making sure the plans and the people you care about don't fall apart if something happens to you. For parents, it replaces income, pays off debts, and ensures that dependents are taken care of. But even if you don't have children, life insurance can play an essential role in your compounding system.

Some people use it to cover business loans or fund a buy-sell agreement. Others use permanent policies as tools for wealth accumulation, estate tax mitigation, or charitable giving. And because life insurance proceeds are generally tax-free, they can also be used to pass on assets efficiently.

Whether you're using term coverage for pure protection or exploring permanent life insurance for a long-term strategy, the goal is the same: making sure your wealth continues to serve your values — even after you're gone.

Your triple-compounding system doesn't end with you. Life insurance helps ensure that it continues intact.

Replacing your income with disability coverage

Of all the essential types of insurance, disability is often the least understood and most undervalued. Yet your ability to earn income is one of your greatest financial assets, and it deserves protection just like your home, car, or investment portfolio.

Many people assume disability insurance is only for construction workers or people in high-risk fields. In reality, most disability claims are due to illness. Autoimmune diseases, cancer, neurological conditions, or chronic fatigue can sideline anyone — from office workers to self-employed professionals.

Disability insurance helps you maintain your lifestyle if you're unable to work due to a covered condition. Some policies are offered through employers, but many don't go far enough — especially for high-income earners, entrepreneurs, or those with inconsistent cash flow. Individual plans tend to offer more flexibility and better coverage.

Consider a dentist who broke their dominant hand. Without disability insurance, their business would have collapsed. Instead, they were able to continue covering their overhead and stay financially afloat while they recovered.

If you rely on your paycheck to fund your compounding strategy, disability insurance isn't optional; it's a lifeline.

Choosing the Right Type of Life Insurance

Once you understand the importance of life insurance, the next step is deciding which kind best fits your needs. Life insurance isn't one size fits all. Some types are designed for short-term protection, whereas others offer long-term growth and legacy planning. Your choice should depend on your goals, cash flow, and where you are in your compounding journey.

Let's explore the most common types and how each one can serve your triple-compounding system.

Considering term life for affordable protection

Term life insurance is the simplest and most budget-friendly option. It provides coverage for a fixed number of years — typically 10, 20, or 30 — at a fixed premium. If you pass away during that term, your beneficiaries receive the payout. If not, the policy expires, and that's that.

Term life doesn't accumulate cash value or offer fancy features. But that's exactly what makes it appealing for people who need a large amount of coverage at a low cost, especially during the years when their family depends on their income most.

For example, a 35-year-old in good health may secure a $1 million, 20-year policy for less than $40 a month. That's enough to cover a mortgage, childcare, and college tuition without breaking the bank.

This is a great first step if you're just starting to build wealth, and it works especially well as a foundational layer of protection while you grow other parts of your compounding strategy.

Term life only pays out if you die within the term. If you outlive the policy and still need coverage, you could be older, less healthy, and facing significantly higher premiums. If you want long-term coverage, have a backup plan in place before your policy expires.

Building long-term value with permanent policies

Unlike term insurance, permanent policies provide coverage for life — as long as you keep paying the premiums. They also come with a built-in savings component called *cash value*, which grows over time and can be accessed during your lifetime.

The following are two types of permanent policies:

>> **Whole life insurance** is the most traditional form. It offers fixed premiums, guaranteed death benefits, and predictable cash value accumulation. Many people use it as a conservative asset class: a place to park cash with tax-deferred growth, asset protection, and estate planning benefits. If term insurance is like renting, whole life is like buying a home. You're building equity while maintaining security.

>> **Universal life insurance** adds more flexibility. With this type, you can adjust your premium payments and even your death benefit, making it suitable for people whose income fluctuates or who anticipate changes in their financial responsibilities. This option is especially attractive for entrepreneurs, freelancers, and anyone with inconsistent cash flow.

Although permanent insurance costs more than term insurance, the additional features can support your compounding system in more advanced ways, especially once your wealth strategy moves beyond protection and into optimization.

Tapping market potential with indexed universal life

If you're looking for long-term protection *and* growth potential, indexed universal life (IUL) may offer the best of both worlds. IUL policies tie your cash value growth to a stock market index, such as the S&P 500, with built-in downside protection. That means when the market goes up, your policy can benefit. When the market drops, you won't lose principal.

IULs have become popular tools among high-income earners, business owners, and those who want to add a tax-efficient, flexible growth vehicle to their financial system. Contributions can accumulate cash value that's accessible through policy loans — often without triggering taxes — while the policy still provides a death benefit.

For example, a 42-year-old executive contributing $15,000 per year may build a sizable tax-advantaged asset that can later be used for retirement income, real estate down payments, or legacy planning.

When used strategically, an IUL can support multiple layers of your triple-compounding system: income protection, long-term growth, and liquidity access.

Permanent policies aren't just about death; they're also about design. With the right structure, they can become powerful tools for legacy, liquidity, and tax-free income.

Indexed universal life policies can be powerful, but only if managed correctly. If you underfund the policy or borrow too aggressively, you can risk policy lapse, reduced death benefits, or unexpected tax consequences. These policies should always be designed and reviewed by an experienced advisor.

Adding an umbrella for asset protection

Most people think of insurance as something you buy for specific things: your car, your home, your health. But what happens when something big happens and your basic policies aren't enough to cover the damages? That's where umbrella insurance comes in.

Umbrella insurance is exactly what it sounds like: extra coverage that sits on top of your existing policies and protects you when things go beyond your standard limits. If your auto insurance covers up to $300,000 and you're sued for $1 million after a car accident, your umbrella policy steps in to cover the gap. Without it, you'd be on the hook for the remaining $700,000, which can mean selling off investments, tapping retirement accounts, or even losing real estate just to pay legal judgments.

This kind of policy is especially important for triple compounders who have built up meaningful assets: rental properties, brokerage accounts, a business, or even just a high income. The more visible your wealth becomes, the more likely you are to attract legal claims. Unfortunately, one big lawsuit can undo years (or decades) of compounding.

Consider the story of a real estate investor whose tenant slipped on ice in their driveway and suffered a serious injury. Their homeowner's policy covered up to $300,000, but the final judgment was $900,000. Because they had a $1 million umbrella policy, they didn't have to liquidate any of their properties to cover the difference.

And the best part? Umbrella coverage is relatively inexpensive. A $1 million policy often costs between $200 and $400 per year. That's a small price to pay for protecting your entire wealth system.

If you own anything beyond your home — like rental units, a sizable brokerage account, or a small business — an umbrella policy isn't a luxury. It's a must-have layer of defense for your compounding engine.

Some business owners use strategies like asset protection trusts or captive insurance companies. These aren't for everyone, but if you're building serious wealth, it's worth exploring with a pro.

Giving Your Money Multiple Jobs

In a traditional financial plan, most dollars have a single job: spend, save, or invest. But in a triple-compounding system, your dollars are expected to multitask. One dollar should ideally serve multiple roles: protecting your future, growing your wealth, and offering access to liquidity when needed.

This is one of the major mindset shifts that separates everyday savers from wealth builders. Triple compounders don't ask, "Where should I put my money?" They ask, "How can this dollar serve three purposes at once?"

You may use a cash-value life insurance policy to protect your family, build long-term equity, and access funds for a business opportunity. Or, you may borrow against a brokerage account instead of selling your stocks, allowing your investments to continue growing tax-deferred. These strategies require thoughtfulness, but when executed well, they give you more control, flexibility, and compounding power over time.

In this section, I take a closer look at how to give your dollars multiple jobs without spreading them too thin.

Borrowing against your insurance

Permanent life insurance policies, such as whole life or indexed universal life, come with a cash value component that grows over time. (I cover indexed universal life policies in the earlier section, "Tapping market potential with indexed universal life.") Once that cash value reaches a certain level, you can borrow against it, often without triggering taxes or credit checks.

These loans are flexible. You typically don't have a fixed repayment schedule, and the policy's full death benefit remains intact as long as the loan is managed properly. It's one of the few places in personal finance where you can access liquidity *without interrupting growth*.

Imagine needing $25,000 to fund a renovation, invest in a deal, or cover medical costs. Instead of cashing out investments or taking on high-interest credit card debt, you borrow from your policy. Your account keeps compounding as if that money were still there, and you regain access to your funds on your own terms.

Borrowing too much or delaying repayment can cause the policy to lapse or shrink your death benefit. Always have a plan — and an advisor — when using policy loans as part of your strategy.

When done strategically, borrowing from your policy becomes a way to self-finance your own life on your own terms.

Using debt as income

Here's a strategy few people talk about but the wealthy use all the time: They borrow against appreciating assets instead of selling them.

Why? Because selling triggers taxes, halts compounding, and can cost you future gains. Borrowing, on the other hand, keeps the asset in place while giving you cash today. This tactic can be applied to assets such as

>> Brokerage accounts (via a securities-backed line of credit)

>> Real estate equity (via a HELOC — home equity line of credit — or cash-out refinance)

>> Insurance policies (via a policy loan)

For example, a tech entrepreneur needed liquidity to expand operations. Instead of selling shares and realizing a huge capital gain, they took a loan against their portfolio, preserving both their ownership and the portfolio's long-term growth. The result? No taxable event. No disruption. Just access to capital when it mattered most.

This is what wealthy people mean when they say, "I don't use income; I use debt." It's not recklessness. It's strategic borrowing, backed by appreciating assets and guided by discipline.

Used wisely, debt isn't the enemy of wealth. It's a bridge between your current goals and your long-term growth that doesn't trigger taxes or break your compounding rhythm.

Layering your financial tools

Triple compounders think in systems. A rental property isn't just real estate. It's monthly cash flow, long-term appreciation, and tax deductions. A permanent life insurance policy isn't just insurance. It's protection, liquidity, and a legacy tool. An emergency fund, when parked in the right place, offers both accessibility and interest income.

Every time you look at a financial product, ask yourself: *What other job could this dollar be doing?*

Here's how this plays out in real life:

>> A family used their cash-value life insurance to fund their child's college tuition. Later, they tapped the same policy for a down payment on a rental property — without dipping into their stock portfolio.

>> A high-income earner structured their policy to grow tax-free, offer critical illness coverage, and serve as a supplemental retirement income stream — all in one.

>> A business owner used an IUL policy to access emergency liquidity during a market dip, avoiding the need to sell undervalued assets.

These aren't tricks. They're intentional moves based on understanding how different financial tools interact. By giving your money multiple jobs, not only do you protect your triple-compounding system, you accelerate it.

Your dollars can wear more than one hat. Don't let them sit idle when they can be working double — or even triple — shifts on your behalf.

Taking smart action to lock in your protection

Understanding how insurance fits into your triple-compounding system is the first step. But knowledge without action is like having a car without ever turning on the ignition. To actually protect your wealth engine, you need to review your setup, adjust your coverage, and build habits that support long-term financial safety.

Use this checklist to make sure your protection plan isn't leaving any gaps:

1. **Auditing your coverage**

   Review your current insurance policies — life, health, disability, and umbrella. Are the coverage amounts enough to replace your income, protect your assets, and take care of your family? If not, it's time to level up.

2. **Building your emergency fund**

   Create a cash buffer of three to six months of living expenses — more if you're self-employed, support dependents, or have an unpredictable income. This is your first line of defense when life throws you a curveball.

3. **Exploring permanent insurance options**

   Look into whether a whole life or IUL policy can play a strategic role in your compounding plan. These aren't one-size-fits-all, but the right policy can protect, grow, and give your money access and flexibility.

4. **Getting a risk assessment**

   Sit down with a licensed professional who understands both insurance and investing. You want someone who can identify blind spots and design a strategy that complements — and doesn't compete with — your wealth-building system.

5. **Planning your legacy**

   Use insurance as a tool for passing down assets tax-efficiently, funding a trust, or making sure your business or loved ones stay financially secure if you're no longer around to run the show.

6. **Revisiting annually**

   Life evolves. Your insurance should, too. Review your coverage every year — or any time you go through a major life change, like having a baby, buying a home, or starting a new business.

Check out a comprehensive video on insurance to see which of these strategies is right for you by going to www.triplecompounding.com/training.

Chapter **18**

Tackling Taxes and Growing Wealth Legally and Strategically

I f you study how self-made millionaires and billionaires create wealth, one truth jumps out: They do everything they can to play the game on net terms, not gross terms.

They don't focus on what they earn. Instead, they obsess over what they get to keep from those dollars. And taxes — for business owners, high-income W-2 employees, and investors alike — are the single largest form of *wealth leakage* most people never properly address.

If you're paying 35 to 45 percent of every additional dollar you earn in state and federal taxes (as many do), the math is brutal:

» You're working almost half of the year for the government, before triple compounding can even start working for you.

» Every dollar unnecessarily lost to taxes is a dollar you can't reinvest, and a dollar that will never compound for you.

Smart tax strategy isn't about "gaming the system" or taking silly risks. It's about understanding the rules of the game so that you can legally and ethically play the game at the highest possible level.

When you finally start playing the game to win, you free up an enormous amount of cash flow to power your triple-compounding journey.

Understanding the Hidden "Tax Drag" That Destroys Compounding

I explain the concept of basic compounding in Chapter 1, which is aligned with most people's understanding of compound interest: If you earn 8 percent per year, and you let it ride year after year, your money grows faster and faster — causing the "snowball" effect.

But here's the part many miss: taxes are the hand constantly reaching in to scoop away part of your snowball, every year, slowing its growth.

If your investments are taxed heavily each year — through interest income, short-term capital gains, or high-turnover mutual funds — you're losing valuable dollars that can otherwise be compounding. I call it *reverse compounding*.

Here's a simple analogy: Imagine you're rolling a snowball downhill. Every few feet, a giant heat lamp melts part of the snowball. No matter how much effort you put into rolling it faster, the heat lamp keeps shrinking it.

That heat lamp is taxes.

To become a true triple compounder, you must find out how to shield your snowball from the heat legally and strategically. This section explores some of these methods.

Leveraging tax-advantaged accounts

One of the simplest yet most powerful ways to protect your triple-compounding system is to use tax-deferred accounts, such as 401(k)s and traditional IRAs.

When you contribute to these types of accounts, you

>> Deduct the contribution from your income for the year in which you make the contribution, lowering your tax bill for that year.

>> Allow investments to grow tax-deferred — no taxes on dividends, interest, or realized capital gains while the assets remain inside the account.

>> Pay taxes only when you withdraw funds from the account at a later date, typically in retirement (when your income and tax rate may be lower).

Tax drag compounds, just like interest does. The earlier you reduce tax drag, the more exponential your results become over time.

Maximizing contributions as a business owner

One of the cool side effects of owning a business (besides generating income and being your own boss) is that it helps you accelerate your triple-compounding system with tax advantages.

As a business owner or solopreneur, you can choose between Simplified Employee Pension (SEP) IRAs and Solo (or self-employed) 401(k)s for your tax-advantaged accounts. Here's how they're different:

>> **SEP IRA:** Simpler to administer, allows large contributions (up to approximately 25 percent of compensation/net income).

>> **Solo 401(k):** More flexible — allows you to contribute as both employee and employer, maximizing total contributions each year. It also allows for spousal participation if the spouse is the only other employee of the business establishing the Solo 401(k) plan, possibly doubling the amount of contributions each year.

In 2025, the maximum employee deferral is $23,500 and the maximum employer contribution is $46,500 per person.

Structuring a business for maximum tax-advantaged retirement savings

Early in 2025, my accountant helped a client set up a business infrastructure that incorporated a multi-member limited liability corporation (LLC) in Wyoming as the holding company for the three businesses the client owns. This holding company is owned by their revocable trust and their spouse's revocable trust. They were the only employees of the holding company.

The accountant established a Solo 401(k) at the holding company, and for 2025, the client and their spouse are able to contribute up to $70,000 each into the Solo 401(k) plan ($23,500 as the maximum employee deferral and $46,500 as the maximum employer contribution).

The compounding effect of $140,000+ per year over the next decade is astronomical and sets them up with substantial financial resources to tap into during their retirement years.

Harnessing the power of tax-free growth

The holy grails of tax-free growth in the United States are typically identified as Roth IRAs and Roth 401(k)s. A Roth IRA and Roth 401(k) are retirement savings options that allow you to contribute *after-tax* dollars and enjoy tax-free access to your money later on. Unlike traditional tax-deferred accounts, Roth accounts offer a unique combination of flexibility and long-term benefits.

Here's the flow:

1. You pay taxes on contributions today.
2. Your investments grow tax-deferred.
3. Withdrawals in retirement are 100 percent tax-free.

REMEMBER

An interesting benefit of Roth accounts is that you don't have to wait until retirement to get access to the amount you've contributed. You can access your contributions at any time. The growth/earnings, however, require a holding period of at least five years and your having reached age 59½ to access such funds both income tax- and penalty-free.

WARNING

On social media these days, you can't scroll too long without finding some supposed financial guru suggesting that an indexed universal life (IUL) insurance policy is the golden ticket to tax-free growth, even better than your Roth. But the fact is that life insurance, although a worthwhile tool in many regards, is never an investment alternative. It is a risk mitigation tool. (For more information about IUL and other insurance policies, see Chapter 17.) It's also important to note that complex policies often come with complex fee infrastructures and varying costs over time that can significantly impact the health of such policies down the road. Don't get hoodwinked by "too good to be true" social media posts.

Activating the triple tax play with HSAs

Health Savings Accounts (HSAs) are perhaps the most underused wealth-building tools available — and they come with a powerful advantage: *triple tax benefits*.

Here's how the triple tax play works:

>> Contributions are tax-deductible.

>> Growth is tax-free.

>> Withdrawals are tax-free if used for qualified medical expenses.

You're able to reimburse yourself for your out-of-pocket qualified medical expenses at any time (even years in the future) so long as the expense was incurred after the HSA was established, the expense was indeed a qualified medical expense, and you retained your receipts for such expenses.

This lets your HSA compound uninterrupted, while still allowing you to retain access to those funds whenever you want to reimburse yourself.

A REAL-WORLD HSA EXAMPLE

A client opened an HSA in 2005, a couple of years after it was first enacted. Every year, they contributed the maximum amount possible.

Instead of tapping into their HSA each year for that year's respective qualified medical expenses, they used their other cash flow to meet those needs and simply retained their receipts, leaving their HSA funds in their investment account to compound.

In 2024, they had accumulated a little more than $17,000 of out-of-pocket medical expenses since establishing their HSA, which they had paid for out of their yearly cash flow and other resources as those expenses were incurred. By that same time, their HSA had grown to a little more than $108,000.

After a bit of discussion, they decided to withdraw $15,000 from their HSA (as a reimbursement for qualified medical expenses that were paid previously out-of-pocket) and use those funds to pay for a cruise — tax-free.

Using Tax-Loss Harvesting and Other Smart Portfolio Moves

Tax-loss harvesting is a tool you can use to turn temporary losses into permanent tax benefits. Here's how it works:

>> You sell an investment that is currently down, lower than the price you initially paid.

>> You use the realized loss to offset gains elsewhere in your portfolio.

>> If losses exceed gains, you can use the excess losses up to $3,000 to offset your other ordinary income and carry forward at the federal level additional unused losses to future years.

An IRS rule called the wash sale rule puts some limitations on tax-loss harvesting.

Navigating the wash sale rule

The way the wash sale rule works is that investors are prevented from claiming a tax deduction on losses from the sale of securities if they repurchase the same or a "substantially identical" security within 30 days before or after the sale in question. Here's how it works:

>> **The time frame.** The wash sale rule applies to transactions within a 61-day period, encompassing the date of the sale plus 30 days before and 30 days after.

>> **The impact.** If you sell a security at a loss and then buy the same or a substantially identical security within this 61-day window, you cannot claim the loss on your tax return for that calendar year.

>> **The loss adjustment.** Instead of you being able to deduct the loss, the disallowed amount is added to the cost basis of the newly purchased security.

The wash sale rule is designed to prevent investors from artificially generating tax losses without making a substantial change to their overall investment position.

At the time of this writing, the wash sale rule applies only to securities. Crypto assets are currently not deemed to be securities by the Securities and Exchange Commission. Therefore, this rule does not apply to them. You can hold a position in a crypto asset that suffers a loss on a Tuesday, sell it Tuesday, realize the loss, and buy it back immediately thereafter, and you will be permitted to use that loss to offset gains elsewhere in your portfolio.

Placing the right assets in the right accounts

Different types of investments are taxed in different ways, and *where* you hold those investments can significantly impact your after-tax returns.

>> Tax-inefficient assets (bonds, REITs, actively managed mutual funds with high turnover) are better held in tax-advantaged accounts.

>> Tax-efficient assets (broad index funds held long term, individual stocks with low turnover) are better suited to taxable accounts.

Asset location matters. The same investment can yield very different after-tax returns depending on where you hold it with regard to account types.

Sequencing withdrawals to optimize lifetime taxes

In some years, drawing more from taxable accounts may make sense. In others, strategically converting traditional IRA assets to Roth IRA assets can lock in lower tax rates, reducing your lifetime tax liability. You can make a significant difference in your total taxes paid by coordinating your withdrawals with the following:

>> Social Security timing

>> Pension income

>> Real estate or business income

Work with a qualified advisor on withdrawal sequencing. It can easily create six-figure lifetime tax savings depending on your overall asset mix and account types.

Here are your key action steps for tax-efficient investing:

>> Maximize contributions to tax-advantaged accounts.

>> Conduct a tax-efficiency audit of your overall portfolio.

>> If you're a business owner, leverage the best retirement plan structures available to increase your contribution limits and reduce lifetime tax drag.

Finding Smart Deductions for Business Owners, High-Income W-2 Employees, and Investors

As a business owner, you may be excited about tax write-offs, but it's important to go about them without raising red flags. That's where the golden rule of *ordinary* and *necessary* comes to play.

Knowing what you can write off without raising red flags

Section 162(a) of the Internal Revenue Code is the golden rule of deductions for business owners. It is a two-part test and is the starting point from which all considerations regarding deductibility should begin.

>> **Ordinary.** Although much more complicated, this aspect of the code section essentially boils down to what is common practice within your respective industry.

>> **Necessary.** This particular aspect of the code section leaves a bit more room for interpretation. However, this most commonly breaks down to what is necessary for generating revenue.

A legitimate deduction lowers your taxable income, thereby subjecting a lower dollar amount to your effective income tax rate.

Applying the reasonableness test

Even if an expense passes the ordinary and necessary test, it must also meet the standard of *reasonableness*. Here's a simple analogy: A bakery purchases an oven. This is clearly an ordinary and necessary expense. But if it's the thirteenth oven purchased, doesn't fit in the kitchen, and ends up sitting in the bakery's front entryway unused, it will not be considered a reasonable expense. In an audit, it will likely be disallowed.

A deduction is not a free lunch — but it is a way to shift dollars from post-tax to pre-tax in certain beneficial circumstances.

Taking advantage of smart deductions

One of my biggest joys as a business owner is the ability to take advantage of the tax code so I can invest the money I would have otherwise given to the government to spend on things that may or may not align with my personal values.

Here are some of the strategies you can use to reduce your taxable income, boost your cash flow, and help you keep more of what you earn:

>> **Home office deduction.** If you have a dedicated space in your home, regardless of whether you rent or own your home, it can be exclusively used for business. Because it is a primary place from which you conduct business, it's highly probable that you'll qualify for deductions for the prorated amount of expenses of your home that directly and indirectly support the use of that space for business.

This doesn't necessarily mean that you must conduct all of your business in this space. It can simply be where you conduct the administrative aspects of your business.

Such expenses can include interest payments on your mortgage, rent, insurance, homeowner association dues, utilities, property taxes, maintenance and upkeep, renovations, and depreciation.

>> **Business travel.** When traveling for business, a portion, if not all, of your travel and lodging expenses may be deductible.

There are rules that stipulate the type of travel that qualifies, along with what may be necessary to permit international travel to be deductible. It may also be possible to have a portion of your expenses be deductible even if some of your overall trip is primarily personal as opposed to business.

>> **Professional education.** Qualifying education can be deducted as a business expense. Here are two general categories of qualifying education that can be deductible as a business expense:

- The first is education that maintains or improves skills for your current trade or business. This can include refresher courses, courses on current developments, or specialized training to enhance your existing expertise.

- The second is education that is required by an employer or law. If the education is required to maintain employment, keep your present salary, status, or job, or is required to maintain a professional license, it is likely deductible.

>> **Professional services.** Legal fees, accounting services, and consulting fees are all examples of professional services that are likely to be deductible for your business, so long as they meet the requirements of Section 162(a) of the Internal Revenue Code and are reasonable.

WARNING

Fees paid to acquire business assets, including real estate, are generally not deductible but can be added to the asset's cost basis as part of your capital investments.

>> **Business vehicles.** Expenses related to vehicles may be deductible up to the percentage of actual business use of the vehicle. You can opt for a simple approach to the deduction that provides a certain amount per business mile driven throughout the year. Or, you can opt for the actual expense method of accounting for your expenses, such as maintenance and fuel charges.

Depreciation is also a significant phantom expense that may be taken into account under the right conditions.

Keep a detailed record of your business and personal miles driven, regardless of the method you use, as you'll be required to produce a mileage log in an audit, in addition to receipts for all of your expenses.

REMEMBER

Be wary of "deducting your lifestyle." That's where many audit flags originate — the results of which typically leave most taxpayers bruised at best.

Optimizing Depreciation for Real Estate and Equipment

Optimizing depreciation for real estate and equipment means strategically utilizing various depreciation methods to maximize tax benefits and improve cash flow.

Optimizing for real estate

Real estate, by default, is considered to be a passive activity, and rental income derived from real estate investment is deemed to be passive income. Since 1986, with the introduction of the passive activity loss rules, passive losses can only be used to offset passive income unless an exception within the Internal Revenue Code applies.

Depreciation in real estate allows investors to deduct a portion of the property's original purchase price (for the improvement upon the land only; land itself cannot be depreciated) each year as an expense, reducing taxable passive income.

As I explain in Chapter 7, real estate investment has a variety of categories:

>> **Residential real estate.** Properties used for dwelling purposes, such as single-family homes, condos, townhouses, duplexes, triplexes, and so on.

>> **Commercial real estate.** Properties used for business activities to generate income, including offices, retail stores, shopping centers, hospitals, restaurants, apartment buildings, and multifamily properties with more than four units.

>> **Industrial real estate.** Properties used for manufacturing, production, distribution, and storage, like factories, warehouses, and data centers.

>> **Land.** Undeveloped land, vacant lots, and agricultural land, including farms and ranches.

REMEMBER

Investment real estate is typically depreciated using the straight-line depreciation method over two different time frames, depending on the classification of the real estate:

- Residential real estate: 27.5 years

- Commercial and industrial real estate: 39 years

TIP

The straight-line depreciation method, when it comes to real estate, is also known as the impermissible method within the Internal Revenue Code. What you're supposed to do is depreciate an item based on its useful life. The IRS recognizes that using the actual useful life for real estate assets is not always easy to determine, so they allow taxpayers to use the straight-line method (see the next section). It is often the case that using the actual useful life method results in better tax reduction in earlier years when viewed cumulatively over the entire holding period of the asset.

Optimizing for equipment

Equipment used in a business can be depreciated to recover its cost over its useful life. There are four common methods of depreciating equipment:

>> **Straight-line depreciation.** The asset's cost is spread evenly over its useful life.

>> **Declining balance and double declining balance methods.** These accelerated methods provide larger deductions in the earlier years.

>> **Units of production.** Depreciation is based on the asset's usage or output.

>> **Sum-of-the years'-digits.** This is another accelerated method with higher deductions in the earlier years.

Avoiding Common Audit Triggers

Most taxpayers don't intentionally raise red flags — but a few common missteps can increase your odds of hearing from the IRS. Knowing what to watch for is key to protecting your peace of mind (and your wallet). Here are common triggers to watch out for:

- **Unusually high deductions relative to income.** Deductions that seem too high compared to your income may indicate that personal expenses are being claimed as business costs.

- **Excessive cash transactions.** Businesses with a high proportion of cash transactions, like restaurants, tend to face a bit more scrutiny year to year. It's generally more difficult to track large cash amounts, and the IRS monitors for discrepancies between reported revenues and industry averages.

- **Home office deductions.** Home office deductions are often misused. The space must be used exclusively and regularly for business to qualify (read more in the earlier section, "Taking advantage of smart deductions").

- **Misclassification of employees as independent contractors.** Misclassifying employees can lead to an underpayment of payroll taxes, so the IRS carefully reviews situations that include high independent contractor payments relative to industry averages.

- **Frequent loss reporting.** The IRS has something called the hobby loss rules, which essentially seek to ensure that your business is actually a business and not something you are just doing for the fun of it. If you report losses consistently year to year, they'll want to dive deeper.

- **Large charitable contributions.** Charitable donations that are significantly higher than normal for your business or industry can raise a red flag.

- **Inconsistent information across forms.** Mismatches between information shared across your filed forms, along with other reporting documents such as 1099s, K1s, and W-2s, put you on a fast track to an auditor reaching out for clarification from you.

- **Math errors or typos.** Simple errors on your return can be enough to cause an audit.

- **Neat, round numbers.** The computers are looking at the numbers reported, and if there's a pattern of numbers ending in 0s or 5s, it can suggest estimation and raise a flag.

- **Handling digital assets.** Guilt by association is still a thing when it comes to digital assets, and simply having digital assets in a given year can be enough to spark a desire on the part of the IRS to want to know more.

The IRS audits patterns, and disproportionate deductions to income can raise red flags.

Despite carefully navigating around these and other common red flags, it's still possible to be randomly selected for an audit. So document, document, document.

Check out a training video on some quick ways you can save money on taxes at `https://www.triplecompounding.com/training`.

The Part of Tens

IN THIS PART . . .

Avoid the ten most common mistakes triple compounders make.

Spot and stop ten things that cause reverse compounding.

Adopt ten habits of highly successful triple compounders.

Chapter **19**

Ten Mistakes to Avoid as a Triple Compounder

Triple compounding is a powerful wealth-building strategy, but only if you execute it correctly. Unfortunately, many investors fall into traps that slow down their progress, sabotage their growth, or cause unnecessary losses.

In this chapter, I cover ten of the most common mistakes triple compounders make and explain how you can avoid them to accelerate your path to financial freedom.

Falling for FOMO

If you've ever heard about an investment "going to the moon" and felt the urgent need to jump in, congratulations: You've experienced FOMO (fear of missing out). This happens when hype, social media, and peer pressure override rational decision-making.

The problem? By the time you hear about a "hot" investment, it's usually too late.

Historically, FOMO has led people to buy *shitcoins* (cryptocurrency with little to no value, no real utility, and no long-term potential) at all-time highs, invest in meme stocks right before they crashed, and overpay for real estate bubbles. Instead of chasing hype, triple compounders stick to their system. They buy assets when they are undervalued, not when the entire world is piling in.

If you feel urgency to buy because "everyone is doing it," that's your first warning sign to stop and reassess. The best opportunities aren't the ones making headlines; they're the ones smart investors plan, for using the Invest Diva Diamond Analysis that I unveil in Chapter 10.

Ignoring the Power of Automation

Many people think they lack the discipline to invest consistently. However, the truth is that they're just relying on willpower instead of automation.

Automation is what allows your money to work for you without requiring constant effort. Triple compounders automate

>> Contributions to their investments (so they never "forget" to invest)

>> Buy and sell limit orders (so emotions don't dictate decisions)

>> Reinvesting dividends and cash flow (so compounding never stops)

The wealthy don't spend their days manually managing their money. They set up automated wealth-building systems and let them run, so they can actually enjoy their lives and do things that make their lives impactful.

If you have to "remember" to invest, you're doing it wrong. Automate your contributions and watch your portfolio grow effortlessly.

Overinvesting in High-Risk Assets

There's a difference between strategic risk-taking and reckless gambling. Many people put too much money into high-risk investments, whether it's speculative stocks, cryptocurrencies, or risky options trades. The issue? If those investments crash, they wipe out years of progress in seconds.

Smart triple compounders balance risk and reward:

>> They allocate a portion of their portfolio to high-growth assets, but never more than they can afford to lose.

>> They focus on assets that compound over time, rather than chasing short-term bets.

Risk is a tool, not a necessity. If you're betting everything on one trade, you're not investing. You're gambling.

WARNING

Forgetting Emergency Funds

Your portfolio may be growing at an incredible rate, but if you don't have cash reserves, you're one unexpected event away from disaster. Without an emergency fund, a job loss, medical bill, or urgent expense can force you to sell your investments at the worst possible time.

A triple compounder never wants to be forced into liquidation, so they keep a cash buffer for unexpected events.

Keep at least three to six months of living expenses in a high-yield savings account. Your portfolio should be compounding uninterrupted — not acting as your emergency wallet.

TIP

Trusting "Too Good to Be True" Gurus and Impersonators

The internet is filled with self-proclaimed "experts" promising guaranteed returns and "secret" investing tricks. Market volatility brings all sorts of clickbait, social media posts, and viral videos of people giving you their take either to create more hype or fear just so they can get more likes or to sell you their WhatsApp or Discord signal.

What's even more disturbing is impersonators pretending to be recognized financial experts, scamming people out of hundreds of thousands of dollars.

There are thousands of impersonators of me popping out on social media, for example, who follow my followers, pretending to be my private account. Through their shady sales tactics, they have successfully scammed some people out of their hard-earned cash.

If someone promises "guaranteed profits," they're lying.

Any social media account with my name or my business name that does not have a verified badge is not me.

Skipping Investments in Yourself

Many people hesitate to spend money on mentorship, books, or education, but those investments yield the highest ROI (return on investment) of all.

Triple compounders invest in themselves before they invest in the markets because they understand that they are the ultimate value asset. Here are some ways you can invest in yourself (read more in Chapter 4):

>> Surrounding yourself with like-minded people

>> Developing a vision

>> Mastering your subconscious mind

>> Becoming your future self now

>> Overcoming resistance

>> Reframing your past

>> Developing a decisive nature

>> Doing what moves the needle the most toward your ideal future now, without delay

The best investment you'll ever make is in your own knowledge. The more you learn, the more you earn.

Overcomplicating Your System

Some investors feel the need to track hundreds of stocks, run complex spread-sheets, and time the market perfectly. However, the reality is, simple beats complex.

Triple compounding is most effective when it's automated, straightforward, and repeatable:

>> A portfolio of high-quality, compounding assets beats daily trading.

>> An automated, subscription-based business beats manual door-to-door sales.

>> A focused, consistent plan beats constantly chasing new strategies.

There are a thousand ways to go from Los Angeles to New York. But you'll never get to your destination if you change your path daily based on what you just heard from a guru on social media.

Pick one strategy that suits your personality, risk tolerance, and financial goals, and focus on that strategy only.

Losing Focus of Your Goals

If you don't know why you're investing, it's easy to make decisions based on emotions instead of logic. And you will never become successful if you don't know where you're going.

Triple compounders set clear goals:

>> They understand what financial freedom means to them.

>> They know how much they need to hit their ideal freedom number.

>> They figure out the deeper reason why they're seeking this financial goal.

Your triple-compounding strategy should be based on your goals, not the daily news cycle. Keep your eyes on the long-term prize and align your everyday activi-ties to what would get you closer to your goal faster.

Neglecting to Adjust for Life Changes

Your investment strategy shouldn't stay static forever. As your income, family situation, and financial goals change, so should your approach.

>> If you earn more, increase your investment contributions instead of falling for lifestyle inflation.

>> If your expenses shift, adjust your risk tolerance. (See Chapter 3.)

>> If tax laws change, optimize your strategy accordingly.

Your financial plan is a living, breathing thing. Reassess it annually or anytime something major happens in your life, like when you get married, lose a job, or purchase a house. Then make adjustments to your triple-compounding system as needed.

Waiting Too Long to Start

The best time to start investing was 20 years ago. The second-best time is today.

Every decade, people look back and wish they had started sooner. People in their forties wish they had started in their thirties. People in their fifties wish they had started in their forties. People in their sixties wish they had done anything in their fifties. The cycle repeats itself because time is the most powerful ingredient in compounding wealth, and every year you delay is money lost forever.

Many people hesitate to invest because they feel like they don't know enough yet. They wait for the perfect moment, thinking they need more knowledge, more savings, or a crystal-clear investment strategy before taking action. But here's the truth:

There is no perfect time, and there is no perfect plan. The only way to truly find out how to triple-compound is by starting. Even if you begin small, make mistakes, and adjust along the way, you'll be years ahead of the people who are still sitting on the sidelines, waiting for some mythical moment when the stars align.

Time in the market beats timing the market. Many people hesitate to start investing because they fear a market crash or want to wait for a better time to buy in.

More money has been lost waiting for a crash than in the actual crash because while people sit on the sidelines, their cash loses value to inflation, and they miss out on years of compounding growth. Meanwhile, disciplined triple compounders who stay in the market continue to collect dividends, reinvest profits, and take advantage of long-term appreciation.

Historically, markets have always recovered from downturns, and those who wait for the perfect entry point often find themselves buying back in at higher prices or never entering at all. Successful investors don't try to time the market. They focus on time in the market.

Chapter 20

Ten Things You May Be Reverse-Compounding

When most people think of compounding, they picture a rocket ship of growth — money snowballing into more money, creating generational wealth while they sleep. But there's a darker side to compounding most people overlook: *reverse compounding.*

Reverse compounding is when something grows against you. Instead of building wealth, it quietly chips away at your freedom. And the worst part? It's often invisible . . . until it's too late.

In this chapter, I walk you through ten sneaky ways that reverse compounding can sabotage your triple compounding journey — and how to stop them in their tracks.

Bad Debt

Bad debt is a liability on something that doesn't make you money . . . like luxury bags, a car that depreciates in value, cable TV, and all the other things poor people go into debt for to look like what they think a rich person looks like.

Poor people and Welfare Divas (see Chapter 4) have debt. And bad debt is a burden on wealth. Every time you carry a balance on a high-interest credit card, you're paying someone else to compound their wealth.

That $2,000 handbag bought on a 24 percent Annual Percentage Rate (APR) card is not a $2,000 handbag. It's a $5,000+ handbag once you finish making minimum payments.

If you're compounding debt instead of investments, you're sprinting in the wrong direction.

Not all debt is bad. But if it's high-interest and funding consumption (not income), it's reverse-compounding.

Good debt, on the other hand, also known as funding or leverage, is defined by the money you may owe to acquire an asset, an investment.

What's an investment? It's something that reproduces itself to make more wealth . . . like a skillset you gain that will keep on giving for years to come.

For example, your investment in this book even if you had to leverage the bank's money to get in, is actually an asset . . . because this is going to put you and your family on the trajectory of taking control of your finances and making your money work for you and keep on compounding for years to come, so that you can become financially free in a reasonable time.

Wealthy people, successful entrepreneurs, and Millionaire Divas and Divos leverage funding to create wealth. Leverage is the means to get to wealth. In fact, if it wasn't for leverage, most self-made millionaires and billionaires wouldn't even have had the chance to get started.

401(k) Hidden Fees

You may think that you're saving for retirement . . . but if you haven't looked under the hood of your 401(k), hidden fees may be slowly eating away your gains. Think: administrative fees, fund expense ratios, and advisory fees — some as high as 2 percent annually.

That may not sound like much, but over 30 years, a 2 percent fee can reduce your retirement nest egg by up to 40 percent.

Use tools like FeeX (Pontera) or Personal Capital's fee analyzer to uncover what you're really paying.

Late Fees

Late fees on bills, rent, credit cards, or utilities may seem minor — until you realize they're quietly compounding your stress and draining your cash flow.

Worse, they can hit your credit score, making future borrowing more expensive.

Compounding isn't just about dollars — it's about behavior. Automate your bills or set calendar reminders to protect your peace of mind *and* your credit.

High-Expense Ratio Mutual Funds

Many traditional mutual funds charge sky-high fees without delivering better performance than index funds. If you're paying 1.5 percent annually on a fund that barely keeps up with the S&P 500, you're not investing — you're overpaying for underperformance.

Choose low-cost index funds or ETFs when possible. And once you become a confident triple compounder following my system, start creating your own investment strategies and stop paying any fees on your investments altogether, like thousands of our members!

Every percentage point saved on fees is a percentage point added to your compounding engine.

Actively Managed Funds

Actively managed funds promise to "beat the market." But most of them don't. And those that do often charge you handsomely for the attempt. According to SPIVA, over 85 percent of active fund managers underperform their benchmark over ten years.

Don't let flashy brochures or glossy performance charts distract you from cold, hard math.

Lifestyle Inflation

The moment your income goes up — and your expenses follow — you're reverse-compounding. You're earning more, but you're not keeping more. That dream home upgrade, car lease, or fancy brunch routine? It compounds too, just not in your favor.

Compound your *savings rate*, not your status symbols. Triple compounders celebrate margin, not materialism.

Poor Tax Planning

If you're not strategically reducing your tax liability, you're likely reverse-compounding with every paycheck. Missed deductions, incorrect business structures, and poor timing on investment sales can cost you thousands every year. Read Chapter 18 for tax planning essentials.

Annuities with High Fees

Not all annuities are evil, but many come with hidden riders, surrender charges, and annual fees that can eat up your returns.

If someone sold you an annuity without fully explaining the fine print, you may be compounding regret instead of results.

Always ask: "What are all the fees I'll be charged over the life of this product — and how do they compare to an index fund?"

Bad Habits

Triple compounding doesn't just apply to your portfolio. It touches every area of your life — *wealth, health, and relationships.*

In each of these three areas of your life, the first and most powerful investment you make is in *yourself.* When you take a small, intentional action and repeat it enough times to automate it . . . it becomes a habit. And habits *compound.*

But here's the kicker: *bad* habits compound, too, in the wrong direction. Skipping workouts. Avoiding your finances. Doomscrolling before bed. These habits may seem harmless in the moment, but over time, they build up not only in your waistline or brain fog, but also in lost confidence, energy, time, and opportunities.

Every habit you repeat is casting a vote for your future self. Are your habits reverse-compounding the life you say you want?

Compounding works in every direction — so build habits that work *for you,* not against you.

Negative Mindset

The most dangerous reverse compounder of all? Your own beliefs. If you constantly think, "I'm bad with money," "It's too late for me," or "This won't work for someone like me," guess what compounds? Inaction. Fear. Stuckness.

But just like wealth, confidence compounds. Courage compounds. Results compound. One empowered action can flip your trajectory forever.

Speak to yourself like you'd speak to someone you love. Your mindset *is* your multiplier.

Reverse compounding is sneaky, but once you see it, you can stop it. Then flip the script. Audit your life. Identify the reverse compounders. One by one, you can turn them into growth engines for your triple-compounding system.

Want to see what this looks like in real life? Check if spots are available at `www.triplecompounding.com/live`, where I walk you through these exact shifts in detail.

IN THIS CHAPTER

» **Building routines that reinforce compounding across wealth, health, and relationships**

» **Using systems, not willpower, to stay consistent**

» **Learning from the behaviors of top triple compounders**

» **Turning tiny choices into lifelong momentum**

Chapter **21**

Ten Habits of Successful Triple Compounders

Triple compounding isn't just about what you invest in; it's how you live. Successful triple compounders don't leave their future up to chance or random effort. They shape their daily actions to generate, automate, and accelerate progress.

And they do it in *all* three domains: wealth, health, and relationships.

This chapter gives you a behind-the-scenes look at the daily habits of real-life triple compounders who are building seven- and eight-figure portfolios, becoming healthier than ever, and creating families they're proud of.

Whether you've just started your journey or you're deep into the compounding game, these ten habits help you stay aligned with your goals and multiply your momentum.

Following Your Highest Excitement without Expectation

When in doubt, follow the energy. That's not just woo-woo talk. It's one of the most effective ways to align your actions with your purpose and accelerate your compounding progress.

Successful triple compounders make decisions based not only on logic but also on what feels most energizing right now. They understand that the things that light you up aren't random. They're clues. They point to your next right step — even if that step doesn't make complete sense yet.

The trick is following that excitement without clinging to what the outcome has to be. This means trusting that

>> The excitement is guiding you toward growth.

>> Even if things don't unfold exactly how you planned, they'll take you somewhere better.

>> You're most magnetic and productive when you're lit up from the inside.

Here are some examples. Instead of saying

"I should post on social media today because I haven't in a while . . ."

ask yourself,

"What would feel genuinely exciting to share right now?"

This shift can look like

>> Filming a short video while you're still glowing from a breakthrough.

>> Scheduling a spontaneous date night because your relationship needs presence, not planning.

>> Diving into a new business idea that energizes you even if it scares you a little.

>> Journaling on an insight that's been pulling at you, even if it's not on your to-do list.

Excitement doesn't always mean ease. Sometimes it means butterflies, nerves, or stretching your comfort zone. The key is to follow what feels alive in you, not just what feels safe.

Following your excitement does *not* mean jumping into every hot stock, crypto coin, or trending asset just because some Wall Street bro on YouTube or TikTok said it's "about to 10X." That's not excitement. That's adrenaline. And if you confuse the two, you'll confuse momentum with mania.

Genuine excitement is grounded. It feels expansive, not frantic. It comes from internal alignment, not external noise.

So, before you buy or sell anything, ask yourself the following:

> "Am I excited because this fits my long-term vision?"

or

> "Am I just afraid of missing out?"

Successful triple compounders trust their excitement and their frameworks. They still run the numbers. They still check their Diamond Analysis. They don't skip strategy in the name of sensation.

Excitement aligned with strategy = powerful, whereas excitement based on hype = expensive.

Investing in Your Future Self Today

Your future isn't something you stumble into. It's something you fund.

Every decision you make today is either a deposit into your future self's bank account or a withdrawal. Triple compounders understand this. They don't wait until they've "made it" to act like the person they want to become. They start now with what they have.

Triple compounders know their future self is not some far-off fantasy. It's the exaggerated result of today's thoughts, habits, and investments.

So, they ask the following:

>> "What would my future self thank me for doing today?"

>> "How would the version of me with a seven-figure portfolio show up right now?"

>> "What habits, assets, and relationships does that version of me already have — and how can I start building those now?"

This may look like

>> Contributing $100 to your investment account even when it feels "too small to matter"

>> Showing up to the gym or taking a walk even when you're tired

>> Having an uncomfortable but necessary conversation in your relationship

>> Hiring a coach, joining a program, or reading a book that stretches your mindset

Investing in your future self doesn't always mean investing money. Time, energy, attention, and decisions compound, too.

Triple compounders don't wait until they're motivated, wealthy, or "ready" to start behaving like their future self. They begin acting like that person now, and reality eventually catches up. You don't get the future you want. You get the future you *invest in.* Start small, start messy, but start today.

Putting your future on pause until you feel more confident or less busy is one of the sneakiest forms of self-sabotage. Time doesn't wait. Start compounding now — even if it's imperfect.

Multiplying Time through Strategic Focus

You can't "make" more time. But you can multiply it.

Triple compounders don't waste energy trying to manage every minute. Instead, they focus on creating leverage — so the time they spend produces results that keep compounding long after they've stopped working.

Think of it like this:

There are two types of tasks in your day.

>> **Linear tasks:** You do the thing; you get the result once.

>> **Compound tasks:** You do the thing once, and it pays you over and over again.

Triple compounders prioritize compound tasks. They build systems, assets, and relationships that keep working even when they're asleep, offline, or on vacation.

Here are some examples of time multipliers:

>> Creating an automated investing plan that grows without you checking it

>> Recording a video or writing a post that continues attracting ideal clients for months

>> Hiring someone to take over repetitive work so you can focus on what moves the needle

>> Teaching your team how to make decisions without you, so your business runs on systems, not stress

The most successful people aren't busier. They've just found out how to spend time in ways that create more time, income, and freedom.

If your calendar is full of tasks that don't scale, don't inspire, and don't compound, you're not multiplying time. You're recycling exhaustion.

Shifting Your Emotional State before Acting

Strategy matters. But emotional *state* comes first.

Triple compounders know that how you *feel* directly impacts how you *act*. You can have the best investment plan, business idea, or relationship tools, but if you're operating from fear, burnout, or resentment, you'll sabotage the result.

That's why before they make big moves — financial or otherwise — they check in with their emotional state and reset if needed.

They understand that

>> A regulated nervous system makes better decisions than a reactive one.

>> Energy is contagious — especially in leadership, love, and wealth.

>> Your emotional state determines what you notice, what you miss, and what you bring into your life.

Instead of white-knuckling through being overwhelmed, they pause and ask

>> "What am I feeling right now?"

>> "What do I have to believe is true in order to feel this way?"

>> "Is this the version of me I want to bring into this decision?"

>> "What would elevate my energy so I can act from power, not pressure?"

Once you find the root cause and the limiting beliefs that are causing you to be in that particular low-level state, you can make a shift. Here are some ways triple compounders shift state:

>> Movement (walks, dance, workouts, breathwork)

>> Music (curated playlists that energize or ground them)

>> Reframing (asking better questions or shifting perspective)

>> Visualization (connecting with their future self before making a move)

Sometimes it takes 5 minutes. Sometimes 30. But that reset can save you hours of backtracking — or years of regret.

Build a *state shift menu* — a personal toolkit of activities that help you get back to center. Keep it handy for stressful days or decision-heavy moments.

Tony Robbins teaches that "emotion is energy in motion." Triple compounders know that if you move your body, breathe differently, or focus on gratitude, you shift your emotional state. And from that elevated place, the right actions become clear.

Making investment decisions, relationship moves, or big business calls when you're in a low state is like texting your ex at 2 a.m. You *can*, but you probably shouldn't.

Aligning Your Identity with Your Future Vision

You don't get *what you want*. You get what you *believe you are*. Triple compounders understand that the fastest way to close the gap between where you are and where you want to be is to stop acting like the old version of yourself.

Instead of asking, "What do I need to *do* to hit my goals?" they ask, "Who do I need to *become* to make those goals inevitable?" This is what Dr. Benjamin Hardy calls *identity-based transformation*. And it's the key to lasting change — not just in your finances, but in your health and relationships, too.

Here's how this looks in real life:

>> You don't just automate your investments. You *become* someone who builds wealth automatically.

>> You don't just work out. You *embody* someone who honors and maintains their energy daily.

>> You don't just go to therapy or on date night. You *own* the identity of a conscious, emotionally intelligent partner.

This shift isn't about faking it. It's about aligning with the future version of you that already exists — and making choices from *that* place.

Try asking yourself each morning, "If I already had the wealth, health, and relationships I wanted, what would I do today?"

Then take one aligned action, even if it feels unfamiliar or uncomfortable. The more you act in alignment with your future identity, the faster it becomes your new normal.

Visualize your future self often. Name them. Describe their routines. Get emotionally connected to them, so you recognize when your current habits are out of sync.

Triple compounders don't wait for external proof before upgrading their identity. They *become* the millionaire, the aligned parent, or the magnetic leader first — and let the world catch up.

Behavior follows identity. If you want different results, start by becoming someone who expects them.

Practicing Gratitude and Celebrating Wins

Gratitude is not just a feel-good practice; it's a performance enhancer. Triple compounders know that the *energy* you bring into your financial, health, and relationship decisions matters just as much as the actions. When you operate from a place of lack, fear, or frustration, everything feels like an uphill battle. But when you lead with gratitude, you create an internal environment where *receiving* becomes easier.

Here's the science-backed truth: Gratitude rewires your brain to focus on what's working. It boosts your resilience, strengthens your immune system, and increases your ability to take bold, aligned action.

And yet, most people skip it. They focus on how far they still have to go instead of how far they've already come.

Triple compounders flip the script by doing the following:

>> Tracking progress, even if it feels small.

>> Celebrating every win (new savings milestone, first dividend, healthier meal, hard conversation).

>> Training their nervous system to feel safe with success — not just with struggle.

>> Practicing gratitude daily — not only when things go well.

If you only celebrate the "big" wins, you'll train your brain to believe progress doesn't count until you're exhausted. That belief kills momentum. Celebrate early. Celebrate often.

Gratitude isn't passive. It's *activating*. When you feel good about what you already have, you're more likely to take empowered action toward what you want next.

Start or end your day by writing down three things you're grateful for and one thing you're proud of. Bonus points if it's something you once *wished* for.

What you appreciate, appreciates. Gratitude is a compounding habit that multiplies your capacity to grow — and to receive more of what you actually want.

Setting Milestones and Rewards

Triple compounders don't just set goals. They set milestones and reward themselves along the way. Why? Because the brain needs wins. If all you do is grind for some far-off finish line, you'll burn out before you ever get there.

But when you break your big goals into *bite-sized victories* and tie them to meaningful rewards, you keep yourself engaged, energized, and emotionally invested in the journey.

Here's how this habit shows up in action:

>> Investing your first $500? Celebrate it.

>> Automating your contributions for three months straight? Celebrate it.

>> Having one hard conversation that brings your relationship closer? Celebrate it.

>> Completing your first workout streak or losing the first five pounds? Yup — celebrate that, too.

The reward doesn't have to be expensive or extravagant. It just needs to feel good and reinforce the identity you're building.

Momentum multiplies when it's emotionally reinforced. Rewards aren't indulgent; they're intelligent.

If you never feel "allowed" to celebrate your progress, you're conditioning yourself to associate growth with deprivation. That's not sustainable. Set the milestone. Claim the win.

Automating Contributions and Investments

Triple compounders don't rely on willpower. They rely on systems.

If your financial growth depends on you remembering to log into your brokerage account every week, it's not going to compound. Life gets busy. You get tired. Things fall through the cracks.

That's why successful triple compounders automate everything they can so their money grows whether they're working, sleeping, or playing at the park with their kids.

Here's what they automate.

- >> **Contributions:** A fixed amount flows from their checking account to their investment accounts on a set schedule (weekly, biweekly, or monthly).

- >> **Investments:** Buy limit orders are in place, based on their Diamond Analysis, so assets are purchased at smart entry points, without needing to babysit the market.

- >> **Dividends:** DRIPs (dividend reinvestment plans) automatically reinvest earnings into more shares.

- >> **Cash flow:** Money funnels into high-yield savings accounts or flexible funds without manual transfers.

This habit is not about being lazy. It's about being *smart*. Automation removes emotion from investing, so you don't freeze when the market dips or spend impulsively when you're feeling flush.

If you're still relying on memory, motivation, or mood to grow your portfolio, you're one unexpected bill or bad day away from falling off track. Automate it. Then watch it work.

Focusing on Priorities That Align with Your Biggest Goals

Not everything on your to-do list deserves your attention. In fact, most of it doesn't. Triple compounders don't confuse *busy* with *productive*. They focus on what matters most — the 20 percent of actions that move them 80 percent closer to their goals.

They know that every "yes" comes with a hidden "no." So, before they commit to a project, conversation, or purchase, they ask the following:

- >> "Does this move the needle the most toward my top three goals right now?"

- >> "Does this support the future I'm building or distract from it?"

- >> "Is this a priority or just a polished-looking procrastination?"

Each week, write down your top three priorities across wealth, health, and relationships. Let those guide your calendar. Filter out the rest.

When you operate from your zone of genius and ignore the distractions, your growth compounds faster and feels easier.

Success isn't just about doing the right things. It's about *not doing* the wrong ones. Alignment is your most underrated productivity tool.

If you're constantly exhausted, overwhelmed, or stuck, it's not a motivation issue. It's a misalignment issue. You're saying yes to things that pull you off track. Start pruning.

Committing to the Infinite Game of Expansion

Triple compounders aren't just playing to win. They're playing to keep evolving.

Although most people chase goals like they're sprinting toward a finish line, triple compounders see life as an *infinite game*. There is no final destination, no magical number that suddenly makes you whole. Just continued growth, deeper alignment, and more capacity to give, receive, and enjoy.

That's why they don't panic when they hit a plateau. They don't quit when things slow down. And they don't shrink just because they already "have enough."

Instead, they commit to expansion as a *lifestyle*. That means

>> Reinventing themselves at each new level of growth.

>> Letting go of identities that no longer fit.

>> Staying curious and humble, even as they succeed.

>> Continuing to compound — not because they *need* to but because they *want* to.

Triple compounders know that true wealth is not just numbers on a screen. It's becoming the kind of person who can generate, automate, and accelerate value in *every* season of life.

They don't fear change. They *expect* it. They don't avoid challenges. They *use* them.

And most importantly, they don't stop expanding just because they've reached one goal. They zoom out and choose a bigger one.

Every time you hit a milestone, pause and ask, "What's the next version of me being called forward? What's the next expansion available here?"

There is no "done." There is only depth, joy, and the next level of alignment. Stay in the game — and let your growth compound forever.

Index

grinder level, 184–185, 188
growth equity, 126
growth stocks, 99, 105–106
guided meditation, 66–67

H

habits, for compounding
  anchoring momentum, 145
    habit stacking, 144
    rewarding for small wins, 144
    small beginnings, 143
hacking, 51
Hardy, Benjamin, 64, 69, 311
Health Savings Account (HSA), 265, 279
high-frequency trading, 213
high-risk investments, 292–293
high-yield savings accounts, 218
Hill, Napoleon, 13, 33, 64, 74, 170
home office deduction, 283, 286
Hormozi, Alex, 153, 190, 221
Hormozi, Leila, 190
house flipping, 121–122
house hacking, 123
HSA. *See* Health Savings Account (HSA)
human-centered communities, 222
hype risk, 51

I

Ichimoku Kinko Hyo, 258
Ichimoku Secrets (Danial), 213
IDDA. *See* Invest Diva Diamond
    Analysis (IDDA)
ideal customers, 153, 195
identity-based transformation, 311
imagination, 65

impersonators, 293–294
income
  acceleration, 17–18, 23, 26
  debts, 271
  and expenses, 41
  influence-driven, 229
  rental, 44
  See also business income; savings,
      income from
  tracking, 44–45
income-generating extensions, 16–18,
    34–35, 52, 75, 92, 97
  businesses, 89–94
  from current job, 85–86
  portfolios, 86–89
  with savings, 76–85
indexed universal life (IUL), 268–269, 278
index funds, 116–117, 301
industrial real estate, 285
inflation, 8, 50, 55
influence (power of), 221
  building audience of people, 224–225
  -driven income, 229
  exploring in real life, 226–228
  mess into message, 223–224
  myths about, 228–231
  understanding, 222–223
in-kind charitable giving, 203
insurance, 261
  agents, 91
  borrowing against, 270–271
  disability coverage, 264, 266–267
  layering your financial tools, 272
  life insurance, 264, 266–270
  medical coverage, 265

outcomes, 155–156

overinvesting, 292–293

overpaying, for convenience, 84

P

Parke, David, 190

partnerships

  compounding legacy,
    203–204

  understanding compounding, 202

passive income stocks, 99

past experiences, 142

past reframing, 68–70

P/B (price-to-book) ratio, 100

peer-to-peer lending platforms, 218

penalty, early withdrawal, 11–12

P/E (price-to-earnings) ratio, 100

perfection, 230

permanent policies, 268, 269, 273

personal brands, 221–222

personalization, 240

physical assets, 42

platform partnerships, 203

Polkadot (DOT), 88

poor financial choices, 50

poor tax planning, 302

portfolio goals, 97–98

portfolios earning

  crypto rewards through staking, 88

  dividend stocks, 87

  interest on investments,
    86–87

  options trading, 89

  swing trading, 87–88

Premium Investing Group (PIG)
    coaching, 197, 199

premium pricing, 240

  cash flow for strategic growth,
    241–243

  impact more with fewer clients, 243

  value ladder, 244

Prepeople, 152–153

Pressfield, Steven, 67–68

priorities, 314–315

private acquisitions, 126

private equity

  buyouts and private acquisitions, 126

  funds of funds, 127

  growth equity, 126

  venture capital, 125–126

procrastination, 67, 73, 198

profits automation

  anticipation, not reaction, 214

  buy/sell limit orders, 214–215, 251

  crowd sentiment, 213–214

  dividend reinvestment plans (DRIP), 216

  dollar-cost averaging, 217

  interest-paying investments,
    217–218

  using market notifications, 217

psychology factor, 250–251

pump-and-dump stocks, 99, 103

put options, 115

R

Ramos, Rowell, 242

Ramsey, Dave, 7, 15, 27–28

rate of return (ROR), 12–13

S

About the Author

Kiana Danial, former electrical engineer and founder of Invest Diva, is an internationally recognized expert in investing, entrepreneurship, and wealth creation. She is the author of seven books, including the *Wall Street Journal* and *USA Today* bestseller *Million Dollar Family Secrets,* as well as *Cryptocurrency Investing For Dummies,* published by Wiley.

Through her signature Triple Compounding method, Kiana empowers professionals to take control of their finances and accelerate their path to financial freedom.

Author's Acknowledgment

To all members of the Invest Diva movement, who inspire me to keep leading as they follow my methods and share their wins.

To present and future triple compounders, who are using this method to become the best versions of themselves, helping me realize my mission of creating a world where everyone thrives as their fullest self.

To my amazing Invest Diva team — the A-players who uphold my high standards and keep the movement going even when it's hard. A special thank-you to Arleny Lopez-Cordero for her continued support and commitment.

To our incredible Invest Diva coaches, who are passing the torch to thousands of members so that they, too, can take control of their financial future — especially Tonya Rideout, who lives and breathes triple compounding and, with her attention to detail, helped keep this book accurate.

To my Accelerators, who keep leveling up and making *giraffe decisions* to accelerate their triple-compounding system. (If you know, you know.)

To my Diamond member Mandie Hunt, founder of Free Nurses, who is helping burned-out nurses become financially free, amplifying the ripple effect of the Invest Diva movement. Follow her journey on Instagram at @Freenursemandie

To my Diamond members Wissam Alherech, Payeman Raja, and May Shawi, who partnered up to help physicians and high-income-earning moms finally take control of their wealth, reduce taxes legally, and build a lasting financial legacy without burnout, exhaustion, or guesswork.

Special thanks to Brett Wible, Hanna Horenstein, and Edward Collins (Instagram handle: @edwardcollins_upleveled), who not only helped me with real-life applications of insurance and tax strategies in my own Triple Compounding system but also contributed to this book so that thousands of others can accelerate their own triple-compounding journey.

And thank you, Tracy Boggier, for making this book happen.

Dedication

To my amazing husband Matt — your unwavering support and the safe space you created gave me the freedom to explore, refine, and fully live the principles of triple compounding.

Because of you, I discovered how this method isn't just about money — it's about integrating masculine and feminine energy in everything we build together and allowing me to continuously become the best version of myself.

Publisher's Acknowledgments

Senior Acquisitions Editor: Tracy Boggier

Project Editor: Charlotte Kughen

Copy Editor: Marylouise Wiack

Technical Editor: Tonya Rideout

Production Editor: Magesh Elangovan

Managing Editor: Sofia Malik

Cover Images: © Palto/Shutterstock, © Artur Marciniec/Alamy Stock Photo

Printed and bound by CPI Group (UK) Ltd, Croydon, CR0 4YY

07/07/2026

14916218-0002